M000228763

Modal Subjectivities

The publisher gratefully acknowledges the generous contribution to this book provided by the Sonia H. Evers Renaissance Studies Fund of the University of California Press Associates.

Modal Subjectivities

SELF-FASHIONING IN THE ITALIAN MADRIGAL

Susan McClary

UNIVERSITY OF CALIFORNIA PRESS

University of California Press
Berkeley and Los Angeles, California

© 2004 by the Regents of the University of California
First Paperback Printing 2019
Library of Congress Cataloging-in-Publication Data

McClary, Susan.
  Modal subjectivities : self-fashioning in the Italian
madrigal / Susan McClary.
      p.   cm.
  Includes bibliographical references and index.
  ISBN 0-520-23493-6 (cloth : alk. paper); 978-0-520-31425-2 (pbk. : alk. paper)
  1. Madrigals, Italian—Italy—16th century—Analysis,
appreciation.   2. Musical form—History—16th
century.   3. Music theory—History—16th century.
4. Music and language.   I. Title.
ML2633.2.M33   2004
782.4'3'0945—dc22   2003025287

CONTENTS

EXAMPLES

ACKNOWLEDGMENTS

It has taken me a very long time to produce this book. My first encounters with the madrigal repertory occurred in the early 1960s at University High School in Carbondale, Illinois. Buried deep in a region best known for cultivating corn and soybeans, U School had a student population made up primarily of faculty brats, and it lavished nearly as much prestige on the members of Dr. Charles Taylor's madrigal group as on cheerleaders or sports stars. I cringe when I remember the fancy costumes we concocted for ourselves (patterned, I suspect, after the ball gowns in Walt Disney's *Cinderella*); those costumes cured me forever of the desire to dress up in Renaissance drag. But Charlie taught us to sing virtually all the pieces (English madrigals, Parisian chansons, a few Italian numbers) collected in an old Novello edition with heavily bowdlerized translations. We traipsed around southern Illinois dazzling the crowds—or so we thought at the time—with our animated renditions of "Sing We and Chant It" and "Matona, Lovely Maiden." (Years later, in a crowded café in Harvard Square, Joel Cohen sang me his own unexpurgated translation of "Matona"—an event I'm not likely ever to forget.)

In graduate school, I had the privilege of singing in Anthony Newcomb's madrigal group, which often worked directly from the hand-scribbled transcriptions later published in his *The Madrigal at Ferrara*. I owe him my deepest gratitude, for it was in the context of his ensemble that I first encountered many of the pieces discussed in *Modal Subjectivities*. I also owe to Tony my abiding intellectual and musical commitment to this repertory. Unfortunately, Tony left Harvard before I embarked on my dissertation, "The Transition from Modal to Tonal Organization in the Works of Monteverdi" (1976), but his influenced permeates it.

To a very great extent, the present book comprises a reworking of the first half of my antiquated dissertation (the parts on modal theory and the Monteverdi madrigals). But it also includes a lengthy backstory concerning the madrigal before Monteverdi. If the dissertation represents a *Siegfrieds Tod* stage of the project, *Modal Subjectivities* subjects you to the whole *Ring:* what you need to know in order to make sense of the ending.

I have not been entirely idle in the years since I finished that first draft. Although I have taught graduate seminars on the madrigal and modal theory at several institutions (the University of Minnesota, McGill University, and UCLA), most musicologists probably assume that I have moved on permanently to other pastures: to the standard eighteenth- and nineteenth-century canon, to feminist theory, to pop music. But in fact, my whole bibliography developed as a way of figuring out an implicit scholarly ideology that resisted my modal analyses when I first tried to get them published in the 1970s. I had left my heart in the Renaissance, however, and it's nice to come home again.

Needless to say, this "revision" differs considerably from its first version with respect to theoretical grounding. In the nearly thirty years since I received my degree, I have immersed myself in the issues and methods developed within cultural studies. Whereas the dissertation stuck closely to treatises and formal analysis, *Modal Subjectivities* brings the madrigal to the interdisciplinary project concerned with tracing the histories of bodies, genders, sexualities, and subjectivities. Whatever its faults, it's a far richer enterprise than it would have been if I had turned it into a book immediately after graduate school.

And, of course, my writing style has changed. I recall how desperately I worked to rein in my language in those early years when I thought that scholarly prose needed to be boring. My turning point occurred in the fall of 1980, when a rejection slip objected to my use of the word *shriek* to describe the high A in Monteverdi's "Ah, dolente partita." I decided at that very moment (with Richard Leppert's encouragement) that if I could not write about music in ways that satisfied me, I would not bother to stay in the field. Well, I persisted. The word *shriek* appears in all its scandalous glory in my introductory chapter, and that's scarcely the beginning.

ONE

Introduction

The Cultural Work of the Madrigal

Ah, dolente partita!
Ah, fin de la mia vita!
Da te parto e non moro? E pur i' provo
la pena de la morte
e sento nel partire
un vivace morire,
che dà vita al dolore
per far che moia immortalmente il core.

> (Giovanni Battista Guarini,
> *Il pastor fido*)

Ah, sorrowful parting!
Ah, end of my life!
I part from you and do not die? And yet I suffer
the pain of death
and feel in this parting
a vivacious dying,
which gives life to sorrow
causing my heart to die immortally.

In this highly concentrated verse, the pastoral lover Mirtillo attempts to put into words the contradictory impulses he experiences in but a single moment.

Multiple passions—longing, abjection, disbelief, anguish, resignation—assail him from within, finally to condense into the oxymoron of "un vivace morire." Banished from Amarilli's presence, Mirtillo hangs suspended between an agony so violent that it ought to bring about his immediate demise but that, because of its very intensity, prevents the release from suffering promised by death. In this brief speech, Giovanni Battista Guarini displays his celebrated epigrammatic style: an economy of means that sketches in a mere eight lines an emotional state comprising opposites that cannot even hope for reconciliation. He manifests his virtuosity particularly well in his successive redefinitions of "vita" and "morte," binary opposites that shift positions back and forth until they become hopelessly (and deliciously) fused.

Imagine, however, having the ability to convey all these sentiments at once, as though one could read the lines of Mirtillo's speech together vertically as a score. The resulting performance, alas, would amount to little more than noise, each string of words canceling out the others; instead of a realistic representation of Mirtillo's conflicting affects we would get something akin to John Cage tuning in randomly to twelve different radio stations. For despite all its potential for precision and sophistication, language relies for its intelligibility on the consecutive presentation of ideas in linear grammatical order. We may marvel at the extent to which Guarini appears to overcome the limitations of additive speech. Indeed, literary figures of the twentieth-century literary avant-garde—James Joyce and Virginia Woolf, for example—labored to push language in these directions through stream-of-consciousness technique, leading some literary theorists to latch onto the concept of counterpoint to explain such experiments; Julia Kristeva even offers double-column prose to simulate the experience of jostling two contrasting thought processes at the same time (a simulation that often leaves the reader feeling little more than wall-eyed).[1]

The very term *counterpoint*, however, alludes to the cultural medium in which such feats occur as a matter of course: namely, music. And in his madrigal setting of Mirtillo's lament, Claudio Monteverdi manages to achieve the simultaneity toward which Guarini gestures. Given the performing force of five independent voices, the composer can actually superimpose the sentiments of the first four lines of text, allowing them to circulate within the same space and time. Thus, in the first motive two voices divide from a

1. Julia Kristeva, "Stabat Mater," in *Tales of Love,* trans. Leon S. Roudiez (New York: Columbia University Press, 1987).

FIGURE I. Monteverdi, "Ah, dolente partita": First four motives

unison to a sequence of close dissonances to enact the searing anguish of separation expressed in the first line; a too-rapid collapse toward premature closure on "Ah, fin de la mia vita!" parallels Mirtillo's futile death wish in the second; a slowly ascending melodic motive that cancels out the would-be closure of the death wish registers the incredulity of the third; and an insistent repetition of a high pitch on "E pur i' provo / La pena de la morte" shrieks out the stabbing pain of the fourth (Fig. I). The dynamic vectors of Monteverdi's motives, in other words, offer analogues to these divergent affects, giving us a visceral enactment of the suffering, resignation, doubt, and protest that surge through Mirtillo's mind and body during this single moment. Moreover, in keeping with Guarini's sense that Mirtillo cannot escape his internally conflicted state, the madrigal moves on in time to yet other combinations that recycle these mutually antagonistic elements but come no closer to resolution.

What Monteverdi offers here is a sound-image of subjective interiority on the verge of psychological meltdown, and he thereby gives us what music can do that language cannot, even at its most ingenious. Of course, not everyone has celebrated this particular strategy. Some of Monteverdi's own contemporaries, including most prominently Vincenzo Galilei (the father of the astronomer), complained that the contrapuntal excesses of late sixteenth-century madrigals prevented the intelligible projection of the words; such critics advocated instead a solo-voice model whereby the music serves primarily to inflect the lyrics, declaimed in an unimpeded fashion approximating public oratory.[2]

To be sure, it takes a leap of faith to accept a five-voice ensemble as reproducing the swooning of a single individual. Musicologists trip all over themselves to explain away this embarrassing convention, so far removed from the realistic expressivity of seventeenth-century solo singing. They gain support from sixteenth-century critics such as Galilei, who likewise detested the contrapuntal artifice of polyphonic text-settings. But this convention should seem quite familiar to fans of gospel, doo-wop, or any of the boy-group collectives that rise to the top of today's pop charts with great regularity. Like madrigal ensembles, these feature simulations of complex interiorities: rational grounding in the bass, melodic address in the middle, ecstatic melismas on the top. No contemporary teenager needs to be told how the various vocal roles in, say, *NSYNC function together to produce a viable representation of the Self.[3]

Even as Monteverdi was delivering "Ah, dolente partita" to the publisher, he and his colleagues were embarking on a style that brought music into the arena of dramatic spectacle we now call opera. The realistic performance of individual subjects afforded by the *stile recitativo* made opera the dominant genre of musical representation for the next three hundred years. But we often forget that recitative accomplished its coup at the cost of harnessing music to the linear imperatives of language: as music attaches itself to the exigencies of rhetorical declamation, it finds itself restricted to speech's limitations. We could thus count "Ah, dolente partita" (to which we will return later in this chapter) as not only Mirtillo's wistful adieu to Amarilli but also as a reluctant farewell to the multivoiced medium honed to perfection in the sixteenth century as a means for depicting the phenomenological interior Self.

Music historians like to start the clock for the early modern period in 1600. Several factors lend support to that date: the first opera, the first oratorio,

---

2. Vincenzo Galilei, *Dialogo della musica antica, et della moderna* (1581); an excerpted translated appears in Oliver Strunk, *Source Readings in Music History*, rev. ed. (New York: Norton, 1998), 463–67. See my Chapter 6 for a more extended discussion of Galilei.

3. I have not included girl groups in my discussion here because their voice parts interact differently. These too find their equivalent, however, in the *concerti delle donne* in late sixteenth-century Ferrara and elsewhere. See Chapter 6.

the first solo sonata—in other words, the first "realistic" musical representations of the individual persona—all appear in that year. Moreover, these emergent genres all rely on the new technology of *basso continuo* responsible for securing the tonal era that still persists to this day, if not in expressions of the avant-garde then at least as the lingua franca that underwrites film, advertisement, and popular music. But the coincidence of all these elements makes it perhaps too easy to draw a line of demarcation whereby all cultural agendas before that point count as radically Other. Nor does this problem arise solely within musicology: witness Michel Foucault's similar partitioning of epistemologies in *The Order of Things* at around 1600 or philosophy's designation of point zero at Descartes's "Cogito."[4] If we take these interdisciplinary resonances as further confirmation, then the early seventeenth century seems irrefutably the dawn of modern subjectivity.

Of course, something momentous *does* occur in European culture around 1600. Yet that break is not so radical that it can justify the flattening out of what happened prior to that time—an inevitable effect of Othering. As Eric Wolf explains in his classic *Europe and the People without History,* our historiographies tend to ascribe Selfhood and complex sequences of significant events to those we choose to regard as "us," and they project everyone else into a kind of timeless, unconscious arcadia.[5] Thus, the decades preceding our countdown year often count as interesting insofar as their cultural practices point toward the advent of the new; but to the extent that they align themselves with soon-to-be-obsolete genres and techniques, they still seem to belong to the old world, the backdrop up against which the innovations under consideration can stand in bold relief.

Truth to tell, some distinctions of this sort will appear in this book: I too wish to trace a history of Western subjectivity and will even refer occasionally to the Cogito as a crucial verbal manifestation of the phenomenon I examine. I also plead guilty to drawing a line for the sake of de-

4. Michel Foucault, *The Order of Things: An Archaeology of the Human Sciences* (New York: Vintage Books, 1973). For Foucault-oriented epistemology within musicology, see Gary Tomlinson, *Music in Renaissance Magic: Toward a Historiography of Others* (Chicago: University of Chicago Press, 1993) and *Metaphysical Song: An Essay on Opera* (Princeton: Princeton University Press, 1999).

5. Eric R. Wolf, *Europe and the People without History* (Berkeley and Los Angeles: University of California Press, 1997). See also Johannes Fabian, *Time and the Other: How Anthropology Makes Its Object* (New York: Columbia University Press, 1983).

limiting my study, such that what lies before my designated time and outside of northern Italy will have to remain suspended (at least for now) in a vague atemporality.[6]

My argument *in nuce* is that from around 1525 the Italian madrigal serves as a site—indeed, the first in European history—for the explicit, self-conscious construction *in music* of subjectivities. Over the course of a good century, madrigal composers anticipate Descartes in performing the crucial break with traditional epistemologies, plunging musical style and thought into an extraordinary crisis of authority, knowledge, power, and identity. They do so, however, not by repudiating the modal edifice they had inherited from centuries of scholastic theorizing but rather by systematizing, allegorizing, and finally blowing it up from the inside. During the process, they move not closer to but instead further and further away from what might qualify as "tonal" (at least in the standard eighteenth-century sense of the word). And they do so in the service of an agenda that interrogates what it means and feels like to be a Self—to be more specific, a morbidly introspective and irreconcilably conflicted Self.

If similar issues also show up in various other cultural media, they need not advance together in lock-step. Indeed, my other work suggests that music often yields a somewhat different chronology of issues such as subjective formations or conceptions of the body than would a study based solely on written documents. On the one hand, the madrigal resuscitates a tradition of vernacular love song—together with its infinitely fascinating ruminations on the affects of passion on identity—stretching from the Moorish courts of medieval Spain, through the troubadours, and climaxing in the works of Petrarch, whose fourteenth-century sonnets prove a major source of texts for the sixteenth-century genre we are tracing.[7] From that point of view, the madrigal might count as a throwback, and indeed, one of the important strands we will follow involves the association of madrigals with individu-

---

6. See, however, Bruce W. Holsinger, *Music, Body, and Desire in Medieval Culture* (Stanford: Stanford University Press, 2001). Kate Bartel is writing a dissertation at UCLA on Josquin and his contemporaries that takes many of these issues back into the fifteenth century. See her *Portal of the Skies: Topologies of the Divine in the Latin Motet* (in progress). Moreover, Elizabeth Randell Upton is developing methods for the critical interpretation of Dufay's love songs.

7. See María Rosa Menocal, *The Shards of Love: Exile and the Origins of the Lyric* (Durham and London: Duke University Press, 1994), and Robert M. Durling, Introduction to *Petrarch's Lyric Poems*, trans. and ed. Durling (Cambridge: Harvard University Press, 1976).

als and/or communities in exile who yearn nostalgically for their homeland in the guise of the Lady. But on the other hand, the musical settings that comprise madrigal composition often articulate astonishingly modern insights into subjectivity, for in the process of converting lyrics into the more corporeal and time-oriented medium of music, they necessarily bring to bear aspects of human experience and cultural assumptions not available to poetry. The historiographer Hayden White has pleaded with musicologists to start paying back for what they have gleaned from historians and literary scholars by offering information not available except through music.[8] This book serves as an installment of that payback.

It is, of course, notoriously difficult (I won't accept the word *dangerous*— dangerous to what? to whom?) to rely on nonverbal media for historical data. Pitches and rhythms reside a long distance away from the apparently solid semiosis of language. Yet if music is to figure as anything other than a mere epiphenomenon (and those of us who lived through the music-driven 1960s fervently believe as much), then we must find approaches that will allow us to examine its meanings.[9] Otherwise, we will continue simply to graft music onto an already-formulated narrative of historical developments; more important, we will fail to learn what music might have to teach us or to question seriously what may be incomplete accounts of the past. At the very least I want in this book to shake loose a version of early modern subjectivity too neatly packaged in recent studies and to encourage a process of historical revision that takes music as a point of departure. I also wish to treat in depth a repertory too long neglected as a site of crucial cultural work: the sixteenth-century Italian madrigal.

The madrigal scarcely qualifies as an obscure genre. Within its own time, it occupied the center of musical production: the aesthetic debates concerning sixteenth-century Italian music revolved around the experiments

8. Hayden White, "Form, Reference, and Ideology in Musical Discourse," afterword to *Music and Text: Critical Inquiries,* ed. Steven Paul Scher (Cambridge: Cambridge University Press, 1992). My book *Conventional Wisdom: The Content of Musical Form* (Berkeley and Los Angeles: University of California Press, 2000) explicitly paid homage to White's *The Content of the Form* (Baltimore: Johns Hopkins University Press, 1987) in its title and project.

9. This slight difference in generation explains, I think, the differences in orientation between those "new musicologists" who search to discern meanings (e.g., Lawrence Kramer, Rose Subotnik, and myself) and those who adopt a more postmodernist approach in their work (e.g., Carolyn Abbate and Mary Ann Smart).

performed by its principal composers,[10] and its success contributed greatly to the viability of the new commercial enterprise of music printing.[11] Moreover, a large number of prominent musicologists have long concentrated their efforts to uncovering its history and making this music available to modern musicians and audiences.

Why, then, this book? In point of fact, I have no new archival sources to offer nor hitherto-unknown composers to tout. Indeed, *Modal Subjectivities* deals only with the most familiar artists and madrigals of the tradition—the ones most celebrated in their own day for their impact on cultural life, the ones most readily available in textbooks, anthologies, and recordings. And it concentrates far more on these musical texts than on the contexts that surrounded their origins. I hope, however, to accomplish three major goals, all of them similar to those pursued in my work on later periods.

First, I want to begin interpreting critically a major repertory that has received mostly stylistic descriptions. By "interpreting critically" I mean interrogating the formal details through which the selected compositions produce their effects—structural, expressive, ideological, and cultural. A few musicologists have previously undertaken projects that link sixteenth-century musical procedures with the social: for instance, Joseph Kerman has written extensively on English madrigals, especially those of William Byrd;[12] Anthony Newcomb's work on the court of Ferrara strongly influenced my own training and much of my subsequent work;[13] Gary Tomlinson and Eric Chafe have examined in detail the music of Claudio Monteverdi;[14] Martha

10. See the account of the tensions between Willaert and Rore in Martha Feldman, "Rore's 'selva selvaggia': The *Primo libro* of 1542," *JAMS* 42 (1989): 547–603; the flap surrounding Nicola Vicentino's enharmonic experiments in Henry Kaufmann, *The Life and Works of Nicola Vicentino,* Musicological Studies and Documents, vol. 11 (Rome, 1966); Galilei's critique of the polyphonic madrigal in his *Dialogo della musica antica et della moderna* (1581); and the Artusi/Monteverdi controversy, discussed at length in my Chapter 8.

11. See Mary Lewis, *Antonio Gardane, Venetian Music Printer, 1538–1569: A Descriptive Biography and Historical Study,* 1:1538–49 (New York, 1988); Suzanne Cusick, *Valerio Dorico: Music Printer in Sixteenth-Century Rome* (Ann Arbor: UMI, 1981); and Stanley Boorman, "What Bibliography Can Do: Music Printing and the Early Madrigal," *Music & Letters* 72.2 (May 1991): 236–58.

12. Joseph Kerman, *The Elizabethan Madrigal* (New York: American Musicological Society, 1962).

13. Anthony Newcomb, *The Madrigal at Ferrara, 1579–97* (Princeton: Princeton University Press, 1980).

14. Gary Tomlinson, *Monteverdi and the End of the Renaissance* (Berkeley and Los Angeles: University of California Press, 1987); Eric Chafe, *Monteverdi's Tonal Language* (New York: Schirmer, 1992).

Feldman in her book on the Venetian contexts of Adrian Willaert and Cipriano de Rore brings into focus the kinds of questions I wish to pursue;[15] and, of course, we all stand on the shoulders of Alfred Einstein, whose monumental *The Italian Madrigal,* while no longer definitive in its details, is not likely ever to find an equal in terms of sheer prodigious learning.[16] These scholars and others will emerge as important figures in the chapters that follow. But although it draws on the work of predecessors, this book will push the enterprise of sixteenth-century music criticism to delineate rather different approaches to theory, analysis, and interpretation.

Second, I want to strengthen the intellectual connection between musicology and scholars in the other humanities. Many of the issues raised over the course of *Modal Subjectivities* bear traces of my engagement with writers such as Michel Foucault, Stephen Greenblatt, Jonathan Dollimore, María Rosa Menocal, Charles Taylor, and Peter Burke, all of whom proceed from the premise that human subjectivity has a history—a history for which modern scholars may receive invaluable insights from the arts.[17] Most New Historicists depend principally on literature, theater, and painting for their evidence; they rarely refer to music as a resource (except in the work of Theodor Adorno or Carl Schorske),[18] in large part because of the specialized training demanded by the task. They sometimes look to musicologists for assistance, but music scholars have concerned themselves only very recently with the questions typically asked by cultural historians. I maintain that the madrigal can tell us all a great deal about constructions of subjectivity—notions of the body, emotions, temporality, gender, reason, interiority—during a crucial stage of Western cultural history. And if some of these notions find direct corroboration in contemporaneous cul-

15. Martha Feldman, *City Culture and the Madrigal at Venice* (Berkeley and Los Angeles: University of California Press, 1995).

16. Alfred Einstein, *The Italian Madrigal,* trans. Knappe, Sessions, Strunk (Princeton: Princeton University Press, 1949; repr., 1971).

17. Foucault, *The Order of the Things;* Stephen Greenblatt, *Renaissance Self-Fashioning from More to Shakespeare* (Chicago: University of Chicago Press, 1980); Jonathan Dollimore, *Death, Desire and Loss in Western Culture* (New York: Routledge, 1998); Menocal, *The Shards of Love;* Charles Taylor, *Sources of the Self: The Making of the Modern Identity* (Cambridge: Harvard University Press, 1989); Peter Burke, *Eyewitnessing: The Uses of Images as Historical Evidence* (Ithaca: Cornell University Press, 2001).

18. See, for example, Carl E. Schorske, *Fin-de-Siècle Vienna: Politics and Culture* (New York: Vintage Books, 1981) and *Thinking with History: Explorations in the Passage to Modernism* (Princeton: Princeton University Press, 1998). For Adorno see *Essays on Music,* ed. Richard Leppert (Berkeley and Los Angeles: University of California Press, 2002).

tural discourses, others do not. Thus, although my work is indebted to Foucault and others, I cannot subscribe in advance to any master narrative against which to map my history of subjectivity, for doing so would foreclose anything I might find in this radically different medium.

Before proceeding further, I should explain why I treat musical texts— here and elsewhere in my other work—as potential sources of historical evidence, why I rely at least as heavily on what I discern in musical procedures as on verbal documents. I do not claim that we can read straight through music to history: without question, many levels of cultural tropes, artistic conventions, and social contingencies mediate between the dots on the page and the complexities of a world now more than four centuries removed. But the same holds true for verbal documents, which likewise require careful contexualization and which never can deliver anything approaching Truth. If we wait for the discovery of a treatise that will tell us everything we want to know about this repertory, we will be able to ice-skate in Hades while we read it. For the questions I ask of this repertory often differ from those posed by its composers and first audiences, all of whom found themselves enmeshed in other cultural debates.

Yet I would not thereby concede that my enterprise qualifies as anachronistic. Take for example the question of sexuality. Renaissance music theorists generally did not discuss strategies for simulating desire, arousal, or climax in their writings; they had (as it were) other fish to fry. Nevertheless, the madrigal repertory deals consistently, obsessively, even graphically with experiences of erotic engagement. I know in advance that those critics who find problematic my ascription of sexual dimensions to Richard Strauss's *Salome* will also balk at this project. And I can also anticipate some who will continue to worry about my hermeneutic incursion into the cultures of historic Others. But if we are ever to move beyond the mere hoarding of old music and enter into cultural interpretation, then we have to take such chances. We must, of course, also take into account whatever documents do happen to survive. But for musicologists (and, if we can make the case, for other cultural historians as well), these documents should also include the music itself. The verbal does not trump the musical.

At issue here is a methodological problem concerning the relative weight of texts and contexts. Music historians have tended to privilege what they know (or think they know) about the historical terrain, then situate their interpretations of music accordingly. But what if—as Jacques Attali quirkily but astutely posits—music frequently registers epistemological changes before they are manifested in words?[19] What if John Cage (as Jean-François Lyotard, among others, claims) sparked postmodernism as it appeared in the other arts, decades before other musicians thought to write what they themselves labeled as postmodernist music?[20] What if Mozart was (as E.T.A. Hoffmann insisted) the first great Romantic—the model for the poets and novelists who followed?[21] And what if the madrigalists anticipated Foucault's seventeenth-century episteme a good seventy years earlier, performed the Cogito when Descartes wasn't even a twinkle in his father's eye? I firmly believe that to demand verbal confirmation for anything we want to say about music assumes that music can add nothing to our understanding of a society that we cannot glean perfectly well from other kinds of sources. And it can lead to grave underestimations of music's impact on structures of feeling in a culture.[22]

I have a third purpose in writing this book. In recent years, most of my efforts have centered on music of the seventeenth century: a period that witnessed the emergence of tonality, the musical system we still too often regard as natural. As I began writing a chapter devoted to musical practices *before* that change, I discovered that I could not do justice to its complexity and vast range of possibilities in the course of a mere introduction, not even in an introduction that threatened to stretch to inordinate length. That chapter clearly needed to become a book in itself—a book necessary if my account of style in the 1600s, *Power and Desire in Seventeenth-Century Music,* were not to seem like yet one more celebration of tonality's inevitable emergence. I hope to demonstrate in *Modal Subjectivities* that there existed no prima facie reason why musical grammar needed to have changed in the 1600s, that the syntactical and expressive sophistication manifested in the sixteenth-century madrigal equals that of any subsequent musical repertory. And, having done that, I can in relatively good conscience proceed to an examination of the transformation, to ask why—given the extraordi-

19. Jacques Attali, *Noise: The Political Economy of Music* (Minneapolis: University of Minnesota Press, 1985); afterword by Susan McClary.

20. Jean-François Lyotard, "Several Silences," in his *Driftworks,* trans. Joseph Maier (New York, 1984), 91–110.

21. E.T.A. Hoffmann, "Beethoven's Instrumental Music" (1813), trans. Oliver Strunk, *Source Readings in Music History* (New York: Norton, 1950; rev. ed., 1998).

22. I owe the expression "structures of feeling" to Raymond Williams. See his *Marxism and Literature* (Oxford: Oxford University Press, 1977), 128–35.

nary capabilities of this modus operandi —composers opted to alter drastically not only their musical procedures but (more important) their fundamental conceptions of temporality and Selfhood.[23]

Now an apology: I would like to be able to assure the interdisciplinary reader that technical music-theoretical jargon will not enter into this text. But my argument proceeds from my conviction that musical procedures themselves constitute an indispensable aspect of the cultural content of any repertory. Formal properties, in other words, operate neither as "purely musical" elements relevant only to music theorists nor as neutral devices on top of which the content gets deposited, inasmuch as the stuff of music is sound and time. And given the extensive grammatical mediation that regulates the relationships between sounds and their temporal arrangements, we cannot hear straight through to the content.

Moreover, our contemporary ears—all long since oriented toward the tonal strategies of the eighteenth and nineteenth centuries—have to be reoriented to hear in significantly different ways if they are to discern the madrigal's expressive and allegorical strategies. This process of rewiring will doubtless prove difficult even for those who have learned to accept as universals the structural and harmonic norms of later musics. But as it turns out (or does so according to the historical narrative I will weave over the course of this book), the cultural agenda of the madrigal's successive stages cannot be disentangled from the successive developments of the highly intricate musical system with which it was allied, which sustained and often inspired its various moments, and which eventually served as the conventional base that needed somehow to be repudiated and sacrificed to the cause of radical individualism.

I will always attempt to translate the principal points I make into language comprehensible to those without specialized musical training. Yet I cannot avoid the formal frameworks within which these pieces unfold without falling back on the assumption that their meanings all proceed directly from the lyrics: an assumption that underlies most accounts of the madrigal, so prevalent that text/music relationships of virtually all varieties are pejoratively termed "madrigalisms" or text-painting. It is as though composers stumbled blindly from line to line, relying for coherence on their chosen verses like children requiring training wheels on their bikes. At best,

23. My *Power and Desire in Seventeenth-Century Music* is now in preparation for Princeton University Press.

then, a composition would reflect its text, and its meanings would reduce to those of the poem. Without question, madrigalists (like later composers of opera or Lieder, for that matter) saw their task as enhancing and interpreting their chosen texts, and we can come to understand their signifying practices in part by following correspondences with words. But if the *music* of the madrigal matters (and I submit that it does), then we must examine how it produces its powerful imagery over and above—and sometimes in contradiction to—the lyrics.

HOW TO DO THINGS WITH MODES

Music theorists of the sixteenth century discussed the formal organization of their music in terms of what they called mode. Yet musicologists have long regarded that penchant as a mere holdover from earlier theoretical traditions designed to classify Roman Catholic plainsong, and they have tended to dismiss sixteenth-century theories as woefully inadequate or fundamentally misguided for purposes of explaining contemporaneous polyphonic practices. Part of the reason for that dismissal is a model of historiography that envisions a teleological trajectory from modal monophony through a gradual breakdown of modality to the consolidation of standardized tonality in the later seventeenth century. Given this intellectual predisposition, music historians often want to hear the music of the sixteenth century as the penultimate step in that evolutionary process: after all those centuries of wandering in the wilderness, we arrive finally within spitting distance of the promised land![24]

Without question, a humanist such as Gioseffo Zarlino—the music theorist upon whom I rely most heavily—blurred the boundaries between his displays of classical erudition, his continued respect for ecclesiastical tradition, and the systems he himself formulated to account for the music of his own contemporaries.[25] The section of Zarlino's *Istitutioni harmoniche* that deals with modes (Book IV) actively works to keep all these very differ-

---

24. See, for example, Edward Lowinsky, *Tonality and Atonality in Sixteenth-Century Music* (Berkeley and Los Angeles: University of California Press), 1962, and Carl Dahlhaus, *Studies on the Origin of Harmonic Tonality,* trans. Robert Gjerdingen (Princeton: Princeton University Press, 1990). Rather than cluttering my exposition with disciplinary debates, I will return to the relevant literature in Chapter 9.

25. Gioseffo Zarlino, *Istitutioni harmoniche* (Venice: 1573; facsimile ed., Gregg Press, 1966).

ent agendas braided together: thus, he appeals to Ancients such as Ptolemy for support of his statements, even as he seeks to explain the music of his own Venetian mentor, Adrian Willaert. Modern scholars rightly despair of Zarlino's universalizing obfuscation of the vast differences between theories borrowed from Greek sources (some of them ostentatiously quoted in Greek) and those appropriate for musical repertories of the High Renaissance. Furthermore, no one would deny that the music of sixteenth-century Italy resembles that of the tonal era far more than it does that of mythologized Dorians and Phrygians. Hence, the sixteenth-century pretense that its composers were reconstituting the musical practices of Hellenic civilization deserves much of the scorn it receives.

But we have too often read Zarlino as a committed antiquarian rather than as the reigning authority on music of his own time who brings in the trappings of classical learning for show and cultural prestige. The fact that he leads off with so much dirty bathwater does not justify throwing out the baby itself, for what Zarlino has to say about mode as a structuring principle provides greater insight into sixteenth-century Italian repertories than does any other source available—not because this music works the same way as does Greek song or liturgical chant (obviously it does not), but because Zarlino constructs his theories with the express purpose of dealing with the most up-to-date practices. In point of fact, his model does not necessarily even help us with much music of the fifteenth century, composed largely without this reworking of mode as part of the precompositional conceptual framework.[26] But beginning with Johannes Tinctoris, who states quite off-handedly and without much further explanation that mode also applies to polyphony, a series of intellectuals—including most prominently Pietro Aron and Heinrich Glareanus, in addition to Zarlino— grappled with formulating theories of modal polyphonic practice.[27] Sub-

26. See, however, Leeman L. Perkins, "Modal Species and Mixtures in a Fifteenth-Century Chanson Repertory," in *Modality in the Music of the Fourteenth and Fifteenth Centuries,* ed. Ursula Günther, Ludwig Finscher, and Jeffrey Dean, Musicological Studies and Documents 49 (Neuhausen-Stuttgart: Hänssler-Verlag, 1996), and "Modal Strategies in Okeghem's Missa Cuiusvis Toni," *Music Theory and the Exploration of the Past,* ed. Christopher Hatch and David W. Bernstein (Chicago: University of Chicago Press, 1993).

27. Johannes Tinctoris, *Liber de natura et proprietate tonorum* (1476); Pietro Aron, *Trattato della natura e cognitione di tutti gli tuoni di canto figurato* (Venice: 1525; partial translation in Strunk, *Source Readings*); Heinrich Glareanus, *Dodecachordon* (Basle: 1547; trans. Clement A. Miller, Musicological Studies and Documents 6, 1965). See my Chapter 9 for a more extensive discussion of modal theory in history and practice.

sequent musicians learned their craft in part by studying such texts, which predisposed them to conceive of their compositional strategies in precisely these terms.

In other words, the sixteenth-century repertory manifests a kind of self-conscious *neo*modality—not the modality of plainsong (let alone that of Greek antiquity!), yet nevertheless a practice that reinhabits and reanimates some of those old and still-prestigious structures of the past for its own purposes. More recent episodes of neomodality—for instance, those of avant-garde jazz or thrash metal—attest to the ways in which those old bottles can serve to ferment entirely new (if quite unlikely) wines,[28] and High Renaissance polyphony counts as another such moment. But just as George Russell and Metallica turned to modes for reasons having little to do with antiquarian authenticity (though the prior existence of ready-made categories such as Lydian and Phrygian helped legitimate and propel their experiments), so too the musicians of the sixteenth century found in these old structures something that appealed to and deeply influenced their own cultural practices. Recall that much of the music of the earlier part of the sixteenth century—the frottolas and dances that enjoyed considerable popularity in northern Italian courts of that time—actually comes much closer to behaving in ways we now call "tonal" than does the more complex music of several subsequent generations. Thus, instead of regarding the music of the sixteenth century as a series of successive attempts to evolve out of modality toward something else, it makes greater sense to see it as a period that deliberately revived, refashioned, and reveled in mode.

J. L. Austin transformed permanently the philosophy of language with his *How to Do Things with Words*, which directed inquiry away from the ontological and toward the performative.[29] So long as we imagine a static entity called "mode" and ask whether or not the Greeks, the early church, Palestrina, John Coltrane, and Megadeth all abide by it in the same ways, the clear answer is: of course not! But although modes do not remain static throughout their various manifestations in Western culture, the very fact

28. For jazz, see George Russell, *Lydian Chromatic Concept of Tonal Organization* (New York: Concept Publishing,1953). I once had the opportunity to hear Russell explain his brilliant ideas of how the Lydian fourth degree freed bop from the imperatives of the tritone that drive tonality. For metal, see Robert Walser, *Running with the Devil: Power, Gender, and Madness in Heavy Metal Music* (Hanover, NH: Wesleyan University Press, 1992).

29. J. L. Austin, *How to Do Things with Words,* 2nd ed. (Cambridge: Harvard University Press, 1975).

that this set of time-honored categories exists has inspired and sustained an unending stream of new possibilities. Thus, we should alter our question and ask instead: What did musicians in the 1500s actually *do* with modes? Why did modes appeal to composers of this particular moment? How did modes (albeit in a very new manifestation) underwrite and facilitate the musical strategies of the time?

Over the course of this book, I will demonstrate how sixteenth-century composers deployed modes in the service of a new cultural agenda that sought to perform dynamic representations of complex subjective states. For the first time in European history, musicians strove deliberately and explicitly to simulate in their work such features of human experience as emotions, bodies, sexual desire, and pleasure. This is not to suggest that earlier music never engaged with such matters: the music of Machaut or Josquin provoke powerful affective reactions in listeners, and the stimulation of such reactions had to have been part of their artistic purpose. Yet most earlier musicians did not appear to have had representations of interiority as their primary goal. Beginning with the madrigal, however, the performance of subjectivity moved to the fore as the dominant and self-consciously acknowledged project.

Stephen Greenblatt, in his important book *Renaissance Self-Fashioning*, demonstrates the ways in which this agenda operated in English literature of the time.[30] It so happens that the moment at which music entered into the representation of what Greenblatt calls "inwardness" was also a moment that regarded inwardness not as a simple phenomenon innocent of the contradictions of modern life but as always already ambivalent and self-divided. The systematization of modality in the sixteenth century became the technology that allowed for the simulations of such conflicted conceptions of Selfhood in sound.

Moreover, inasmuch as these pieces highlight the fundamentally unstable status of the Self, they produce images of "modal"—that is, always provisional—subjectivities, which is why they do not translate easily into the imperative sense of centered subjectivity that grounds eighteenth-century tonality ideologically. Indeed, we might even fail to recognize their configurations as relating to subjectivity. In his *Aesthetic Theory*, for instance, Theodor Adorno grants subjective consciousness to the Hellenic Greeks

---

30. Greenblatt, *Renaissance Self-Fashioning* (see again n. 17).

and to Renaissance sculptors, but he ascribes this attribute to music starting only with Bach.[31]

After a recent talk, in which I had discussed the considerable expressive range in the music of Hildegard von Bingen, I was asked by a nonspecialist whether I would characterize her music as "happy" or "sad." The question took me aback for a moment, but like all good questions, this one stimulated far more than the simple information requested. Of course, the "happy/ sad" dichotomy does not even adequately serve the needs of the tonal music within which it developed: the idea of reducing any given movement to one or the other of these alternatives has driven many critics to advocate the banning of adjectival description altogether. Yet the major/minor polarity of standardized tonality does often operate to reinforce something of this pair of options—especially in pieces by composers such as Schubert that depend heavily on fluctuating mediants for their meanings.

But the binary opposition between major and minor fails to engage effectively at all with earlier repertories, not because these musics lack expressive dimensions, but because their expressivity is conceived up against a grid offering at least eight and sometimes twelve possible categories—or subjective modalities. In other words, we cannot interpret this music through the dualisms that orient the emotional landscape of so much later music, for the technologies underlying modal composition presuppose a much broader range of possible expressive grammars. Just as (according to linguistic mythology) the Arctic languages that possess dozens of words for *snow* cannot find equivalents in English, so the affective qualities of the various modes correspond to no readily identifiable types in later music. The implications of this untranslatability not only involve musical procedure but also bear witness to significantly different structures of feeling. By pointing to alternative ways of experiencing affect than the ones we often assume, they also may lead us to interrogate the reasons behind the radical reduction of this more multifaceted emotional syntax to one with two principal options: major (positive) and minor (negative).

I will not set out here an elaborate theory of modal practice; instead, I will present only the minimal amount of information necessary for understanding

31. Theodor Adorno, *Aesthetic Theory* (1970), trans. and ed. Robert Hullot-Kentor (Minneapolis: University of Minnesota Press, 1997).

the compositions that I examine over the course of this book, providing more detail for specific pieces as needed. The brief expositions offered by most theorists of the sixteenth century prove ample, for they aim only to delineate the basic framework within which to comprehend the enormous variety of strategies available within this practice; they opt for a deliberately baggy concept that lends itself to an infinite number of possible arrangements. I will concentrate for most of *Modal Subjectivities* on the strategies exemplified by a series of madrigals, though those seeking a more detailed discussion of sixteenth-century sources and present-day debates may consult the final chapter. For purposes of the book, I will assume the following general guidelines:

1. Modes are *not* the same as scales. Modern misunderstandings concerning this practice in sixteenth-century music stem in part from our misconceived notion that modal identity requires scalar purity, that accidentals testify to the inadequacy of the system and thus point toward the dissolution of mode and the inevitability of tonality. But most sixteenth-century accidentals no more weaken modal identities than they do in their corresponding places in tonality; it's just that we have internalized a wide range of extensions, loopholes, and techniques for explaining departures from scalar purity in tonal pieces. We must extend the same courtesy to the Renaissance repertory, instead of defining mode by means of the narrowest possible criteria (criteria not ratified, incidentally, by theorists of the time) and then seizing onto accidentals as evidence of the modal system's increasing incoherence and impending demise. Indeed, as we will see, accidentals in the madrigal more often than not operate to distinguish one mode from another and thus to consolidate identity.

2. Modes involve the melodic and structural projection of a particular · species of octave (diapason), fifth (diapente), and fourth (diatessaron) throughout a composition. (I make use of Aeolian for these examples because it is the mode within which Monteverdi's "Ah, dolente partita"— the example for this chapter—operates.) The boundaries of the species usually emerge as the most frequent sites for cadences. Moreover, they define the grammatical implications—that is, the relative degree of tension and repose, the sense of direction—of each pitch in the principal melodies and imitative motives (Fig. 2).

3. The syntax of sixteenth-century modal music is primarily horizontal, presented through the melodic patterns of the surface. The clearest pro-

FIGURE 2. Aeolian species

FIGURE 3. Diapente descent

final

FIGURE 4. Harmonizations of diapente

Passamezzo antico   Romanesca

gression available involves the stepwise descent from the fifth degree to the final (designated in my schematic examples with a double whole note) (Fig. 3). Harmonization matters: for instance, a melodic cadence may be confirmed or frustrated by the extent to which the other voices concur with its primary implication. But it functions as a secondary, inflectionary parameter; the example in Figure 4, for instance, presents two standardized harmonizations—known respectively as the Passamezzo antico and the Romanesca—of this fundamental progression. This principle proves true even in relatively diatonic passages with the most obvious harmonies, which frequently end up sounding very much "tonal" to our modern ears but for which linear explanations provide more reliable accounts. Otherwise, we end up with patchwork analyses that posit tonal islands surrounded by seas of incoherence, instead of consistent interpretations of strategic choices within a single practice.

4. The diapente (or fifth) underwrites the most stable sections of a composition, and its pitches usually remain unchanged. Especially crucial to identity are the boundary pitches and the third degree (the mediant)— the pitch that determines major or minor quality. Chromatic inflections may occur for the sake of leading tones to secondary-area cadences (for instance, in Aeolian, a cadence on the fourth degree, D, will de-

mand a temporary C♯), but such inflections are regarded literally as "accidental"; they may even remain unnotated, though assumed by *musica ficta*—a performance practice that allowed for and sometimes even required such pitches but that did not clutter up the score with theoretically "irrational" pitches. Otherwise, the pitches of the diapente cannot be bent chromatically without disrupting modal certainty. (Note, however, that such disruptions often operate as the expressive crux of particular compositions.)

5. Within a stable section of a composition, the diatessaron (or fourth) often submits to considerable inflection *for the sake of enhancing modal identity.* Thus, both the sixth and seventh degrees in Aeolian will be raised to F♯ and G♯ at cadences to provide a heightened sense of direction (Fig. 5). Yet the actual diatonic pitches of the fourth become hardwired in at the structural level, where they may be altered only for the sake of temporary leading tones or for purposes of signaling irrationality. Consequently, the Aeolian modes differ from Dorian on the higher level of available secondary areas: while the inherently high sixth degree of the Dorian diatessaron facilitates authentic cadences onto the fifth degree (for which it serves as scale-degree $\hat{2}$), the low sixth degree of Aeolian does not for allow such cadences. In those cases in which an Aeolian sixth degree is inflected upward to F♯ to provide the second degree for an authentic cadence on E, the alteration counts as a significant violation and should be regarded as such (Fig. 6).[32]

6. The modal species may be arranged with either diapente or diatessaron on top, producing two possible systems. When the diapente and the modal final occur at the bottom of the range, theorists classify the mode as authentic; when the diapente occurs on top with the final in the middle of the range, they label it plagal (Fig. 7). Clearly, when the composition involves genuinely equal-voiced polyphony, some of the voices will occupy the plagal range and others the authentic. Theorists such as Zarlino recommend that composers and analysts privilege tenor and soprano above the other voices, and they assign mode accordingly. The

32. See, for instance, John Dowland's song "In darknesse," especially on the words "The walls of marble black." In his *L'Orfeo,* Monteverdi uses the F♯ in Aeolian contexts to manifest extreme grief.

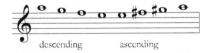

FIGURE 5. Diatessaron

descending   ascending

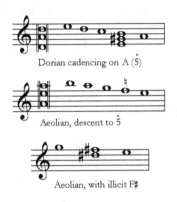

FIGURE 6. $\hat{5}$ in Dorian vs. Aeolian

Dorian cadencing on A ($\hat{5}$)

Aeolian, descent to $\hat{5}$

Aeolian, with illicit F♯

FIGURE 7. Authentic and plagal

authentic   plagal

very fact of the mixture complicates easy classification, of course. But music does not exist for the sake of mere pigeonholing, and we do better to ask why and how such strategies proved useful in the production of musical meaning at this time. As we will see in the analyses that follow, mixtures of this sort facilitate the articulation of internal conflict, making such complexities not a sign of theoretical weakness but rather a factor contributing to the richness of modal practice.

7. On the structural level, a composition may visit the same three or four pitches repeatedly for cadences, in contrast with tonal pieces, which typically follow a linear and nonredundant trajectory on the background. The recurrences of cadences on a few pitches do not, however, imply an arbitrary or primitive approach to structure. Quite the con-

trary: the tensions among cadence points operate to define the text-related allegories central to the strategies of individual pieces. In other words, the structure of each piece corresponds to a particular reading of its text and is tailor-made to dramatize its meanings. The extraordinary variety of modal designs could even be counted as evidence of *greater* formal sophistication within the sixteenth-century repertories than those of the eighteenth, in which most pieces delineate more or less the same background trajectory in their unfoldings. In contrast with what is often relegated to the status of the "purely formal" in standard tonality, the structural features of a modal piece function among the dimensions of the piece concerned most expressly with articulating idiosyncratic meanings.[33]

8. Sixteenth-century modal theorists differ greatly from one another mostly with regard to their respective numbering systems. The scholastics had maintained eight modal types: two each (authentic and plagal—the latter with the prefix *hypo-* to designate its arrangement) for D, E, F, and G, numbered one through eight. But as Pietro Aron discovered when he attempted to analyze contemporary practice, some compositions of the time also shape themselves around C and A as apparent finals. Glareanus and Zarlino solved that inconsistency by positing two extra modal pairs, respectively on C and A, that operated just like the others of the system except for their newly recognized finals. Alas, the two dodecachordans chose to locate their added categories in different arrangements: Glareanus started with A, then runs the gamut stepwise from C to G, while Zarlino decided to offer a more symmetrical, aesthetically pleasing series from C to A. Consequently, what a traditionalist would label as Mode 1 (authentic, with D as the final), Glareanus would label as Mode 5, and Zarlino would count as Mode 3. Although composers continue to title their pieces with respect to mode numbers (e.g., *Missa sexti toni*), these numbers become very confusing, given the competing systems—even though the theorists concur on most other matters concerning modal practice. Accordingly, I prefer to refer to modes by their traditional Greek names, which sidesteps the confusion over numbers: in other words, an authentic mode with D as the final

33. For an extended discussion of eighteenth-century tonality along these lines, see my *Conventional Wisdom: The Content of Musical Form* (Berkeley and Los Angeles: University of California Press, 2000), chap. 3.

FIGURE 8. Twelve modes

(Hypo)Dorian   (Hypo)Phrygian   (Hypo)Lydian   (Hypo)Mixolydian   (Hypo)Aeolian   (Hypo)Ionian

will count for me as Dorian (a label, incidentally, endorsed by Zarlino and others) (Fig. 8).

I do not wish to belabor the theoretical aspect of this study; indeed, it must seem strange that someone so associated with the critique of formalism would spend so much time discussing abstract syntactical matters. But in my studies of the tonal repertory, I have found it necessary to counter the exclusively structuralist accounts that characterize scholarship in those areas so as to introduce some consideration of content. The opposite situation obtains, however, in early and popular musics: most writers have been all too happy to deal only with what they term the "extramusical"—that is, lyrics, biographies, social contexts, and even encrypted references—with virtually no serious engagement with critical analysis. Thus, in order to pursue the same kinds of interpretations of these theoretically neglected repertories that I regularly offer of tonal pieces, I have to shore up the formal side this time. For my concerns have always centered on the interrelationship between form and content—on how structural procedures themselves contribute to the production of expressive and cultural meanings. The discussions of the madrigals that make up the larger part of this book require some amount of knowledge concerning the conventional practices within which they operate. As we shall see, the too-common habit of labeling chords in this music frequently obscures some of the most significant moments in a piece; it may even so misconstrue the basic framework of a piece as to prevent recognition of the fundamental tensions upon which its governing allegory relies. I am not, in other words, insisting on this theoretical sidetrack for the sake of historical pedantry, nor am I casting sixteenth-century pieces as mere examples in the service of an analytical project. Yet we do need a sufficient grasp of the theoretical principles underlying this music if we are to have access into the cultural work performed by each piece.

And I can best demonstrate the efficacy of the guidelines just presented by turning to the music itself. The remainder of this chapter deals, consequently, with the madrigal that opened this chapter: Monteverdi's "Ah, dolente partita."

AH, DOLENTE PARTITA

For his musical setting of Mirtillo's lament (Book IV, 1603), Monteverdi chose the Aeolian mode: a mode that offers even in the abstract certain formal predispositions that the composer perceived as parallel to Mirtillo's condition. We often assume that Aeolian operates much as tonal minor does, in that its scale—including even the location of its sixth degree a half step above the fifth—is exactly the same. But scale does not equal mode; as we saw above, mode also entails a whole package of melodic tendencies, structural demands, and probable ambiguities that convert mere scalar properties into dynamic potentialities.

Like all modes, Aeolian features an octave (A to A) divided into a species of fifth (the diapente, A to E) and of fourth (the diatessaron, E to A). The boundary pitches of these species should appear in prominent positions— at cadences, as principal melodic points—if the mode is to maintain its identity. A glance at the motives in the first half of "Ah, dolente partita" (see again Fig. 1) confirms that the composer complies with this basic criterion of modal propriety.[34]

But Aeolian also brings with its pitch arrangement certain idiosyncrasies, the most critical of which involves the relative weakness of its fifth degree. Whereas the fifth degree in Dorian often threatens to usurp the authority of the final, that same boundary pitch in Aeolian cannot establish itself through temporary finalization: the F♯ needed for a cadential confirmation of E does not occur within the system. By contrast, Dorian has access to both versions of its sixth degree, in that the higher one (the one responsible for tonicizing the fifth degree) exists within its species, while the lower one may be annexed through principles of *musica ficta*. We learn to wink at these "fictional" pitches, to regard them as not *truly* there, even as they perform undeniably important functions; leading tones both count and don't count because of this "just kidding" status. But although *musica ficta* freely grants Aeolian any number of chromatic leading tones, it cannot legitimately supply the F♯ needed as second degree to E.

---

34. Monteverdi alludes in some of his motives to Giaches de Wert's setting of the same text, though their concepts—including choice of mode and all that implies—differ radically from one another.

FIGURE 9. Emphasis of $\hat{5}$

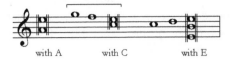

FIGURE 10. Alternative divisions of A octave

final on A   final on D

This difference—which only emerges as significant at the structural level—accounts largely for the affective distinctions between Dorian and Aeolian. For lacking the gravitational pull in Dorian toward the fifth degree, Aeolian can assert that boundary pitch only with considerable difficulty: as part of a stable Aeolian configuration; as part of the area on the third degree, C; or as an unstable half cadence, arrived at by equivocal Phrygian movement. It can never shore itself up as a temporary region in and of itself (Fig. 9).

What Aeolian offers instead is a tendency (also available, incidentally, in Dorian) to divide its octave at the fourth degree (Fig. 10). Depending on context and harmonization, the Aeolian fifth degree, E, may sound as though it is poised to confirm D as the stronger pitch. And because D lies to the flat (i.e., less dynamic) side of the Aeolian center, this propensity to collapse over onto the fourth degree lends a quality of passivity to many Aeolian pieces—passivity answered with an uphill struggle to reassert E as the proper boundary pitch, however limited its systemic resources to do so.

Here we may begin to appreciate the relevance of Aeolian to poor Mirtillo's inner turmoil. He never musters the energy to take action (as an aggressive move to the fifth degree might register, making Dorian the preferred mode for recriminations) but rather draws the conflict down within himself. He wills himself dead (often on D) yet ends up somehow always in the same position: that is, with his whiny, ambivalent E, confirming his ineffectual identity even as it always seems ready to collapse in keeping with his death wish. In other words, Aeolian already maps out in its formal predispositions an analogue to Mirtillo's psychological state (as we shall see in Chapter 8, Amarilli's psychology turns out to be far more complex than Mirtillo's—or at least it is so in Monteverdi's hands).

When introducing the various components of Mirtillo's simultaneous yet contradictory feelings, Monteverdi follows Guarini's sequence. One could even envision a monodic setting of the text for solo voice, in which the reactions succeed each other in linear, speechlike fashion: Monteverdi does as much in his celebrated *Lamento d'Arianna*. But, as we saw at the beginning of this chapter, the five-voice idiom characteristic of the madrigal allows for the gradual layering of these sentiments. They can do so, however, only if the materials that initially make sense in horizontal arrangement can also accommodate themselves to vertical stacking.

As it happens, all the motives associated with the first lines of text feature some configuration of Aeolian's sore pitches, E and D, with F always ready to follow the lead of the others. As the new layers enter, the entire complex begins to waver back and forth between A and D orientations: a mere fictive C♯ can cause the even the most stable of Aeolian configurations to tilt dangerously toward octave division on D, whereas E (the rightful divisor) has nothing more in its arsenal for purposes of stabilizing itself than an equivocal half cadence (Fig. 11). Thus, the ambiguities of this section are not limited to just the incompatible vectors of the various motives; in addition, the superimposition of motives alters the syntactical implications of each, injecting self-doubt and slippage into even those ideas that seem completely clear at first glance. They come to affect—indeed, to *in*fect—each other to an extent only hinted at in Guarini's generating text.

The madrigal opens with two high voices singing a unison E, a pitch initially undefined with respect to mode—though stylistic probability would argue for a beginning on either final or fifth degree (see Ex. 1). Only on the last syllable of "dolente" do the voices start to distinguish themselves, as the canto moves to produce a painful half-step dissonance above the quinto— the sorrowful parting mentioned in the text. But Monteverdi's sorrowful parting extends itself through a suspension chain: if the quinto moves reluctantly down to relieve the tension, the canto (as if already regretting the separation) returns, only to find itself now dissonant with respect to its partner. At this point, the quinto leaps to the F previously occupied by the canto, but it finds there a lonely void. It writhes slowly around E (F-E-D-E) in belated imitation of the now-absent canto, striving in vain to restore the unity of the opening sonority. The music thus tracks the parting of the two would-be lovers, with their clinging hesitations, misunderstandings, failures to synchronize, and futile attempts at reconciliation. But it also de-

FIGURE 11. Combinations of E, D, and F

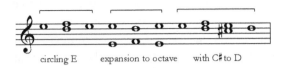

circling E   expansion to octave   with C♯ to D

picts Mirtillo's internal anguish, his feeling of being torn apart on the inside. The quality of being identical with himself, suggested by the unison E of the first measures, has disappeared, never again to be restored. Yet his condition of equanimity always was (at best) extremely tenuous, hovering as it did on that high, unsupported, undefined pitch.

While the quinto is twisting around E to complete its verbal phrase, the canto launches into the next line of text, "Ah, fin de la mia vita," with a gesture that plunges downward suddenly into the abyss—toward cadence or (given the words) toward death. Whereas the canto lands in a position of relative powerlessness (the opening E now reproduced at the octave below), the alto (a new voice) succeeds in tracing a linear descent to A: the final that would spell closure in Aeolian. But in contrast to the excruciatingly slow motion of the opening, this motive moves too quickly—more quickly, in fact, than the half-note pulse (or *tactus*) that marks the rate of actual progression. Because its pitches occur at the level of diminution or ornament, it counts technically as a throwaway, an exasperated and fruitless wish to escape the entire situation. Despite its impetuousness, it cannot break free from that tortured web of motives that continues on, quite oblivious to these attempts at bailing out. Mirtillo might as well will himself out of his own skin.

Still, "Ah, fin de la mia vita" does register as a motivic unit, and as the madrigal progresses, this gesture will repeatedly rip—even if impotently— against the exquisite languor of the other voices. Indeed, following its initial appearances in canto and alto, the canto and quinto take up the motive, elevate it to various pitch levels until they find one that guarantees at least the linear cadence on A in m. 15, bringing to a conclusion the first section of the piece.

Meantime, however, another idea has slipped in, disguised at first as a mere supporting bass. The motive on "Da te parto e non moro?" not only casts verbal doubt on the self-deluded attempts at cadence in the upper voices but also unravels their apparent progress: while the canto is plummeting down confidently to A, the bass reverses the action as it climbs inexorably from C back to the opening E. Monteverdi here masks skepticism as affirmation—a paradox only perceptible when the lower voices complete their motivic mission and fall silent right at the moment when they should, if they were *only* harmonic in conception, advance to solidify A. (Performance decisions make all the difference here: the bass and tenor must crescendo through their lines to the moment when they break off if they are to convey successfully their double-edged functions.) The sighing upper voices consequently arrive on their A without external corroboration; the cadence presents itself as a classic case of false consciousness.

But Monteverdi *does,* of course, supply an A to greet and support (at least provisionally) the canto's conclusion: the tenor enters with the missing pitch—if only to begin a concentrated passage on "Da te parto e non moro?" involving the three lower voices. Up to this point, the madrigal's ambiguities have centered on the fact of simultaneous yet contradictory impulses, but these impulses at least all point to A as final. And although none of the voices presents anything other than full-fledged motivic materials, certain of them have appeared more prominent with respect to modal definition, while the others seemingly acquiesce to the role of harmonic support.[35]

This slight comfort now evaporates as the three lower parts all trace exactly the same motive—that statement of incredulity, "Da te parto e non moro?"—at different pitch levels. At first, the alto might seem to qualify as the one with the "real" modal information; like the bass in the phrase just completed, it ascends from C to E: $\hat{3}$-$\hat{4}$-$\hat{5}$ in Aeolian. Moreover, it gets to present this material in the uppermost voice instead of getting buried in the mix. But then there's that worrisome bass, trailing behind and offering the same tune a fifth below—an odd harmonization of the alto's line, to say the least. If all three voices concur in their verbal sentiment, which now mounts in a veritable chorus of skepticism, together they instill syntactical unease. The first presentation of that skepticism in the bass brought us circling back to the opening position, but this rising tide of doubt in mm. 15–18 threatens to destabilize any clear sense of pitch orientation: it's not just that we return to the disappointment of the beginning, as did the bass

35. Note that mm. 9–10 have what appear to be clanging parallel fifths: one of the great taboos of sixteenth-century contrapuntal practice. The fact that the bottom pitches belong to different voices mollifies the situation only slightly. I would argue that Monteverdi deliberately plants this stark parallel progression in order to emphasize the descent to $\hat{4}$ in the reigning modal line.

in the previous phrase, but now the reliability of that anchor point is itself in question.

The dark-horse voice, the tenor that was threading its way along apparently as harmonic filler, suddenly takes control with its C♯ and follows through to D in m. 21, causing the entire complex suddenly to pivot disastrously. Even though the two upper voices have recommenced their opening gambit of "Ah, dolente partita," their once-secure boundary pitch, E, now registers as a second degree prepared to cadence on D. Indeed, all motives here find themselves twisted on their axes: the alto's E likewise reads as second degree, the bass's A sounds like a harmonic dominant that stops short of the implied resolution onto D. It is as if that growing realization of doubt fed on itself and led beyond mere rejection of the false closure of "Ah, fin de la mia vita" to an even greater horror—one that severely undermines Mirtillo's subjective center. Note that Guarini's lyrics convey none of this directly; we owe the psychologizing of this moment (which draws for its effect on the innate dynamics of the Aeolian mode) to Monteverdi. Thus, the apparent repetition of materials that begins in m. 18 is colored with a quality of panic: whereas the soprano voices originally luxuriated in their sweet torment, now they hang on to a quickly unraveling rationality, their D or F escape notes now spelling capitulation to the tenor's paranoiac *musica ficta*. Who could have guessed that the situation could become worse than that of the beginning? Mere unadulterated separation now sounds in retrospect like a picnic.

No sooner does the crisis break, however, than another motive enters with the words "E pur i' provo / La pena de la morte"—which lends verbal confirmation to precisely the sentiment already rendered so vividly by the swerve onto D that has just occurred. This motive jumps to the octave above the final and literally shrieks out in anguish on repeated, stabbing tones; if the alto part is sung by a man, it anticipates the quality of vocal strain heard when the tenor enters on the same pitch two measures later.[36] But the motive loses heart and ultimately droops back to the neutral E of the beginning. Indeed, its protest submerges itself into the mix that now includes all four other motives, as one reaction among many (yearning, resignation, incredulity) to the calamity at hand. The alto soldiers onward, stating the en-

36. In his long-definitive edition of Book IV (1927), Gian Francesco Malipiero marks this motive pianissimo, no doubt to pull this shriek back into the unbroken serenity expected of madrigals during his own day. It should, however, register as a shriek.

tire motive twice, but the tenor—following its first outburst—swallows its indignation, abjectly drops in register, and ends an octave below the actual bass voice. The alto maintains some sense of protest, but the tenor converts Guarini's line into a resentful whine.

Yet this motive has served some productive purpose syntactically, for its insistent A, coupled with the disappearance of C♯, gradually allows Aeolian to fade back in as the probable mode, confirmed with the cadence in m. 31. Although this cadence sounds stronger than the one in m. 15, it too has liabilities, most obviously the tenor's E that prepares the arrival in the three lower voices—the pitch that ought by right to lead to A but that emerges as a defeated termination, unable even to make the causal leap from dominant to tonic. The A in the bass that greets the sopranos' moment of closure merely initiates the next futile cycle.

This time the sorrowful parting occurs in the lower voices, while the sopranos take up the affects of incredulity and protest. The bass voice at first seems only to be supplying the final, A, to lend harmonic support the rest of the voices. But even this most reliable of functions—a sustained tonic in the bass—proves deceptive as its move to B♭ in m. 37 suddenly reveals our anchor pitch to be a double agent: all along, that A was actually serving as the fifth degree of D, and in collusion with the tenor's C♯, it leads to another arrival on D in m. 39. As before, the traumatic swerve to D triggers howls of protest, death wishes, and incredulity. And once again, the Aeolian mode gradually coalesces and manages a third halfhearted cadence in m. 47, this time with the soprano changing the usual conclusion (E) of the protest motive to the bitter confirmation of A. The lower voices refuse to participate in this arrival. Instead they embark on a series of short ruminations on the third and fourth motives, and in each case, the energy drains away in Phrygian approaches to E: the starting position Mirtillo can neither escape nor confirm as a viable alternative. The last of these approaches, which edges its way along through equivocal *fauxbourdon* voicing (parallel chords in first inversion), culminates in m. 56 with a sonority that even lacks a mediant, so empty is its arrival, so devoid of fervor its complaint.

A few words about the madrigal up to this point. Although it may seem that I have twisted and turned every pitch in these fifty-six measures, I have in fact omitted many that might well serve as the beginning of yet other readings. For Monteverdi presents here a process nearly as organic as any by a latter-day serialist, except that he has a commitment not only to the saturated integrity of his piece but also to the conventions that make it publicly intelligible. No voice in this first half sings a throwaway pitch or presents a line written for the mere sake of harmonic support or filler. At the same time, the simultaneous appearances in the five voices of mutually antagonistic affects, coupled with the ways in which they change their modal implications in context, produce a web of unwilling (though invariably consonant) fellow travelers.

Once these motives begin to interact, they generate whole chains of meanings that go far beyond Guarini's verbal blueprint to chart an interiority pulled not just between the pain of living and the impossibility of death, but also in directions not specified by the words. For instance, if the madrigal starts by suggesting allegorical links between E as unresolved agony and A as wished-for death, then what do all those swerves toward D signify? I have based my reading of these moments (which do not align themselves with any particular line of text but rather surge through the entire complex, capsizing the orientation of every single motive) on the modal dynamics themselves. The binarisms of Guarini's lyrics map fairly easily onto the A/E axis of basic Aeolian identity, to which Monteverdi then adds a third dimension. It is as if the cumulative pressure of these competing emotions pushes Mirtillo to the point where reason itself becomes unhinged, and he struggles not just between the poles of life and death, but also with an increasingly frayed sanity and a tendency to tip over into madness. In each case, the symptoms (C♯ or B♭ chromatic alterations) trigger a frantic pull back toward the proper boundaries of Aeolian. But the ease with which a single voice can veer over the edge and hence pollute the whole ensemble makes rationality particularly precarious. Although Guarini may hint at such ramifications, Monteverdi makes them fundamental elements of his structural logic.

Later music has conditioned us to situate ourselves according to sequences of verticalities or chords. Indeed, the great technological breakthrough of the early seventeenth century involved new notational conventions—figured bass—based on this conception. One may easily listen to "Ah, dolente partita" as a succession of chords, for the individual lines have been contrived in such a way as to yield perfectly consonant sonorities during their superimpositions. But this reduction eliminates much of the madrigal's effectiveness. Moreover, although these pieces were presented before select audiences, they were designed not only for spectators but also for the performers themselves. Each singer would have had a part book inscribing only a single vocal line, and each would have seen at a glance that her/his score made modal sense independent of the others; in fact, each singer might well have anticipated leading the ensemble as *the* mode-bearing voice. Only in performance would that part's susceptibility to the contrary impulses of the other voices have become manifest, as each singer experienced something of that unbidden and unanticipated log jam of emotions about which Mirtillo complains.

This multifaceted representation of conflicted interiority requires, in other words, the contributions of five separate performers; utterly private feelings come to voice only by virtue of this communal effort. Seventeenth-century musicians (though not our more recent *a cappella* pop groups) would soon balk at the artificiality of this construct and exchange this representational convention for the greater realism of the solo singer. But in doing so, they would sacrifice the capacity for paradox and troubled inwardness cultivated in the polyphonic madrigal. In effect, a culture focused on the hidden secrets of the inside will give way to one oriented toward the outward, theatrical display of the public figure. And while I would not want to decry the arrival of tonality (the conventions that emerged to sustain the semblance of rhetorical speech), I do insist that we acknowledge the heavy price paid for that change.

Meanwhile, back to Mirtillo, whom we left lying depleted on his open-E sonority. In Guarini's text, the next line—"E sento nel partire / Un vivace morire"—offers the flip side of the previous line ("E pur i' provo / La pena de la morte"). Monteverdi might well have superimposed these two lines, causing them literally to cancel each other out, but he has already played that card throughout the first section of the madrigal. Instead, he opts for a new strategy: a controlled, homophonic recitation that proceeds to a strong cadence on A in m. 61. Mirtillo seems to marshal his powers of reason and to pull himself from the morass of contradictory impulses in which he has wallowed thus far, as though he thinks that stating his dilemma calmly and succinctly will solve the problem. He puts his faith in logical discourse—or so Monteverdi suggests in this most speechlike passage of the madrigal.

But despite all the homophonic clarity of this passage, it harbors some very odd internal convolutions. In Monteverdi's setting, Mirtillo strives to hold the elements of effect and cause apart from each other; he calmly acknowledges his phenomenological state (OK, so I feel . . . a vivacious dying) while trying to bracket the memory of the separation that has thrown his world into havoc. Monteverdi achieves this double-level effect by tracing a linear descent from E to A, but embedding along the way a paren-

FIGURE 12. Expansion process

Romanesca

E sen - to nel par - ti - re   Un vi - va - ce mo - ri - re.

"Ah, dolente partita," mm. 56–61

thetical expansion of D, thus recalling the unforeseen difficulty of the first half. He isolates and even tonicizes briefly this treacherous pitch,[37] then steps gingerly around it and secures the cadence on A, almost as though Mirtillo is inoculating himself against the threat of further contagion.

What makes this detour possible is Monteverdi's use of most familiar improvisatory progression in sixteenth-century music, the Romanesca,[38] which allows the listener to keep track of the implied goal despite the balloon embedded along the way (Fig. 12). Of course, that balloon never sounds entirely innocuous. With the broken-off leading tone in m. 58, the floor

37. Monteverdi's intricate part writing marks this parenthetical effect. He leaves the C♯ by leaping down, thereby compromising its force as a leading tone to D. Within the parenthesis, the collection on D sports an edgy F♯, which suggests that it might return to the G of m. 57. Both these potential areas—D and G—are redefined as provisional, however, with the reappearance in m. 59 of the canto's D, which resumes the diapente descent and the principal thrust of the sentence.

38. Standardized harmonizations of the diapente descent, such as the Romanesca and the Passamezzo antico, count as the blues progressions of the Renaissance. Working musicians improvised thousands of dances and songs by means of these patterns, and they eventually became the background framework for common-practice tonality. I will take this topic up at much greater length in my *Power and Desire in Seventeenth-Century Music.* See also my discussions of tonality in *Conventional Wisdom* and "Constructions of Gender in Monteverdi's Dramatic Music," *Feminine Endings: Music, Gender, and Sexuality,* 2nd ed. (Minneapolis: University of Minnesota Press, 2002), chap. 2.

seems to drop out from under us, and we hover along with Mirtillo in that space of alienated suspense. But when in m. 61 the passage arrives (as promised) on A, the danger seems to have been successfully quarantined.

Alas, Mirtillo is simply in denial: he cannot arrest so easily the logic already set in motion over the course of the first section, and this crystalline presentation of Aeolian merely gives way to an identical presentation of the same materials transposed to D, all the more chilling for its apparent lucidity. At this point in the madrigal—the moment that presents its dilemma in its most condensed form, its *mise-en-abîme*—A has no greater claim over the meaning of events than its Other; both have acquired equal status, as sanity and insanity become indistinguishable, unreason speaks with the voice of reason itself.

As before, the swerve toward D precipitates a shriek of protest, this time in the highest soprano range and with the very words with which the lower parts are cadencing: "Un vivace morire." The motive purposely recalls the repeated stabbing A of "E pur i' provo," the motive that entered to counteract earlier moves to D. But whereas the earlier motive usually ended slumped on E (an Aeolian boundary pitch, even if not the strong conclusion desired), the soprano now dithers and finally confirms through linear descent in m. 68 the very D that had provoked the outburst. The problems the middle section purported to have untangled—simultaneous but incompatible utterances, modal identity—snarl up again, now more virulently than ever because of the false hopes raised by mm. 57–61. Thus, although the quinto and alto coax the soprano back to a reiteration of that descent, now to the "correct" pitch of A (m. 70), the damage is done: from here to the end, the madrigal will list back and forth between A and D orientations, granting both equal weight and authority. The pitch A, because it is common to both areas, cannot decide the matter, and without the possibility of shoring up E as a powerful counterbalance, the piece has difficulty asserting A as final instead of fifth degree. The foreign element introduced by Monteverdi in m. 19 is now so entangled with its host that it constitutes half of a permanently hybrid identity.

It remains only for the final phrase of Guarini's verse ("Per far che moia immortalmente il core") to specify what we already know from the musical process: Mirtillo is locked in a condition whereby he dies yet doesn't die—in perpetuity. This final motive returns to the intertwining yet irreconcilable serpentine lines of the opening measures. Whereas initially they performed the painful separation of the title, here they just flicker among those sore pitches (D-E-F), now favoring one interpretation, now the other;

they duplicate each other (as do Mirtillo and Amarilli) yet remain forever out of phase. Cadences punctuate the last section of the madrigal, but they mechanically alternate between confirmations of A and D. At last, as if to set the matter straight once and for all, the two top voices undertake an octave scalar descent from A to A, and a prolonged dominant preparation in the bass allows for an unequivocal arrival on A in m. 89. If only the floodtide could be stopped here! But the twisted logic of Mirtillo's subjectivity cannot halt; it continues on inexorably, as the tonic A in the bass now comes to function as a dominant preparation, prepared to cadence on D. The diapason descent from A to A recurs in the alto and tenor, but against voices that make the octave seem to divide at D rather than E.

How does one conclude such a piece? Can the composer satisfy both the integrity of the materials and the powerful rule that one must cadence within the mode? As we shall see in subsequent chapters, Monteverdi did not invent the solution he deploys here, but he uses it to great effect. He breaks the piece off on the stipulated A sonority, thus confirming the mode. But that sonority contains a C♯, which can be—indeed, given the context of this piece, *must* be—heard doubly: as the conventionally raised mediant in a final chord (the *tierce de Picardie*) or as the dominant of D, poised to resolve all the weight of the madrigal onto the rival final. By halting there, he produces a musical equivalent of Mirtillo's immortal undeath: a freeze-frame that stops while implying like an ellipsis that the flip-flop between A and D will go on forever.[39]

What Monteverdi accomplishes in this final gesture is very difficult to do within standard tonality, which creates its long-term structural effects at the expense of forgoing these sorts of ambiguities. Yet we do on occasion find this strategy resuscitated—most obviously in Bach's C♯-Minor Fugue from *WTC* I and in Beethoven's C♯-Minor String Quartet, Op. 131, and his "Moonlight" Sonata of the same key. Why did this Aeolian problematic come to be identified with C♯ minor?[40] That would be a different

39. Of course, performance matters enormously here. If the ensemble chooses to mark the arrival on A in m. 89 as a moment of genuine closure, followed by a plagal extension, we will hear the madrigal as having reached conventional resolution. But if the singers render the section starting in m. 89 as I have described it, they can produce an electrifying effect: one that both matches the burden of Guarini's text and counts as the payoff for Monteverdi's strategy over the course of the entire madrigal. In other words, we *can* hear this culminating ambiguity— but only if it has been made audible by the performers.

40. I have traced this key association back to a ricercar in C♯ minor by Johann Jacob Froberger, the final composition in his *Libro di capricci e ricercati* (c. 1658). This ricercar's theme

project. But it would require that we take mode rather more seriously than we have in the recent past.

Within the context of Guarini's play, Mirtillo would deliver his soliloquy passionately but within the codes of decorum appropriate to theatre. If he went through the spasms and conniptions of Monteverdi's score, he would look like an epileptic speaking in tongues. In retrospect, it is as though the Guarini's character can only put bland verbal labels on the warring affects Monteverdi causes to be heard and viscerally experienced.

Monteverdi has long received more than the lion's share of attention in madrigal studies. Many factors contribute to his prominence, including his fame among his contemporaries, his pivotal role in the change from sixteenth- to seventeenth-century cultural enterprises, and the ways in which his compositional priorities happen to coincide with those of later periods—especially, as we have just seen, his penchant for organic economy. We also often think of him as having progressive or radical qualities, in contrast with his lesser known predecessors. But as impressive as "Ah, dolente partita" unquestionably is, it does not really break new ground. Quite the contrary, it hearkens back in its contrapuntal density, allegories of inwardness, and willingness to operate strictly within the exigencies of his chosen mode to the music of, say, Adrian Willaert. He thereby brings to an aesthetically satisfying close the era of the madrigal.

But the radical edges reside elsewhere in the repertory. It was Monteverdi's forebears who opened up this arena of conflicted Selfhood for cultural elaboration and scrutiny, who defied the long-standing authority of Pythagoras, who developed musical analogues to the entire range of affects, who experimented with the graphic simulation of sexual experience. Monteverdi reaped the benefits of this heritage, but he did not invent its principles. And his relatively conservative reinhabiting of the madrigal even makes the genre appear tamer, more classically bounded in retrospect, than it actually was.

In this introduction, I hope to have whetted the reader's appetite for the kinds of things that can be done with mode: the conceptions of subjectivity that shaped its procedures, the ways its procedures informed represen-

---

bears a striking resemblance not only to Bach's C♯-Minor Fugue but also to the theme of his *Musical Offering*. Of course, tracing the problem back to Froberger only defers the question of why C♯ minor. I include a chapter on Froberger and his C♯ ricercar in *Power and Desire in Seventeenth-Century Music*.

tations of Selfhood. As the book proceeds, I also hope to encourage a sense of aesthetic connection between the contemporary listener/reader and the madrigal, for the tunes I discuss in *Modal Subjectivities* count among the great artworks of all time. Without question, an enormous gulf lies between us and the individuals who composed, sang, and first heard this music; no one survives to testify for them as we try to interpret their cultural artifacts. But to the extent that we still study, perform, and record these works, their meanings should matter to us, no less than do those of their contemporary Shakespeare. With the next chapter I will move back in history to the works of earlier practitioners, to those who first began exploring the possibility of revealing how emotions feel in music.

TWO

Night and Deceit

Verdelot's Machiavelli

It has become customary in musicology to situate the madrigal and music of the sixteenth century within a neoplatonic framework, with particular reliance on the Italian pythagorean Marsilio Ficino.[1] Within that framework, concepts undeniably crucial to Renaissance culture (for example, *harmonia*) dominate. As we will see in Chapter 8, these concepts rise explicitly to the surface in polemical debates over compositional propriety in the fin de siècle madrigal.

But a wide range of intellectual contexts coexisted in the sixteenth century, some complementary but others mutually antagonistic. For instance, this same period also nurtured Baldassare Castiglione's *Book of the Courtier* (1528), a self-help guide for those who would pass themselves off as members of the élite, and Niccolò Machiavelli's *The Prince* (1513), which marks the beginning of modern political theory. Whereas Ficino's neoplatonism exalts unities and resemblances as ideals, both Castiglione and Machiavelli actively encourage divisions between public demeanor and private intention, the consistent masking of feelings behind a carefully fashioned façade

---

1. For accounts grounded in Ficino, see particularly Gary Tomlinson, *Music in Renaissance Magic: Toward a Historiography of Others* (Chicago: University of Chicago Press, 1993), and *Metaphysical Song: An Essay on Opera* (Princeton: Princeton University Press, 1999), chap. 2.

of nonchalance or (as Castiglione terms it) *sprezzatura*. They advise those who would succeed in the world of political and social intrigue to play their cards close to the chest, to perfect a dualistic subjective construction based on a split between inside and outside.[2]

Although Castiglione and Machiavelli seek to influence external behaviors, they do not (except as they gesture toward some unruly essence that requires masking) deal with subjective "reality." The Italian madrigal, which develops in precisely these same hothouse environments, rushes into that vacuum by offering elaborate mock-ups of inwardness for public delectation. As we saw in the discussion of Monteverdi's "Ah, dolente partita" in Chapter 1, this genre revels in the simulation of complex inner feelings. Within the context of these pieces, individuals get to experience vicariously—and in public—the kinds of impulses they work so hard to keep under wraps; they can give voice to otherwise suppressed sentiments and still disavow them as nothing more than musical pastimes. As Castiglione himself writes, describing the interactions of skilled courtiers: "Using various means of concealment, those present revealed their thoughts in allegories."[3] Later on, several northern Italian courts will form cults around what they called *musica secreta,* concerts of avant-garde madrigals performed within an exclusive inner sanctum. Designed as mere entertainment, the madrigal involved the collusion of four or more singers in the social performance of hidden interiorities.

I begin my story of the madrigal with the peerlessly pragmatic Machiavelli, in part because his intellectual agenda resonates more satisfactorily than Ficino's with the kinds of divided subjectivities I perceive in this musical repertory. But a closer link exists as well: some of the first madrigals were composed for Machiavelli's 1526 production of his play *La Mandragola* (The Mandrake), among the most celebrated comedies in the Italian language. Those who know Machiavelli only from *Il Principe* and his other political treatises will easily recognize his imprint in this extraordinarily cynical work—a bedroom farce in which the clergy, the medical authorities, a woman's mother, and even the duped husband himself conspire in arrang-

2. For more on this side of the sixteenth century, see William J. Bouwsma, *The Waning of the Renaissance, 1550–1640* (New Haven: Yale University Press, 2000); Norbert Elias, *The Court Society,* trans. Edmund Jephcott (New York: Pantheon, 1983); and Jon Snyder, *Dissimulation and the Culture of Secrecy in Early Modern Europe* (Berkeley and Los Angeles: University of California Press, forthcoming).

3. Baldassare Castiglione, *The Book of the Courtier,* trans. George Bull (London: Penguin Books, 1976), 44.

ing an adulterous liaison between Lucrezia, a paragon of chastity, and Callimaco, her scheming suitor. Lust, self-interest, and ruthless strategy win out over every abstract virtue, as Callimaco finds a way to satisfy his desires with the full sanction of family, church, state, and, finally, even Lucrezia herself.

When the playwright revived his play of 1518 for a special performance in 1526, he added a canzona at the conclusion of each act. Musical settings of three of these survive, one attributed to and the others also probably written by Philippe Verdelot, the most prominent composer of lyric verse in Florence at the time.[4] Like Machiavelli and their Florentine colleague Michelangelo, Verdelot sympathized with the Republic, and he often found himself in the delicate position of negotiating between Medici and Republican partisans. The performance of *La Mandragola* in 1526—together with its new poetry and music—was dedicated to the Medici pope Clement VII;[5] it took place right on the cusp on political intrigue and turmoil.

A French musician who had brought with him to Florence his experience as a composer of motets, masses, and chansons, Verdelot figures among the earliest practitioners of the new genres of vernacular Italian music soon collectively known as madrigals.[6] From the French chanson (and perhaps also the Italian frottola) he borrowed homophonic text declamation, and from the sacred domain he lifted strategic uses of imitative counterpoint. With respect to style per se, he seems to have invented little to call his own but chiefly to have deployed in the service of a somewhat different music type the devices already developed by Josquin and his followers.

Yet Verdelot's ability to manipulate his musical materials (especially mode)

---

4. All three appear in the so-called Newberry Partbooks, edited without the missing alto by H. Colin Slim as *A Gift of Madrigals and Motets*, 2 vols. (Chicago: University of Chicago Press, 1972). Slim made use of corroborating sources, when they existed, for his alto parts; when no such sources existed, he composed them himself. When the alto part came to light some years later, Slim published the missing voice for those pieces for which he had supplied the missing voice himself. See his *Ten Altus Parts at Oscott College Sutton Coldfield* (n.p.: n.d.). My editions put together Slim's two versions, with the alto parts for the two Machiavelli pieces he had composed—"Chi non fa prova, Amore" and "Sì suave è l'inganno"—now joined with the parts from the Newberry Partbooks. "O dolce notte" already appeared intact in Slim's *A Gift* because of additional sources. For arguments for why these pieces may have resulted from a direct collaboration between Machiavelli and Verdelot, see Slim, *A Gift*, vol. 1, 92–104.

5. For the play and its history, see *Opere di Niccolò Machiavelli*, ed. Ezio Raimondi, 8th ed. (Milan: Ugo Mursia, 1983), 981–1289.

6. At the time Verdelot's music was compiled for the Newberry Partbooks, he and his contemporaries would still have differentiated madrigals from canzone on the basis of versification. For more on the generic distinctions, see Slim, *A Gift*, vol. 1, 81–5.

to produce internally divided structures of feeling rises admirably to the challenge of Machiavelli's morally ambivalent verse. He rarely indulges in the word-painting variety of expression we associate too indiscriminately with the madrigal genre as a whole; rather, he responds to his texts at the level of affect and allegory, thus establishing the terms I will pursue throughout this book. By starting my narrative with the Verdelot/Machiavelli collaboration, I want to emphasize the fact that the madrigal emerged at the same time and from the same crisis of subjectivity—the discrepancy between interiority (thought, feeling, desire, intention) and public behavior—that also spawned modern political theory.[7]

To be sure, Machiavelli's abstract verses do not purport to express any particular individual's subjectivity, unlike the madrigal texts examined in other chapters. Consequently, they may seem a bit out of place in a study that seeks to explore representations of Selfhood in Italian vernacular music. But Verdelot's settings of these canzone already engage the apparatus for simulating the divided subject: the very essence of the madrigalian project. For although Machiavelli does not designate a specific persona for his lyrics, Verdelot nonetheless simulates the structures of feeling identified with such ambivalence in his settings, which (conveniently for our purposes) lead us step by step through a succession from modal/moral certainty to a degree of ambiguity scarcely surpassed in the entire repertory. Neither poet nor composer indicates explicitly his target subject in the *Mandragola* canzone, in part because both of them strive to produce those uneasy ethical conditions inside us—their spectators and listeners.

Moreover, insofar as Verdelot exploits a still-vague conception of polyphonic mode, his compositions help to kick-start the project of modal theory: Pietro Aron's treatise on mode, which appeared at just this time (1525), puzzles over precisely the kinds of the modal dilemmas Verdelot offers in his settings of the canzone from *Mandragola*.[8] Music historians have tended to disregard sixteenth-century modal theory as irrelevant to its pretonal repertories, in part because so many aspects of these pieces—the simultaneous presence of authentic and plagal versions of modes, the "failure" of the compositions to orient themselves around clear pitch centers—sound

---

7. I wish to thank Andrew Berish for first bringing these compositions and the importance of the Machiavelli/Verdelot collaboration to my attention.

8. Pietro Aron, *Trattato della natura e cognitione di tutti gli tuoni di canto figurato* (1525). A partial translation appears in Oliver Strunk, *Source Readings in Music History*, rev. ed. (New York: Norton, 1998). See my Chapter 9 for a more extensive discussion.

incoherent to modern ears. But these very ambiguities became distinct advantages at Verdelot's cultural moment: mode provides the technical basis for simulating a Self internally divided and irreparably equivocal. If we like to identify the Renaissance with a sense of balance and reason, then the madrigal—with its intensive explorations of damaged subjectivities in the wake of Florentine civil disturbance and exile—qualifies right from the outset as a postlapsarian genre, always already obsessed with loss.[9]

CHI NON FA PROVA, AMORE

Mandragola does not start out in a murky, morally compromised position. Early on in the play, when the option of proper behavior still obtains, the playwright takes the opportunity afforded by his *entr'acte* to deliver a sermon on the perils of romantic love:

Chi non fa prova, Amore,
della tua gran possanza, indarno spera
di far mai fede vera
qual sia del cielo il più alto valore;
né sa come si vive, insieme, e muore,
come si segue il danno e 'l ben si fugge,
come s'ama se stesso
men d'altrui, come spesso
paur' e speme i cori agiaccia e strugge;
né sa come ugualmente uomini e dèi
paventan l'arme di che armato sei.

He who has not experienced, Love,
your great power, hopes vainly
truly to see
what is in heaven the highest good;
nor knows how at once one lives and dies.
how one seeks the bad and flees the good,
how one loves oneself
less than others, how often
fear and hope chill and destroy hearts;
nor knows how both humans and gods
fear the weapons with which you are armed.

9. See Bouwsma, *The Waning of the Renaissance.*

FIGURE 13. Dorian species

And Verdelot responds to Machiavelli's preachy text with corresponding modal bluntness; he elects to operate within the most stoic of modes, Dorian (see Ex. 2).

Indeed, the version of Dorian exploited for "Chi non fa prova, Amore" refuses even the multiple layers of ambiguity readily available within that modal type (see Chapter 9). In keeping with the didactic quality of Machiavelli's text, however, Verdelot restricts himself to emphatic hammering on the bald modal species; only the occasional—and fully licit—cadence on A, the upper boundary of the diapente, offers a modicum of variety. Just as the playwright seems to uphold the law in his extended warning, the composer abides strictly within the confines of traditional authority, with none of the equivocation that will make the subsequent canzone so disturbing with respect to affect (Fig. 13).

Wasting no time at all, Verdelot opens his setting with a direct diapente descent in the tenor, balanced by the ascent through the diatessaron in the canto.[10] Boom! As of m. 2, we're already locked into a world of ethical certainties, with absolutely no wiggle room. The composer matches each of Machiavelli's lines with powerful cadential confirmation—half arrivals for some of the lines that do not conclude sentences, full ones for most. Notice, for instance, the tenor's sweeping descent for the end of the first thought—"what is in heaven the highest good"—with a scalar descent through an extended octave (the F that also marks "gran" in m. 5) to the final a tenth below. Only twice in the entire piece—the cadences on "fugge"

10. Note that the canto operates within a plagal arrangement of the species, with the final in the middle of its range, in contrast with the tenor. More often than not, canto and tenor part share the same arrangement. I am following the tenor of "Chi non fa prova, Amore" as the principal mode-bearing voice in part because contemporaneous theorists advise us to do so but also because Verdelot locates most of his crucial syntactical moves within the tenor. Finally, Hypodorian (the canto's implied mode) more often appears transposed to G with B♭ in the key signature. The canto in this canzona does participate fully in the presentation of diapente descents, however.

(m. 22) and "strugge" (m. 30)—does Verdelot give us cadences briefly tonicizing the fifth degree, A: the first in the context of flight from the good (i.e., D), the second in the destruction that results from moral deviance (i.e., departure from D). When in his last two lines Machiavelli throws in his final pessimistic appraisal of the human ability to withstand Love's assaults, Verdelot waxes even more legalistic; he battens down the hatches, offering repeated, strongly harmonized diapente descents from there to the end.

If I were to encounter this piece in an anthology, separated out from the other *Mandragola* canzone, I might suspect that a relatively unimaginative composer had written "Chi non fa prova, Amore." After all, Machiavelli's verse holds out many opportunities for word reflection, and even law-abiding Dorian allows for much more variety than we get from this prudish musical setting. In fact, "Chi non fa prova, Amore" invites the description of "neutral" often given to Verdelot's style. In the context of the *Mandragola* series, however, it stands as an articulation of traditional values—ethical and musical—before we get sucked into the downward spiral of the subsequent acts. As we proceed through the play, this certainty (which surely sounds overblown and overemphatic, even here at the outset) drains away until we end up wallowing in the delicious and corrupt world of "O dolce notte."

SÌ SUAVE È L'INGANNO

The halfway point in the series follows Act III. Whereas the characters in *Mandragola* are still wrestling with the propriety of their ambitions and strategies when we encounter "Chi non prova, Amore," they are encouraged to embrace their moral turpitude in "Sì suave è l'inganno"—"How sweet is deceit!" Within the context of the play, they will eventually persuade themselves that even the cuckolded husband will benefit from their chicanery.

Sì suave è l'inganno
al fin condotto imaginato e caro,
ch'altrui spoglia d'affanno,
e dolce face ogni gustato amaro.
O rimedio alto e raro,
tu mostri il dritto calle all'alme erranti;
tu col tuo gran valore,
nel far beato altrui, fai ricco Amore;
tu vinci, sol co' tuoi consigli santi,
pietre, veneni e incanti.

FIGURE 14. A-process ending on E

How sweet is deceit
leading to a dear and imagined goal,
which lifts suffering from others,
and makes sweet every tasted bitterness.
O worthy and rare remedy,
you show the straight path to errant souls;
You, with your great prowess in making
another happy, make him rich, Love;
You defeat alone with your blessed counsel
stones, poisons and incantations.

In place of the powerful assertion of D-Dorian in the previous canzona, this one introduces us to what appears to be a mode based on A, though it will eventually end on E (Fig. 14). For the most part, "Sì suave è l'inganno" unfolds as though in a wholly consistent, "normal" A mode (albeit oriented around a final still untheorized and unauthorized at this time):[11] its cadences usually confirm A, its melodies adhere to species with A and E as boundaries. Indeed, the tenor's first two phrases (repeated immediately for phrases 3 and 4) dutifully wend their way between E and A, punctuated with a series of four cadences in a row on A (see Ex. 3).

At the same time, however, the canto merely circles equivocally around E, suggesting a Phrygian orientation. When it does finally deign to move, to participate in noncommittal cadences in mm. 9 and 18 (note the weak stepwise descents in the bass), the canto infuses those moments of would-be arrival with a tinge of disingenuousness. The degree of cynicism rises exponentially with the canto's inflections of the mediant (either through direct instructions in the partbooks or through the practices of *musica ficta*)

11. Aron would have labeled this piece as Phrygian in keeping with its conclusion, but also because he has no modal category with a final on A. He tells us in other instances—for situations in which judging from the final would suggest a nonexistent category—that we should assign mode on the basis of its unfolding, just as Aristotle advises us to judge a man's life from his deeds rather than his death. See also n. 13.

to C♯ at these cadences: a taunting "butter wouldn't melt in my mouth" quality emerges to heighten the masked bitterness referred to in Machiavelli's text. One thinks of those portraits of Machiavelli, with his cruel, thin-lipped smile.

A moment of apparent transcendence occurs in the setting of "O rimedio alto e raro" (m. 19), as though briefly we addressed the Holy Sacrament, recalling such popular Communion texts as "O admirabile commercium." But of course Machiavelli's appeal for succor is addressed to Deceit. As the text continues with its appeal for guidance along the right path, the canto suddenly makes explicit just which path is here under consideration: not the straight and narrow but a sudden plunge directly into the lowest rungs. For the first time, we get in mm. 22 and 26 unambiguous cadences on A in all voices.

But from that point to the end, the clarity that has prevailed thus far begins to fade away. When the canto plunges again to A in the lower depths in m. 32, it receives a D harmonization, in keeping with the tenor's decisive D-diapente descent. The penultimate line recalls in its salient details the canzona's opening (the canto warily circling around E, stepwise descent in the bass, a smiley-face C♯ at the cadence), and the last phrase hangs us up on a question mark: the canto's descent halts on E, and the other voices find themselves unable to pull away toward their usual A habitat. Instead, they sustain Phrygian, at which the canto had hinted since the outset.

The transparency of the musical syntax in "Sì suave è l'inganno" before its final gambit should beguile us into accepting Machiavelli's verbal arguments. Only with the explicitly Phrygian twist at the end does Verdelot deny us the security and comfort he had proffered up until then. This secular motet in praise of deceit finally throws the moral dilemma into the listener's lap. We can hear the last sonority as a dominant preparation for A that never gets fulfilled or as unmasking the deceptive, duplicitous harmonization of an entire piece that had operated surreptitiously within Phrygian all the way along but that only revealed its true nature at the very end. Yet whichever interpretation one chooses, nothing gets resolved. The sweetness of deceit lingers on.

O DOLCE NOTTE

But it is "O dolce notte," the canzona that appears at the conclusion of *Mandragola*'s fourth act, that truly ushers us into the subjective world that madrigals will continue to plumb. The machinations of Machiavelli's plot have worked to put Lucrezia, the virtuous wife, in bed with Callimaco, our conniver who has managed to win the support of the entire community for his enterprise. When Act V begins, the night has passed, and we soon learn of the unalloyed success of Callimaco's nefarious scheme. The canzona serves the purpose of invoking the moment's ambivalent ethical situation: yes, the triumph of romantic love, but at the expense of every criterion of human decency. We may cheer the exploits of Machiavelli's hero (indeed, the lyrics out of context seem but a standard celebration of Eros), but Verdelot's noncommittal musical strategies, which respond far more strongly to the implicit irony of Machiavelli's text, refuse to give us the pleasures of certainty. Instead, he suspends his listeners between bliss and wrenching doubt, between teleological clarity and the obscurity that attends both "night" and (in the canzona just discussed) "deceit."

O dolce notte, o sante
ore notturne e quete,
ch' i disiosi amanti accompagnate;
in voi s'adunan tante
letizie, onde voi siete
sole cagion di far l'alme beate.
Voi, giusti premii date
all'amorose schiere, a voi amiche,
delle lunghe fatiche;
voi fate, o felici ore,
ogni gelato petto arder d'amore.

O sweet night, O blessed
nocturnal and quiet hours
that wait on ardent lovers;
in you are joined so many
delights, from which you
alone make souls happy.
You bestow just gifts
upon companies of lovers, your friends,
deserved by long trials;
you make, O happy hours,
every chilled breast burn with love.

Verdelot's setting begins—and ends—on a radiant A-major triad (see Ex. 4). But no such mode existed at the time, of course, making it improbable that this can qualify as an unequivocal center. Complicating the

FIGURE 15. Hypophrygian

FIGURE 15. Hypophrygian

Hypophrygian on E   Hypophrygian on A

situation even more is the key signature of one flat, which informs the eye that A *major* can never stand as a reliably stable point of reference. Moreover, the very first harmonic shift, in which both canto and bass creep up by half step before returning to their starting positions, renders this internally uncomfortable configuration fully audible. Whatever we make of this unsettling opening, we're clearly not in Kansas anymore.

Leaving aside for the moment the C♯ of the first sonority, the most obvious modal designation would seem to be Hypophrygian, transposed up a fourth to A by means of the B♭ key signature (Fig. 15). The bass's initial movement of A-B♭-A—a configuration that echoes repeatedly in all voices over the course of the madrigal—makes this the likely choice. But the C♯ puts a kind of torque on this always-unpredictable modal type: as the B♭ pulls downward, the C♯ strains upward.[12]

Part of this confusion is endemic to the Phrygian/Hypophrygian pair, which does not have its own consistent syntax: its flat second degree above the final does not allow for the authentic (i.e., V-I) cadences available for purposes of definition within all the other modes. As a consequence, Hypophrygian pieces typically alternate between hovering paralyzed on their home base (as does the first line of "O dolce notte") or seeking refuge within the syntax of borrowed or subordinate species, most commonly, the area on the fourth degree (D in this case). The final, A, remains constant in both these areas, but the octave itself (bounded by E in transposed Hypophrygian) slips downward, and it takes a formidable effort to shore up the proper species in such a way as to make them sound convincing. In fact, the dia-

---

12. Several recent popular songs have exploited this same bizarre configuration. Robert Walser has observed, for instance, that Alanis Morissette's "Uninvited" operates within a Phrygian context with a major tonic triad and thereby produces something of this same strange effect as "O dolce notte." Some examples of this pattern seem to refer to the descending tetrachord of flamenco, which arrives at its final sonority—a major triad—through a half-step descent. Most such songs (including Morissette's "Uninvited") have exoticist resonances. Verdelot's canzona has no such leanings. My thanks to Rob for this comparison.

FIGURE 16. A-Hypophrygian with D subregion

FIGURE 17. D mode with B♭, ending on A

pente boundary, E, usually sounds in this canzona as though it is functioning as a second degree, poised to resolve to D (Fig. 16). Given the preponderance of internal cadences on D (and on F, the alter ego of D) in "O dolce notte," we might well be tempted to interpret D as the final, with the termination on A as a conclusion on the fifth degree of a D mode (Fig. 17). In that case, we could hear the enigmatic initial sonority—that A-major triad—as a precadential dominant of D, the top voice announcing its urgent desire to resolve to D right at the outset with that signed-in C♯ leading tone. But this would qualify as an unusual opening, even if D were the designated final.[13]

Verdelot's madrigal was not waiting for analysts to put it in its proper pigeonhole, however, nor is it the product of inchoate musical procedures. Rather, "O dolce notte" makes its home quite deliberately within this exquisite cluster of tensions that refuses for strategic reasons to disclose a definitive identity. Many of his ambiguities revolve around that slippery A-B♭-A melodic configuration, which focuses the attention directly on the Phrygian problem. Yet despite the ubiquity of this characteristic figure, Verdelot offers a wide range of harmonic interpretations, none of which can finally

---

13. I hesitate to give this D mode a name. Pietro Aron would have labeled it as Dorian, despite the flat in the signature, because the alternative—that this is Aeolian transposed to D—was not available to him. Accordingly, Aron decides that such compositions are probably just D-mode pieces after all, even though (never mind!) they have a signed-in B♭. This theoretical inconsistency—around which Aron tap-dances and waves his hands, clearly wishing it would just go away—attracts the attention of his successors like sharks scenting blood. More than any other snag, this one seems to have compelled the expansion of the system to include modes on C and A.

FIGURE 18. Harmonizations of A-B♭-A

ground it (Fig. 18). It is by means of those conceptual ambiguities that Verdelot manages to create his queasy opening configuration, which is still unwilling to divulge its intentions even with its last sonority.

"O dolce notte" begins already painted into a corner, poised either to conclude on D or just to extend the edgy suspended animation of A-Hypophrygian (exacerbated here with that raised mediant). If we regard the complex as pointing toward D, then the tenor and canto both appear in precadential guise (the tenor alternates between 2 and the final, the canto slips up to tap the final from the leading tone), while the bass moves deceptively from A to B♭ and back; only the alto provides a modicum of mobility. But all voices end up right back where they began, and the second phrase starts off just like the first.

Verdelot offers some relief as he moves on the word "quete" past the impasse to a far more congenial move through D (implied in some of the vocal contours) to F: the bottom voice seems to accept its conventional role as harmonic bass as B♭ drops to F in m. 6, and the canto leaves its edgy perch to descend through B♭ to A, which now operates as a sweet, wistful mediant. If the provisional cadence on F in m. 7 is not quite what we expected from the opening A-major sonority, it presents us with a far more manageable context—a context that allows room for maneuver after the dense, obscure constriction of the first four measures.

For a while (up through m. 16), Verdelot allows us to luxuriate in F: a sustained moment redolent of shared desire, unimpeded motion, and apparent fulfillment—except that it refuses any of the places foreshadowed by the opening gambit (though A and B♭ continue to resonate throughout the F area here prolonged). Night may accommodate such activities as love, along with its more mundane functions, but it still holds itself aloof, as mysterious and impenetrable as ever.

The paean to night continues to assert F until the canzona reaches its midpoint phrase, "Sole cagion di far l'alme beate." And here Verdelot sneaks us back into that opening enigma: an A-major triad, now positioned so as to sound like a half cadence on D. An apparent attempt at solidifying D in the following phrases leads instead to an emphasis of D's secondary area on G: these long ordeals and fatigue lead to a half cadence—deceptive "happy hours," to be sure, though the point of arrival on V/G only gives us yet another harmonization of the A-B♭-A figure that haunts the canzona.

In its setting of the final line of text, the tenor presents as clear a Hypophrygian melodic line as we have heard. But its characteristic twists around A and B♭ are harmonized by the alto and bass in a rigid *fauxbourdon* ("a frozen heart"), before breaking open onto D, with the tenor stranded in the middle on A. And when the canto repeats the tenor's line, the harmonizations point in every conceivable direction: if someone were to supply an F♯ underneath the canto's last pitch in m. 38, we would hear it as V/G; the inner voices seem, however, to be concerned with establishing D through their melodic and harmonic shapes, and all the while the canto refuses to budge from its A. Eventually the whole complex subsides to accommodate the canto's A—but in what capacity? The final gasp of the tenor, with his cramped diminished fourth from F to C♯, and the alto especially want to align themselves with D. But the canto's Hypophrygian conclusion casts an aura of mystery over the coda, which ends on the same ambiguous sonority that opened the piece.

In an important sense, Verdelot's madrigal offers us Night as a nocturnal arch consisting of A-B♭-A, which may be interpreted and made to accommodate any number of worlds (A, D, F, G), but which never yields fully to any one of them.[14] Machiavelli's words for this canzona appear only to praise night as an opportunity for love and repose, even if his dark comedy calls "love" very much into question. Through his modal machinations, however, Verdelot manages to bring to the ear the ironies of Machiavelli's plot, with its cynical eroding of the ideals associated in conventional verse with romance and human integrity. Yet his musical setting is gorgeous in its equivocations. He seduces us sensually into the trap Machiavelli has contrived not only for Lucrezia but also for us.

"O dolce notte" ends with a coda that waffles back and forth between the pitch that will serve as its ultimate bass pitch (A) and the pitch a fifth below (D). I am reluctant, however, to describe this as an alternation between tonic and subdominant. Not because of the anachronistic tonal

---

14. I am reminded strategically here of *Prélude à l'après-midi d'un faune*, in which Debussy harmonizes the opening flute chromatic line in a variety of ways, none of which manages to rationalize or defuse the mystery of the faun's erotic leitmotiv.

vocabulary—other pieces by Verdelot (for instance, "Italia mia," discussed below) situate this alternation in such a way as to invoke tonic and sub-dominant in all but theoretical terminology—but because this madrigal never has really decided which pitch counts as its center. Accordingly, this alternation at the conclusion just keeps taunting us, fanning the coals of ambivalence all the way to the end, with the suggestion of infinite itera-tions. "O dolce notte" begins balanced as though on the blade of a knife. It might pivot to one side or the other, exploring more normative solutions before rejecting them one after the other as not viable. But end it must, still balanced precariously on that same knife blade from which it first started.

Of course, this sequence of events—from a securely centered and pontificat-ing D-Dorian in "Chi non fa prova, Amore" to the treacherous A/E com-plex of "Sì suave è l'inganno"—culminates in the extreme expression of "O dolce notte," which begins and ends in utter surrender to mixed-mode obscurity. No wonder Verdelot's theoretically inclined contemporaries sought to unravel these sites that served as breeding grounds for modal per-versity, to set straight in their treatises a consistent, rational way of work-ing through all possible configurations. This briar patch of evident A-mode pieces perplexed Pietro Aron and threw his otherwise clear and consistent paradigm into disorder, while his immediate successors announced the so-lution by simply positing additional modal types on A and C.

But the new paradigm announced by Glareanus and Zarlino solves noth-ing with respect to Verdelot's Machiavelli settings. The crisis precipitated by pieces such as Verdelot's leads both to a new self-conscious articulation of modal theory and to a new genre that reveled in the divided consciousness Verdelot's modal strategies helped to pioneer. In the wake of Machiavelli's *Il Principe*, many traditional ethicists rushed in to undo the havoc his writ-ings threatened to wreak on accepted moral standards, though we now ig-nore them and concentrate instead on the modernity of their nemesis. Sim-ilarly, music theorists of the decades following the first glimmer of madrigal composition attempted to preempt such tactics by manufacturing new on-tological categories. But Verdelot and others had already shown musicians how to seep down through the crevices, how to ferret out and exploit the vulnerable points within the system. The new modal theory really only offered additional types within which madrigalists could construct their ever more daring explorations of morally and musically ambiguous notions of the Self: recall Monteverdi's "Ah, dolente partita" (Chapter 1), which per-forms equivocations nearly as unsettling within a fully justified Aeolian.

The historical record loses traces of Verdelot after 1530; some believe that he died in a plague that devastated Florence that year, others suggest that he too fled Florence to seek patronage in less troubled political environments. Most narratives situate him in the early phase of the Italian Renaissance, before the great classical flowering of Willaert or Palestrina, long before the rowdy *seconda prattica* began to call traditional values into question. But Verdelot's Machiavelli settings—mere incidental music in a *commedia dell'arte*—should give us pause. This music already testifies eloquently to a prior Fall from Grace; it cannot qualify as a pastoral Age of Innocence up against which the indulgences of the Mannerists act out their transgressions. The early modern Self—with all its insecurities, its arrogance, its narcissism, its skepticism, its dualisms—already stands here fully formed in these canzone.

ITALIA MIA

In her brilliant *Shards of Love*, María Rosa Menocal argues that lyric poetry often emerges as a response to exile, posing the object of longing simultaneously as Lady and homeland.[15] Her examples—the troubadours of Languedoc whose world was shattered by the Albigensian Crusade, the Jews and Arabs dispersed from the Iberian peninsula during the Reconquest, Dante ejected in political disgrace from his beloved and despised Florence—all package their expressions of homesickness as unrequited love songs, thus converting political anguish into apparently innocuous amorous sentiment.

I have already mentioned the ways in which Machiavelli and Verdelot both brought with them memories of past and fears of future exile, and although *La Mandragola* purports to deal only with sexual malfeasance, it lends itself quite readily to political interpretation. Moreover, as Martha Feldman has demonstrated, the madrigal in its first several stages found its most enthusiastic patrons among the Florentine exile community in Venice.[16] This most influential genre of secular song thus emerges from and remains identified with the political crises of the early sixteenth century. Of course, the madrigal does not continue to exploit poets as obviously saturated with those crises as was Machiavelli. Instead, Petrarch—the

15. María Rosa Menocal, *Shards of Love: Exile and the Origins of the Lyric* (Durham and London: Duke University Press, 1994).

16. Martha Feldman, *City Culture and the Madrigal at Venice* (Berkeley and Los Angeles: University of California Press, 1995).

fourteenth-century Florentine writer of sonnets—became the poet of choice for the next generation of composers.[17] Because he predated this particular moment of crisis by a couple of centuries, Petrarch appeared to transcend its particular debates and antagonisms while still celebrating Florence.

One of Verdelot's most familiar madrigals turns for its text to Petrarch—not Petrarch the unrequited lover of Laura but the Petrarch who in his own day bewailed the animosities that threatened to decimate his homeland. In his multistanza lament "Italia mia," Petrarch decried the violence wreaked on the peninsula by warring factions around 1345; self-consciously alluding to the song of the Hebrews in Babylonian captivity, Petrarch sits himself down by the waters of the Po and weeps when he remembers his own Zion. Verdelot chose to set only the first of these stanzas, probably as a response to the sack of Rome in 1527 by imperial forces. In doing so, he drew on an irreproachable and timeless canonic text, even as he engaged quite explicitly with the political tensions he and his contemporaries still continued to suffer, two centuries after Petrarch first penned this plaint over Italy's internal strife.

Italia mia, ben che 'l parlar sia indarno
a le piaghe mortali
che nel bel corpo tuo sì spesse veggio,
piacemi almen che' miei sospir sian quali
spera 'l Tevero et l'Arno,
e 'l Po, dove doglioso et grave or seggio.
Rettor del cielo, io cheggio
che la pietà che ti condusse in terra
ti volga al tuo diletto almo paese:
vedi, Segnor cortese,
di che lievi cagion' che crudel Guerra;
e i cor' ch' endura et serra
Marte superbo et fero,
apri tu, Padre, e 'ntenerisci et snoda;
ivi fa' che 'l tuo vero,
qual io mia sia, per la mia lingua s'oda.

My Italy, though speaking is useless
for the mortal wounds of

---

17. Petrarch figures prominently in Menocal's book, not only because of his position as the last of the dispersed troubadour tradition, but also because of his deliberate and successful attempt at concealing the debt European vernacular poetry owed to Moorish verse.

FIGURE 19. F-"Lydian"

which so many I see on your lovely body,
I wish at least that my sighs be such
As the Tiber and the Arno hope for,
and the Po, where I now sit, sorrowful and sad.
Ruler of Heaven, I beg
that the mercy that made You come to earth
may turn You to Your beloved, holy land:
behold, gracious Lord, from
what trivial causes comes such cruel war:
the hearts that proud, fierce
Mars hardens and holds fast,
Father, make them open and soften and free;
there cause your Truth (though I am not worthy)
to be heard by means of my tongue.

For purposes of setting "Italia mia," Verdelot moves far to the other extreme from the opacity and ambivalence he exploited for the Machiavelli canzone. Although the madrigal conveys its sorrow, it does so within F: the most stable, least ambiguous of modal types (Fig. 19).[18] No double meanings, half-truths, or divided consciousnesses arise here; instead this lamentation maintains the highest degree of lucidity in keeping with the gravity of the events Verdelot commemorates. Cadences occur on the most secure of modal pitches—F and C—to punctuate the lines of Petrarch's text, which maintains its integrity and its ability to convey its appeal, no less urgent in Verdelot's day than in that of the poet.

Because of the length and relative clarity of "Italia mia," I will not proceed through a detailed analysis at this time.[19] But it is worth noting that if sixteenth-century composers had been striving for tonal stability, they

18. We would classify this mode—final on F with signed-in B♭—as Ionian, a category that did not exist for Verdelot or Aron. Instead, they would have called it Lydian, for most compositions on F coincided with the soft hexachord and the regularized B♭. Only after the designation of a mode on C does Lydian begin to require that aberrant B♮ a tritone above its final.
19. For a full score, see Slim, *A Gift*, vol. 2, 398–406.

already had the necessary means available to them in the 1520s, and they understood rhetorically what such stability would signify. For the most part, however, they deliberately chose opacity over transparency: they pursued a path that plunged inwardly, into the swamp of self-divided subjectivity.

Neither laments such as "Italia mia" nor the unrequited plaints of the madrigals altered the harsh conditions of the real world: Italy continued to disintegrate, and cruel ladies still refused to submit to their lovers' desires. In the madrigal, the anxieties that attend fully conscious Selfhood serve as an irritant, which has the effect of bringing expression into being. Its dilemmas rarely hold out the possibility of solution, for the genre revels in the exploration of suffering. The resulting turn inward to the morbid nurturing of wounds—simultaneously spiritual, amorous, and political—becomes the discursive nexus for a generation of Florentines contemplating or enduring exile.

THREE

The Desiring Subject,
or Subject to Desire

Arcadelt

What is desire? Does it emanate from that part of the individual recognized as "the Self"? Or does it spring up unbidden as an independent force and drive the Self in directions contrary to "the will"? And, given that these and still other possible understandings may occur at various times—or even simultaneously, as in Mirtillo's battle-torn soul—within the boundaries of a single human organism, what do they imply with respect to the definition of subjectivity?

The twentieth century put such questions in the foreground of psychoanalytic theory, which trickled down quite rapidly into the arts and cultural criticism, even if ultimately dismissed from the realm of scientific endeavor initially aspired to by Freud and some of his disciples. But this recent history does not mean we must put a Lacanian trademark sign beside the word *desire*,[1] for the problem of understanding desire and its varying solutions predated formal psychoanalysis by millennia. Cupid's arrow—a favored metaphor in antiquity—constitutes but one answer to the question of how one may be smitten suddenly and devastatingly by powers seemingly ex-

---

1. See particularly Jacques Lacan, *Écrits: A Selection*, trans. Alan Sheridan (New York: Norton, 1977), and Julia Kristeva, *Desire in Language: A Semiotic Approach to Literature and Art*, ed. Leon S. Roudiez, trans. Thomas Gora, Alice Jardine, and Leon S. Roudiez (New York: Columbia University Press, 1980).

ternal to the Self.[2] Because the madrigal from the very outset seeks to simulate through music the interiority of desiring subjects—or selves subject to desire—it offers an extraordinary site for investigating the history of Selfhood.

In this discussion, I will concern myself very little with recent theoretical models—such as those of Lacan—that some critics grant a nearly universal status. I am interested instead in a particular historical moment and the ways in which its musicians understood subjectivity: how sixteenth-century composers rendered *in music* notions of Selfhood, interiority, and passions.[3] Recall how Monteverdi's setting of "Ah, dolente partita" reaches far beyond the meanings of Guarini's lyrics in simulating contradictory internal feelings (Chapter 1). Monteverdi could do so in part because he had inherited a rich inventory of strategies honed over the course of the previous seventy years. This chapter focuses on one of the earliest architects of musical desire, Jacques Arcadelt.

We know little of Arcadelt's life, except that he enjoyed an unusually cosmopolitan career. His name suggests that he probably belonged to that flood of Flemish composers imported as stars to virtually all parts of Europe during the fifteenth and sixteenth centuries, though he may have been French by birth. He worked within the court of Duke Alessandro de' Medici in the mid-1530s, then moved to Rome as a protégé of Pope Paul III later in the decade. After Pope Paul's death in 1549, Arcadelt joined the French court in the service of the Cardinal of Lorraine. Yet despite all his high-profile positions and widespread influence, he led a rather shadowy existence—at least one that attracted little public comment.

The commercial interests of the burgeoning printing industry contributed heavily to Arcadelt's popularity. Beginning with Antonio Gardano's publication of his *Primo libro di madrigali* in Venice in 1539, Arcadelt's madrigals occupied a central place in Italian culture.[4] More so than any other collection, Arcadelt's *Primo libro* put the madrigal on the map: the collection itself went through an astonishing fifty-eight editions; its

---

2. See Roberto Calasso, *The Marriage of Cadmus and Harmony,* trans. Tim Parks (New York: Vintage Books, 1993) for a wonderful consideration of desire in Greek mythology. My thanks to Christopher Small for introducing me to this book.

3. For a brilliant survey of structures of desire through European history see Jonathan Dollimore, *Death, Desire and Loss in Western Culture* (New York: Routledge, 1998).

4. See T. W. Bridges, "The Publishing History of Arcadelt's First Book of Madrigals" (Ph.D. diss., Harvard University, 1982).

madrigals provided the basis not only for mass cycles and intabulated variations but even of pedagogical lessons on how to improvise, and they found their way into anthologies far more frequently than any other pieces in the genre. They formed, in other words, a core repertory of sixteenth-century "standards," the tunes all performers—vocal and instrumental, professional and amateur—had tucked away in their memories to draw upon at a moment's notice.

As their fledgling industry first started to take shape, madrigal publishers sought both to instill and feed a growing demand for music viable for private performance by amateurs, and the relatively simple, easy-to-execute pieces in Arcadelt's *Primo libro* satisfied their needs to perfection. Some of Arcadelt's avant-garde successors came to insist on musical complexity and vocal virtuosity, and in later decades, the performance of madrigals fell increasingly to specialists and professionals. Within this trajectory of spiraling difficulty and deliberately alienating styles, madrigals such as "Il bianco e dolce cigno" and "O felic' occhi miei"—both discussed in this chapter—remained readily recognized titles that served to push new collections to a more general public, rather the way the appearance of a favorite 1960s soul number can boost the marketability of a new movie-soundtrack CD. Although Arcadelt published four additional collections of madrigals within the five years following 1539 while others of his compositions circulated in manuscript, the *Primo libro* stands as his Greatest Hits album—then and now. Consequently, we have ample evidence that sixteenth-century Italians embraced these pieces as successful renderings of their own idealized sensibilities. It is in no small part because of what Arcadelt achieved within his *Primo libro* that the music-printing industry became economically viable when it did and that the madrigal became the musical site par excellence for public explorations of subjectivity for at least the next seven decades.

IL BIANCO E DOLCE CIGNO

I will begin with the all-time favorite of the madrigal repertory, Arcadelt's "Il bianco e dolce cigno." Part of its status stems from its extraordinary elegance: it unfolds with a sense of balance and grace scarcely surpassed in either its own day or any other. More important, however, is the actual content of Arcadelt's composition—the cultural agenda it announces. For despite the surface simplicity of "Il bianco e dolce cigno," the madrigal presents an extraordinarily complex model of Selfhood that touches on many of the most important themes of the next several centuries: tensions between a speaking subject and an inner core of exquisite sensitivity, simulation of the experience of sexual bliss, implied homologies between erotic and religious ecstasy, anxiety over the loss of control entailed in passionate transport, and the mysterious mechanism of desire, which fuels a sense of agency even as it seems to come unbidden from a source nonidentical with the Self.

Our tendency to reduce the content of madrigals to "word painting" has led us to overlook the more consequent dimensions of expressivity in this repertory. Without question, the poetic texts of madrigals allowed composers a far greater degree of specificity than would have been available to them otherwise. Yet the words and musical settings of madrigals relate to each other in ways that remain fluid and unstable; even in this repertory that relies so heavily on lyrics, the notes and verbal images rarely correspond on a one-to-one basis with one another. For words and music operate on the basis of very different phenomenological economies: if music always falls short of language's denotative capabilities, it often outstrips language in its ability to produce precise images of feeling—especially (as we saw with the discussion of Monteverdi's "Ah, dolente partita" in Chapter 1) feelings that involve simultaneous contradictory impulses.

Even in the case of the most obvious musical reaction to the words— say, the chromatic dip to E♭ on "piangendo" in "Il bianco e dolce cigno"— the composer's response is not determined by the text and can never be anticipated fully in advance; indeed, a great many possible choices for musical analogues to "weeping" would have presented themselves to musicians at the time. We need to recognize that the word "piangendo" triggered this particular musical solution in Arcadelt, but we must also ask which experiences of weeping the composer has drawn upon for purposes of this particular passage (eighteenth-century composers could scarcely read this word without delivering chains of "sighing" appoggiaturas, for instance). And if we interrogate the complexity of Arcadelt's representation, we can sometimes catch a glimpse not only of the early history of musical semiotic encoding, but also of the history of assumptions concerning emotions, the body, and subjectivity itself.

> Il bianco e dolce cigno
> cantando more et io
> piangendo giung' al fin del viver mio.
> Stran' e diversa sorte,
> ch' ei more sconsolato
> et io moro beato.

Morte che nel morire
m'empie di gioia tutto e di desire.
Se nel morir' altro dolor non sento
di mille mort' il dì sarei contento.

The white and gentle swan
dies singing, and I,
weeping, approach the end of my life.
Strange and diverse fates,
that he dies disconsolate
and I die blessed.
Death, that in the [act of] dying,
fills me wholly with joy and desire.
If in dying I feel no other pain
I would gladly die a thousand times a day.

Drawing on the old canard that swans sing for the first and only time at the point of death (ergo, the "swan song"), the first-person speaker in this verse compares his lot with that of the proverbial bird. But whereas the swan dies singing and disconsolate, the narrator dies weeping—and yet, somehow, "beato." Another canard: the mysterious dying that fills the narrator with such joy that he gladly dies "a thousand times a day" plays on the conventional association of sexual release with death (*la petite mort,* as the French still call it). An apparent paradox thus resolves itself as double entendre, the expiration of the poor swan serving as a setup for the confession of libidinal excess that gradually emerges over the course of the poem. But despite the fact that Arcadelt gives us at the end of his madrigal an extended musical simulation of orgasm, he produces something far more significant here than just a dirty joke. We should resist, in other words, reducing the madrigal to its punch line. If the poem nearly exhausts its meaning once it has divulged its secret, the madrigal—lyrics and music together—sets up far more than the final line can dispel (see Ex. 5).

A homophonic style of declamation prevails in "Il bianco e dolce cigno": the tight ensemble presents the verse as though simply reciting it with an occasional touch of rhetorical inflection. Only when the established homophony threatens to splinter into multiple and contradictory impulses do we appreciate how it functions within this piece, how its ability to maintain that quality of unanimity operates within the economy of this madrigal. For the simultaneous recitation of text in all voices assists in creating the illusion of a single centered subject who speaks directly to us in an expository manner. By contrast, those moments that disrupt this illusion seem to betray some element operating below the surface, in excess of the rational exigencies of public speech.

The poem itself sets up a dichotomy between the swan and the Self: the swan dies singing, while I, weeping, approach the end of my life. Note that the too-early arrival of "et io" through enjambment rudely displaces the swan's position as ostensible subject of this poem, even before the conclusion of the two lines devoted to it. In his setting, Arcadelt chooses to overlook the enjambment, instead giving the swan a rounded musical statement, to balance as a counterweight against the statement beginning with "et io." He sets the description of the swan with restrained but exquisite poignancy—suspended animation on "BIAN-co"; parallel-sixth chords (considered a sign of "sweetness" since the early fifteenth century) on "e dolce"; lingering dissonance on "more." So long as it concentrates on the swan, the madrigal unfolds in a decorously diatonic fashion: that is, its pitches all belong to the F-Ionian mode without any chromatic alterations, and all its moves can be accounted for in terms of standard practice.

"Et io" too receives a stable consonant setting. But when "piangendo" appears, the voices swerve into a darker domain, marked by a lowered seventh degree, E♭, first in bass and alto, then spreading its contagion even to the canto. Diatonic normality returns in m. 8 and perseveres as far as the cadence in m. 10. But Arcadelt chooses to underscore this moment of the text by repeating the line concerning the Self ("et io"), and the E♭ appears once again as a musical sign of weeping. His breaking of the rules of modal propriety, compounded by his pointed reiteration of the offending line, shifts the attention away from the swan and toward the speaking subject—the "I" of the text.

Musicologists usually (and rightly) justify this violation by interpreting it as a deliberate depiction of emotional expression. But what kind of depiction is it? How does an E♭ represent emotion, and which emotion is it meant to signal? In fact, we might be dealing here with something better theorized in terms of "passion," the concept favored up through the eighteenth century, which underscores the *passivity* of the individual subjected to such overwhelming tides of feeling. If the protagonist of this piece exercises full discursive control over the elegant description of the swan, he suddenly falters when he turns to an account of his own situation, opening up a gap between the "I" that speaks and the "I" that feels.

As the madrigal unfolds, we learn that this "weeping" is not (as we might have assumed initially) an expression of grief, but rather the experience of intense sexual *frisson*. Arcadelt has little interest in this madrigal in drawing distinctions among emotional types (a project crucial to the semiotic project of seventeenth- and eighteenth-century musicians); he seeks rather to register the fact of these disruptive impulses per se. And within the economy of this opening gambit, he defines "emotion" as that which stands in excess of speech, that which destabilizes rational order, that which shorts out the ability of the subject to maintain the carefully wrought illusion of centered unity. He offers us a model of subjectivity that combines a public façade that orates and a private core that experiences feelings so strong that they threaten to seep out and betray the individual's inside to the outside world, even as he speaks.

I am not suggesting here that this model of outside/inside, speaking/feeling is somehow true or universal. Quite the opposite: I wish to emphasize its appearance at a certain moment in cultural history and to examine the ways in which composers marshaled the medium of music to articulate such a construction. In subsequent chapters, other constructions—based on significantly different premises and different notions of Selfhood—will be examined in their turn. But for now, back to Arcadelt.

As I mentioned above, most of Arcadelt's madrigal maintains a homophonic style of delivery: that is, all four voices declaim the text at the same time to produce the image of a single speaking subject. Although homophony counts as one of several common modes of deploying voices in Renaissance music, Arcadelt enlists it here to stand in contrast to another common device: staggered entries among the voices. Stylistically, he does nothing unusual in alternating such textures; indeed, one could easily write off this aspect of his piece as generic practice. But again, the economy of this piece—its specific relationships between music and text, its particular succession of events, and the implicit allegory that begins to emerge—invites the listener to hear this set of alternations as highly significant.

One more detail worthy of attention in this opening section. The tenor serves as the lowest voice in the statement concerning the swan, and its initial rising fourth encourages us to hear it as a functional harmonic bass. Indeed, as it continues, with its drop from C to F in mm. 2–3, it seems even more to present itself as unobtrusive support for the more prominent melody in the highest voice. Yet it is the tenor—not the canto—that traces the entire diapente descent. Moreover, the tenor's rising fourth figures heavily in the motivic structures that gradually coalesce over the course of the madrigal. The bass voice enters only with "et io," thereby strengthening the contrast between the swan (presented in relatively unsupported higher voices) and the masculine Self—a persona that features stronger harmonic motion but that also bears the still-unexplained wound of the chromatic E♭.

In the second section of the madrigal, the voices begin to fall out of phase with one another with the words "Strange and diverse fates, / that he dies disconsolate / and I die blessed." Not only do they present the words in overlapping sequences, making the lyrics difficult to discern by ear, but they also suggest disconcertingly different syntactical impulses. Whereas the opening section offered the image of a centered (if deeply feeling) subject, here the speaker becomes riddled with inner conflict. The tenor, for instance, reiterates his opening rising fourth, thus implying a structural parallel between this section and the first, and the bass shores up this motive by imitating it immediately, converting its initial modal implication (a leap from the final to $\hat{4}$) to that of a powerful descent through the Ionian diatessaron. When the emphatic bass drops out, however, the three upper voices proceed, each presenting the same hovering, noncommittal reciting formula, but each at a different pitch level, each suggesting its own modal center:[5] the canto seems to circle around the mediant of F, the C in the tenor to serve as an unstable dominant pedal, and the alto mostly to fill in the harmonic gaps.

But other readings of these lines turn out to be possible and more accurate. When the voices suddenly converge on a D-minor cadence in m. 24, they invite us to realize in retrospect that the alto was tracing out the diapente on D and thus was functioning all along as the mode-bearing voice. This simultaneity of several possible trajectories reflects the paradoxical sentiment of the text at this point, producing an extended moment of queasy unease before an unexpected pivot suddenly requires us to grasp the enigma underlying surface clarity. The strong authentic cadence on "beato" sounds unambiguous to tonal ears—and, it must be said, it also would have carried that implication within the norms of Arcadelt's time.

Yet the most exquisite feature of this passage is the tenor, which disregards the context produced by the other voices and ascends through the F-Ionian octave to cadence on F. This is his moment of beatification, of mystical transcendence, all the more poignant because it escapes "rational" understanding—that is, the surrounding context fails to confirm its insight. Note that Arcadelt goes out of his way to make this detail audible: the tenor

5. Compare this strategy with that of mm. 15–21 in Monteverdi's "Ah, dolente partita," discussed in Chapter 1.

ascends up past its proper tessitura, crossing over the alto to complete this gesture. The composer also keeps the canto in a neutral position: the top voice participates in neither arrival, yet harmonizes ambiguously with both. The downbeat of m. 24 thus counts as simultaneous cadences on D and F, and it is in the tension between the two implications that the meaning of the passage resides.

Of course, this extraordinary moment cannot be discerned if the performers do not grasp and project it. Most recordings of "Il bianco e dolce cigno" sound as though the tenor has been coached to sing this arrival as quietly and apologetically as possible, as though Arcadelt had made an error in judgment when he suddenly had the tenor rise to that exposed, vulnerable position just to sing a mediant. If, however, the tenor's voice is allowed to ring with the conviction that he alone has now glimpsed Truth with his fulfilled octave, the complexity of the passage—the most loaded moment of the sacred/secular allegory—can shine through. The passage will still sound ambiguous (just why is the tenor having that ecstatic experience there in the middle of the texture, while everyone else is arriving on a lugubrious D-minor triad?), but it will also up the ante of the paradox, which is approaching its moment of resolution. Now we see in a glass darkly, then face to face—a thousand times a day.

Following this passage of greatest ambiguity, Arcadelt returns to his normative position of homophonic declamation and modal clarity: the temporary D orientation gives way to F, while the tenor reestablishes unequivocal activity within the F diapente. Communicative speech takes over for this explanation of the paradox, and although the words "se nel morir'" echo the sudden dip to VII♭ on "piangendo," Arcadelt has positioned the gesture within the diatonic mode (the bass moves not from I to VII♭ but from V to IV), thus seeming to give Reason control over what was initially an irrational swoon.

But if Reason seems to have regained its dominance in this explanatory passage, it now surrenders itself to the most spectacular display of decentered subjectivity in the madrigal. For after the settings of three lines that restore the homophonic dignity of the opening, we reach the moment of Truth: "If in dying I feel no other pain / I would gladly die a thousand times a day." The voices that had been held together so tensely up until this point suddenly split apart; each in turn peaks then cascades downward. The parts enter at spaced time intervals, such that the unified subject now dissolves into multiple overlapping performances of climax and closure. Each line seeks desperately the sweetness of the cadence, yet their phased superimposition causes them to cancel each other out: every moment of would-be conclusion is swept along in the delicious flood of release, until gradually they all subside—rocking to a point of repose over an extended plagal cadence in what sounds like a sustained and pious "Amen."

Note that Arcadelt bases this final point of imitation on the motive that had continually threatened to break through the surface from the very beginning of the madrigal: the rising fourth of the tenor in m. 1, the "false start" between tenor and bass for the second section, and especially the bass's transformation of the tenor's line for its presentation of "Stran' e diversa sorte" (compare the bass in mm. 17–18 with his mm. 35–36). The paradox has been present musically throughout the madrigal, though its eventual solution lies disguised as harmonic bass, as an element unworthy of critical attention. We could, consequently, hear the entire piece right from the beginning as an attempt of a rational canto to speak—to explain or justify—and yet suppress (or at least delay) the impulse to faint away in sexual bliss that always lurks just beneath the surface, even during the innocuous description of the swan. What takes the poet the whole length of the verse to set forth appears already in embryo in Arcadelt's deceptively simple opening gambit. We might also link the concluding ecstasy with that moment of premature closure enacted by the tenor in m. 24, where he manages to trace his way stepwise through the ascending fourth or diatessaron of the mode.

Throughout the madrigal, Arcadelt offers us occasional glimpses of interiority (through the E♭ *frissons,* through nonsimultaneous declamation), held in check by the speaking subject until the end, when this emotionality overflows in torrents. Irrational disruptions of speakerly decorum—and a complex mixture of desire for and fear of that disruption—are at stake, rather than the constitution of any particular emotional type. This final passage brings us to fully satisfying formal closure, even as it dissolves the ego boundaries that had been so carefully held in check up until this point.

So far as I know, Arcadelt offers here the first graphic simulation in music of orgasm. The device he uses to produce this image, however, was common imitative counterpoint: a fugal technique practiced by composers since Guillaume Dufay in the 1400s. Needless to say, not all points of imitation in Renaissance music intend to represent sexual transport; indeed, the device appears most often in the austere sacred music of the Netherlandish School, and it is usually regarded as evidence of intellectual complexity. But Arcadelt did not have to invent *ex nihilo* all his compositional techniques for simulating emotions and passions. He seems to have detected sensual analogues in the music of, say, Josquin and harnessed such devices for his own very different purposes.[6] Only the poetic text in "Il bianco e dolce cigno" makes explicit the erotic connotations of its musical imagery: without the words, the concluding sequence counts as nothing more than an extended point of imitation. With the words, however, Arcadelt's madrigal becomes a paradigm of erotic expressivity: emotions understood as that which stands in excess of normative standards of reason.

O FELIC' OCCHI MIEI

The subject of "Il bianco e dolce cigno" declares himself content in the end to display his self-division, his split between the rational, public persona who speaks and the interiority that experiences sexual ecstasy at the expense of centered control. But other versions of self-division in Arcadelt operate according to different and far less pleasurable premises. In "O felic' occhi miei," the speaker bitterly chastises his own eyes, the desire of which to gaze on an unobtainable beloved drive the Self repeatedly to his own undoing.

O felic' occhi miei, felici voi,
che sete car' al mio sol
perchè sembianz' havete
de gli occhi che gli fu si dolc' e rei,
voi ben voi sete voi, voi, voi felici
et io, no, che per quetar vostro desio,
corr' amirar l'onde mi struggo poi.

O my happy eyes, happy you,
who are dear to my sun
because you bear resemblance to the eyes
that to [her?] were so sweet and treacherous;
you, to be sure, *you* are happy
and I, no, for to quiet your desire,
I run to look at that from which I then languish.

Like "Il bianco e dolce cigno," "O felic' occhi miei" appeared in a large number of anthologies during the sixteenth century, and it also served as

---

6. Compare Arcadelt's strategy with, for example, the conclusion of the Kyrie in Josquin's *Missa pange lingua*.

the basis for many instrumental intabulations: for instance, the Spanish pedagogue Diego Ortiz chose it as his example for demonstrating how to improvise on a "standard."[7] Some of these manifestations indicate that contemporaries valued the madrigal at least as much for its elegant melodic contours as for its relationship to its text: even if some listeners would have supplied the missing lyrics when following an ornamented performance on Ortiz's solo viol, the piece had to be able to carry itself as coherent without the words. Despite its power to communicate as "purely musical," however, "O felic' occhi miei" also presents an extraordinary allegory of subjective anxiety. Indeed, its performances as an accompanied melody mask some of the most significant features of the madrigal as a four-voice complex (see Ex. 6).

To set his allegory, Arcadelt chose G-Hypodorian—probably the most common and affectively neutral of modes. Composers of the time often set carefree pastoral texts within this mode, and it rarely exhibits the internal conflicts typical of other types. Ordinarily, the diapente controls G-Hypodorian pieces, with the diatessaron engaged for the occasional cadence on the fifth degree, D, in which case some tension may develop between whether G (the final) or A (the upper boundary of the D diapente) should emerge as the rightful divisor of the D octave. But many G-Hypodorian compositions avoid conflict altogether. Strangely enough, "O felic' occhi miei" features no rival pitch centers but stays entirely within the species identified with G-Hypodorian. And that is because—or so Arcadelt's strategies suggest—the problem lurks within the Self's own constitution (Fig. 20).

Arcadelt opens his madrigal with a point of imitation in alto and tenor, each of which begins on D, then moves up through E to G. Deliberately ambiguous and vague, this motive will turn out to be tracing the diatessaron of G-Hypodorian, but the listener cannot know that for a while. Even after subsequent phrases and cadences have established the mode, this motive will maintain its ambiguity, for the diatessaron—especially in the Dorian modes—is subject to the vagaries of *musica ficta*. Indeed, only the boundary pitches of the diatessaron, D and G, remain dependably uninflected. The inner pitches, the sixth and seventh degrees, waver chromatically according to the gravitational pull of their immediate contexts,

---

7. Diego Ortiz, *Trattado de glosas* (Rome, 1553), ed. M. Schneider (Kassel, 1967). Jordi Savall's performances of Ortiz's examples, however, make a powerful case for their musical worth.

FIGURE 20. G-Hypodorian diapason

Octave divided at G   Octave divided at A

producing vectors of greater or lesser desire at the will of the performers. For instance, the fifth pitch of both alto and tenor looks like F on the score; but the configuration within which Arcadelt situates it would have conjured forth a leading tone from most singers at the time. The resulting F♯ would have the effect of cementing G as final and also of rendering the motive as an image of rising hope very rapidly locking onto its object of desire.

But then the canto appears, and this voice—the one that dominates most of the madrigal—has nothing to do with the motive that had just begun its fugal entries. Instead, it presents the most rational of diapente-based melodies, arching up three times from the final to fifth degree, then tracing a linear descent to cadence. If the diatessaron continually lends itself to the whims of the moment, the canto's tune imposes reason over the entire complex, rather like a wet blanket thrown over a smoldering fire. And the other voices quickly submit to the canto's hegemony: the tenor takes up this melody and likewise presents the diapente three times, and when the bass enters for the first time in m. 4, it too lends its support to the canto's magisterial motive.

Note that contemporaneous sacred polyphony sometimes offers something resembling this setup: a motet may feature a cantus firmus entering in slower motion over an unrelated point of imitation; J. S. Bach's chorale preludes and cantata movements also frequently proceed in just this manner. In other words, Arcadelt's lofty canto recalls the strategy of superimposing a fragment of liturgical authority over newly composed contrapuntal display. If the opening point of imitation lunges too quickly for a still-undefined goal, the canto—with its confident opening fifth—grounds the madrigal within the bounds of coherent grammar.

This brilliant opening presents to us two conflicting impulses: the first representing the "happy" and willful eyes (two of them, in close imitation!) that leap to grab onto the object of their gaze, the second the voice of wisdom that attempts to rein in the unruly desires of the eyes. In the first section, which cadences securely in m. 11, Reason hastens to curtail the initial exuberance of the lower dimension of the mode: the equivalent here of Bakhtin's unregulated lower body, for even if the eyes are located in the face, they operate within the economy of this poem and musical setting as the opponent of the mind.

Yet at the moment of the cadence in m. 11, we still have no verbal cues for making sense of Arcadelt's allegory, for the lyrics thus far have only hailed the "happy eyes" without further explanation. Indeed, the significance of the opening passage unfolds only gradually over the course of the madrigal. We may even forget the first two measures for a while, given that the voices all decide to join ranks with the canto, as if the alto and tenor had started to sing a different composition before the canto came in literally to change the subject. And we may well fail to notice that the bass in mm. 7–8 refers back to that aborted motive, in part because its flexible inner pitches conform to the exigencies of the canto: Arcadelt signs in a flatted sixth degree to harmonize with the canto's B♭, and this E♭ cancels out the possibility of the fictive F♯ that had contributed a sense of urgency to the alto and tenor performances of the motive in mm. 2–3. Moreover, the basso starting in m. 7 sounds like a functional harmonic bass line—nothing more; its motivic implications of potential arousal lie abject, drowned out beneath the multiple renditions of the canto's far less ambiguous melody.

The verbal explanation for this state of affairs begins to emerge in a stammering series of phrases beginning in m. 11: you who are dear to my beloved, *you who are dear to my beloved*—but only because you resemble the eyes of a former lover. The first half of the statement apparently cedes the reciprocity of the eyes' desires, then bitterly douses this illusion with cold water. The Beloved does not actually return these amorous feelings but only remembers those associated with a previous affair.

To deliver this moment of truth, Arcadelt starts far from the certainty of the cadence in m. 11 on an undefined open fifth on C. In one of those gorgeous but completely ambiguous *fauxbourdon* passages that also mark transitions in "Il bianco e dolce cigno," he sidles down to a cadence on B♭— the alter ego of G within Hypodorian, the most common support for D, the fifth degree, after G and D. Having arrived at a position of some clarity (relative to that open-C sonority in m. 11), the upper voices then repeat the same line of text, entirely within B♭—with greater confidence, as though to reinforce the verity of this concession. But the emphasis only sets up all the more cruelly the turnaround, for the second B♭ arrival serves as the platform from which the canto can once again impose reason, its unequivocal double descent through the G diapente on the words that bring bitter reality to the situation. If the sixth degree still exercised some flexibility in the setup (E♭ in the tenor in m. 14 but perhaps not in the alto, one last attempt at rising in the bass in m. 16), the gravity of the Romanesca-harmonized descent (mm. 17–21) drags everything down in its wake. It is difficult to imagine how anything could follow this show of rational force, which will brook no opposition, no more fantasizing.

But the poem has not concluded. Arcadelt had begun to exhibit a tendency to stammer in the previous passage—a tendency that anticipated the next line of text, which simply sputters in frustration, lashing out accusingly at "voi," the eyes that will not behave (note the alto's incorrigible return to its initial motive in m. 21). Still, the canto maintains its aloof stance, as it delivers this verbally shaky line with the supreme confidence that has marked its previous proclamations.

The pivot comes at a moment of extreme poetic vulnerability: an elision between "felici" and "et io," whereby the last syllable of the eyes' happiness merges seamlessly with the confession of the "I." As in m. 11, where a stable G cadence gave way to an underdefined C, the canto finds its cadential G suddenly undercut, reharmonized with C. And as it reveals the source of the speaking Self's unhappiness, the canto sinks fatally down into the diatessaron. Despite all its rational protestations, the Self cannot, in fact, immunize itself against the greater libidinal energy of the eyes. Notice especially the canto's E♮ in m. 29: a quiet admission of complicity. And the motive associated with the eyes first heard in mm. 1–2 erupts gleefully in the bass to drive the now-powerless canto (which attempts desperately to reestablish its dominance through its run that falls just short of its requisite melodic D) to a cadence on B♭ in m. 32.

From here to the end Arcadelt gives us repeated performances of the canto trying to regain its elevated position of authority up against a rapid-fire version of the "eyes" motive. But each time, the canto fails to catch onto its anchor and falls abjectly down into the lower body. To be sure, the tenor does deliver the expected diapente descents to produce closure. But this is not the voice featured in arrangements, nor is it the voice that bears the weight of the affective allegory. And after it has reached closure on the downbeat of m. 38, the tenor sneaks up through a tetrachord again (actually imitating the bass, which has just fallen silent at the moment when it ought to have cemented the cadence), giving us yet another way of hearing the hopeless inseparability of the low desires of the eyes and the rational "I." In this madrigal, the "eyes" have it.

Throughout this final passage, Arcadelt leaves the sites eligible for *mu-*

sica ficta up for grabs. Performers can tweak the pitches in the direction of quick arousal (F♯ in mm. 32 and 35) and/or wallowing abjection (E♭ in the canto in mm. 34, 37, 39). But in either case, the utter devastation of sovereign reason by the mindless desires of the body comes through loud and clear. Any attempt at cordoning off those dueling aspects of the Self from each other—manifested in the poem in the impotent stammering, in the Othering of the eyes—proves futile.

What can Arcadelt's music in "O felic' occhi miei" tell us that the poem cannot? I have referred continually to the lyrics to make sense of Arcadelt's musical strategies, for he locates his endeavor dialectically between this particular text and his setting; even if instrumentalists could perform the melody without its generating words, the music was composed so as to illuminate the particular tensions articulated by the poet. But Arcadelt does not simply respond to words as they appear. Instead, he designs his modal allegory to parallel from the very outset the problem the poem will reveal only gradually: thus the collision between conflicting trajectories in the first two measures of the piece, at a time when the text is simply addressing the eyes. Even the symptomatic stammering that foreshadows the breakdown of the Self's control appears earlier in Arcadelt's madrigal than in the poem, and it becomes more thematic within the music.

Finally, just as Monteverdi's Mirtillo finds that his modal constitution is always already divided, so Arcadelt's persona plots his psychological difficulty within the components of G-Hypodorian: the upper portion of the octave holds to its rational diapente, while the lower, more volatile portion undermines its authority. As the madrigal winds to its conclusion, the canto slips over and over again without traction down through its octave, lacking the willpower that would allow it to seize its final. Within the context of Arcadelt's compositional strategy, the Self's G-Hypodorian identity proves unable to maintain the fictional separation between reason and desire, and its naked display of helpless passivity at the end—even if it stems from the poetic text—pulls the listener into this sense of attempted control melting down into utter abjection.

Before I leave this madrigal, I want to comment on one element I have carefully tiptoed around until now. The poet of "O felic' occhi miei" designates no gender for the Beloved, who is called metaphorically "my sun." When the poem refers back to this person, it uses the male pronoun, in keeping with the Italian "il mio sol"—a masculine noun. Most translations into English assume heterosexuality and call the Beloved "she." But occasionally a canny student will ask why the Italian text seems to say "he," at which point I (like most of my colleagues) go into a song-and-dance routine about the gender of Italian nouns. The goal of this standard explanation is to head off at the pass any potential misunderstanding concerning sexual orientation. And surely, we should hesitate to embrace the opposite position—namely, that the masculine noun "sol" must prove that the Beloved is male.

Still and all, we probably rush in too quickly to "set straight" this ambiguity. The other madrigals considered in this chapter likewise have only other male referents: "cigno," "viso," "ben," "tesoro." And although Arcadelt set many texts addressed explicitly to a "madonna," the ones most famous maintain an undesignated stance. Recall that sixteenth-century Florence was infamous as a hotbed of humanism and of male same-sex eroticism.[8] Michelangelo, some of whose lyrics Arcadelt set, was only the most famous of those referred to as sodomites at the time. Many of these madrigals would have been performed in homosocial settings, often with all-male participants singing even the uppermost part.

This is not to suggest that Arcadelt himself was gay. As I explained above, we do not know his place of origin or all of his professional gigs, let alone anything about his personal life. But his job was to write music for influential patrons and other artists, some of whom did prefer men as sexual partners. The very lack of clarity on this point may have helped launch these madrigals into the "best of" category. If we cannot know that "il mio sol" is male, we have no greater evidence to assume that the Beloved is female.

AHIME, DOV' È 'L BEL VISO

Psychoanalyst Jacques Lacan explains desire as a trajectory of energies deployed in search of something always, by definition, absent. The "lack" perceived at the moment when infantile plenitude is discovered as forever lost becomes a driving force throughout life. It may shift its focus from one designated object of desire to another, but the drive itself never can be truly satisfied inasmuch as plenitude remains out of reach.

Arcadelt's subject in "Il bianco e dolce cigno" seems to have had fulfillment always within its grasp, so to speak (the swan being the only other entity mentioned in the text); it faces only the challenge of postponing gratification long enough to get to the end of the piece. "O felic' occhi miei"

---

8. James M. Saslow, *Ganymede in the Renaissance* (New Haven: Yale University Press, 1986).

does refer to an object of desire, but its battle concerns the warring factions within the economy of the Self. In "Ahime, dov' è 'l bel viso," however, Arcadelt simulates in music something like Lacan's structure of desire, this yearning for something permanently absent (see Ex. 7). The text recalls the last section of Petrarch's *Il canzoniere:* the poet longs for the face of a beloved, now apparently deceased. He may labor to reconstitute the aura of the face by describing it and its effect on him; he may rail against Death, which has robbed him of his Love. But the face stays ever absent—the generator of an obsessive pattern of repetition that may gesture toward fulfillment but can never achieve it.

Ahime, dov' è 'l bel viso,
in cui solea tener suo nid' amore,
E dove ripost'era ogni mia speme?
Dov' è 'l bel viso,
ch' ornav' il mondo di splendore,
il mio caro tesoro, il sommo bene?
Ohime, chi me 'l ritien', chi me lo cela?
O fortuna, o mort'ingorda,
cieca, spietat'e sorda!
Chi m'ha tolto 'l mio cor, chi me l'asconde?
Dov' è 'l ben mio, che più non mi risponde?

Alas, where is the beautiful face
in which alone Love made its nest,
And where resided all my hope?
Where is the beautiful face
that gilded the world with splendor,
my dear treasure, the highest good?
Alas, who deprives me, who conceals it?
O fortune, o greedy Death,
blind, merciless, and deaf!
Who has stolen my heart, who hides it?
Where is my dear, who no more answers me?

To capture the overriding impulse of the poem, Arcadelt configures yet another modal analogy. The madrigal seems at first glance to operate with G as its final: it starts and finishes on G, and most of its internal cadences conclude on G. Yet despite the prevalence of G, the details of the piece point to a rather different reading. The opening line, for instance (the one that returns throughout the madrigal), presents both B♭ and B♮ in prominent po-

FIGURE 21. Incomplete diapente descent to C

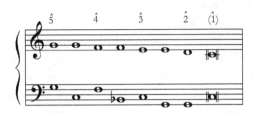

sitions. If this were a G-based mode, it would need to have a consistent mediant; it certainly would not flaunt this indecision over and over in the very passages most concerned with definition. If, however, we take the canto as a mode-bearing voice, we find a direct—if ultimately interrupted—descent from G to D, with D poised as a second degree ready to confirm C as an Ionian final (Fig. 21).

The anomalous pitches also confirm such a reading: as in "Il bianco e dolce cigno," $\hat{4}$ receives a harmonization with VII♭. The accidentals, in other words, affect only the diatessaron, and they serve to contribute extra gravity to the modal descent. Note that Arcadelt does not arrange the arrival on G as a real cadence: the bass reaches always G only by step (ready to move up to the always-absent C), and tenor and canto collaborate in a precadential appoggiatura (I^6_4 to V), ready to contract onto the final that never materializes.

Or almost never, in any case. A few passages actually allow for implied confirmations of C, though these always are riddled with voice-leading problems that undermine their authority. Measure 10, for example, offers something that *sounds* like a cadence on C—but only if we take the interrupted G in the tenor as a dominant that moves to the bass's C, which begins a new line. Again in m. 19 Arcadelt grants us an arrival on C, but with a weak stepwise approach in the bass and an incomplete melodic descent in the canto. But this is no cadence on C, even if it offers a faint glimmer of the otherwise missing object of desire. The next phrase returns to the obsessive progression that drives the madrigal, and it ends (as usual) in a precadential configuration to have the bass enter on the elusive C in the silence that follows its truncation. From here on out, Arcadelt simply reiterates—without possible success—the fruitless trajectory. If C remains out of reach, it nonetheless launches and sustains the energies of the entire madrigal. It serves as the perspectival vanishing point, that imaginary spot beyond the canvas that allows for the illusion of dynamic space; it is the telos that never arrives.

The allegory underwriting "Ahime, dov' è 'l bel viso" permits a composition of exceptional concentration, in which every pitch contributes to the central theme of obsessive longing for an always-absent object of desire. It is not just that the piece works within a modal framework; rather, it depends on a particularly strong reading of that framework to provide its *raison-d'être*. In doing so, it confirms the dynamic capabilities of mode even more than a piece such as "Il bianco e dolce cigno," which resides quite contentedly within its diatonic framework. When a system is sufficiently powerful that it can control an entire complex with a pitch never truly present, it needs no improvement syntactically or expressively.

As was the case with the D/F cadence in "Il bianco e dolce cigno," the meanings of "Ahime, dov' è 'l bel viso" depend on informed performance. An ensemble that weights each termination on G as though it counted as the final will convey nothing of what I have just described. Just as the poet holds in his mind's eye the image of that vanished face, so the singers must always imagine they will actually cadence on C—then fall silent just before that seeming inevitability. In other words, the structure of longing Arcadelt creates is readily audible: it need not be an abstract theoretical device accessible only to those with esoteric knowledge. But desire not performed is desire not heard. With tight allegorical compositions such as this one, it is incumbent upon performers to discern the underlying web and to project it in sound.

The melancholy of "Ahime, dov' è 'l bel viso" emerges from Arcadelt's awareness of the impossibility of closure. Yet the experience of desire invoked by this madrigal is, if anything, more powerful by virtue of its acknowledgement of futility. The inaudible C of the "bel viso" lingers on; like Mahler with his unresolved "ewig" at the end of *Das Lied von der Erde,* Arcadelt leaves it to the listener's imagination to complete the interrupted descent.

At the beginning of this chapter I posed the question, What is desire? Many of us conceive of desire in terms put most blatantly by Mick Jagger when he sang: "And I try, and I try, and I try, and I try, I can't get no . . . Satisfaction!" Indeed, this particular principle underlies virtually all the music of the tonal era, which produces its structures by setting up expectations and then thwarting them until such time as satisfaction has been attained.[9]

---

9. See discussions in my *Feminine Endings: Music, Gender, and Sexuality,* 2nd ed. (Minneapolis: University of Minnesota Press, 2002) and *Conventional Wisdom: The Content of Musical Form* (Berkeley and Los Angeles: University of California Press, 2000), chaps. 1 and 3.

Not only is this the way "desire" works for us, but also the way "music" works, which is one reason why compositions from the sixteenth century often sound arbitrary and rudderless to our ears. Only at strategic points do leading tones enter to sharpen the appetite for some immediate goal before dissolving back into the ambiguities of a context that refuses to reveal its orientation.

But Arcadelt's notions both of desire and musical process operate differently from the ones to which we have become accustomed. In "Il bianco e dolce cigno," desire actually serves to decenter the subject rather than to focus it. Similarly, in "O felic' occhi miei" the teleological and rational canto finds itself unseated by the quirky, unpredictable whims of the lower body, such that it seems to end in the wrong place: desire derails the kinds of expectations that fuel later musical formal schemata. And in "Ahime, dov' è 'l bel viso" the pitch that ought to ground the entire complex remains conspicuously absent, motivating obsessive returns with no feasible solution. Only near the end of the tonal era do compositions flirt again with missing tonics.

Modal procedures, by contrast, allow for—indeed, even encourage—constructions of the Self that question the very possibility of centeredness. They bear witness to a moment of crisis that demands the examination of Selfhood and that delineates in exquisite detail the trauma that gave rise to early modern subjectivities: the irreparable fissure between an imagined past that promised security along with unconditional authority and a free-standing identity that refuses all outside support to ground its infinitely fascinating (if neurotically constituted) inner landscape. Sexuality, that domain left largely unarticulated by earlier generations of musicians, becomes the focus of these celebratory explorations, because it speaks most powerfully to privatized feelings.[10] But sexuality always acts as a wild card, inevitably dethroning the very will that seeks to stage these performances of the emancipated Self. The madrigal from the very beginning made its nest within that fissure.

10. For more on confession and place of sexuality in modern identities, see Michel Foucault, *The History of Sexuality*, vol. 1, trans. Robert Hurley (New York: Vintage Books, 1980).

FOUR

Radical Inwardness

Willaert's Musica nova

Scholars have long acknowledged Adrian Willaert's *Musica nova*—a collection of motets and madrigals—as one of the great monuments of Western art. Indeed, musicians and connoisseurs of Willaert's own time so regarded it, sometimes on the basis of hearsay alone, for it circulated privately for years before Willaert finally consented to its publication; in the meantime, Duke Alfonso of Ferrara resorted to espionage and bribery to have a copy delivered into his hands.[1] Zarlino based much of the modal theory in his *Istitutioni harmoniche* on Willaert's masterwork, and the examples he cites refer his readers to *Musica nova*.

Recent research by Martha Feldman reveals that the collection seems to have been commissioned by and for a cluster of Florentine exiles living in Venice, and the madrigal genre—especially Willaert's Petrarch-oriented compositions—served to cement cultural memory and to guarantee the continuation of their version of Florentine ideals.[2] As Michèle Fromson has argued, this group sought to transmit not only their aesthetic priorities but also (through surreptitious references scattered throughout the collec-

---

1. See Anthony Newcomb, "Editions of Willaert's *Musica nova:* New Evidence, New Speculations," *Journal of the American Musicological Society* 26 (1973): 132–45.

2. Martha Feldman, *City Culture and the Madrigal at Venice* (Berkeley and Los Angeles: University of California Press, 1995).

tion) their now-outlawed political and religious positions.[3] Finally, in its close identification with the literary principles formulated by Pietro Bembo, *Musica nova* stands as a pinnacle of classic Renaissance art.[4]

Yet despite all the lip service paid concerning the collection's historical significance, its madrigals and motets rarely find their ways into concerts, recordings, or critical interpretation. When one of these pieces is discussed, it is usually treated as an example of the complex mid-sixteenth-century contrapuntal style, as evidence of Willaert's adherence to Bembo's stringent formulations, or as the site of deliberately hidden meanings—that is, meanings other than those of the manifest surface. By contrast, Willaert's own lighter pieces, his villanescas, receive book-length studies,[5] painstakingly researched performances, and frequent CD releases. That these relatively transparent, often-bawdy pop numbers attract greater commercial attention is not too surprising: now, as then, sex sells.

Nonetheless, the silence that continues to surround *Musica nova* puzzles me. The nineteenth-century fetishizing of contrapuntal skill as an end in itself may have contributed to our simultaneous admiration of and ultimate indifference to music of this sort. If the recording industry has developed a small but avid audience for the transgressive expressivity of the Mannerist repertory, it does not seem ready to nurture in this same audience a taste for the dense web of Willaert's rule-abiding polyphony. Even music historians who specialize in Renaissance repertories usually write these pieces off as tedious. Too closely aligned with the *prima prattica* to appeal to latter-day rebels, *Musica nova* languishes on its pedestal, absent even from anthologies designed expressly for budding musicologists. So allow me to write the one of the few puff pieces on Willaert's serious compositions since Zarlino canonized him in his treatise.[6]

We marginalize Willaert in part because of our tonally oriented view of music history, in terms of which Willaert's adherence to mode and Zarlino's

3. Michèle Fromson, "Themes of Exile in Willaert's *Musica nova*," *Journal of the American Musicological Society* 47 (1994): 441–87.

4. Feldman, *City Culture*.

5. See, for instance, Donna Cardamone [Jackson], *The Canzone Villanesca alla Napolitana and Related Forms, 1537–1570* (Ann Arbor: UMI, 1981), and Nino Pirrotta, "Willaert and the Canzone Villanesca," in his *Music and Culture in Italy from the Middle Ages to the Baroque*, trans. V. Bartolozzi (Cambridge: Harvard University Press, 1984), 175–97.

6. The masses and motets have fared somewhat better than the madrigals. See the entry on Willaert in the *New Grove Dictionary of Music and Musicians* (London and New York: Macmillan, 2000).

apotheosis of him as the very pinnacle of modal practice appear to make him a throwback. As I argue throughout this book, however, systematized neomodality only began to coalesce in the 1530s. Willaert's music attracted the attention of theorists because he demonstrated—perhaps more so than any single individual—how this new conception of mode could sustain the immense structure needed for setting an entire Petrarch sonnet. As he proceeds through sonnet after sonnet in *Musica nova,* Willaert reveals the variety and long-term coherence of the processes contemporaneous theorists were just starting to formulate. When Monteverdi identifies him with the *prima prattica,* he does not thereby relegate him to the dustbin of history (Monteverdi's respect for his great predecessor shines through in his statement and, I would claim, in his own aesthetic commitment to formal control) but rather distinguishes him from those who will make their marks by violating modal and contrapuntal propriety.

I suggested in my discussion of "Il bianco e dolce cigno" that Arcadelt establishes a crucial dichotomy between his homophonic, speechlike passages and those that—by virtue of the imitative nonsimultaneity of voices—create a simulation of conflicted interiority. I submit that Willaert's intricate counterpoint does more than simply display his extraordinary technical prowess. If Arcadelt's persona inhabits a region hovering somewhere between public oratory and private feeling, those of Willaert reside more or less exclusively on the inside—a hidden stage on which warring impulses battle, shielded from public view by a veneer of patrician decorum. Like the closed society of Willaert's patrons—that community of exiled Florentines whose carefully guarded memories of the past constituted their chosen reality, these madrigals eschew direct address and instead cultivate the contradictory tensions characteristic of inwardness. Willaert's choice of Petrarch as the poet who dominates the collection is thus overdetermined: Bembo had just canonized the fourteenth-century lyricist as embodying the most perfect of styles; the Florentine expatriates revered the poet as an emblem of their former civic glory; and Petrarch had perfected within poetry the claustrophobic world of introverted subjectivity that provided Willaert with his principal secular agenda.

This chapter deals with Willaert's settings of three very different Petrarch sonnets. The sonnet genre itself demands far greater formal control than the short epigrammatic verses more often chosen by Arcadelt: each sonnet-based madrigal comprises two parts—the first presents the two quatrains, the second the two terzets. Both halves operate within the same mode; indeed, the two-part structure more or less demands that the composer produce something of a musical argument corresponding to the verbal conceit of the sonnet itself. Willaert never fails to rise to the occasion, though (like Petrarch) he treats the sonnet's conventional shape in a wide variety of ways; he takes a potentially rigid formal outline and reveals the rich plasticity that made the sonnet the genre of choice among so many generations of poets and composers.

GIUNTO M'À AMOR

Giunto m'à Amor fra belle et crude braccia
che m'ancidono a torto, et s' io mi doglio
doppia 'l martir; onde pur com' io soglio
il meglio è ch' io mi mora amando et taccia;

ché poria questa il Ren qualor più agghiaccia
arder con gli occhi, et rompre ogni aspro scoglio
et à sì egual a le bellezze orgoglio
che di piacer altrui par che le spiaccia.

Nulla posso levar io per mi' 'ngegno
del bel diamante ond' ell' à il cor sì duro,
l'altro è d' un marmo che si mova et spiri;

ned ella a me, per tutto 'l suo disdegno
torrà giamai, né per sembiante oscuro,
le mie speranze e i mei dolci sospiri.

Love has brought me between lovely, cruel arms
that unjustly kill me, and if I complain he
redoubles my torment; whence then, as is my wont,
'tis better if I die loving and remain silent;

for she could the Rhein when it is most frozen
burn with her eyes and shatter every icy ridge
and she has pride so equal to her beauties
that it seems to displease her that she pleases.

With my own wit I can take away none of the
lovely diamond with which her heart is so hard,
the rest is of marble that moves and breathes;

nor will she ever, for all her disdain
take away, nor with her dark looks,
my hopes and my sweet sighs.

Petrarch's Sonnet 171, "Giunto m'à Amor," revels in the paradoxical tension between tender desire and bitter frustration. The poet ascribes both sublime beauty and inhuman cruelty to the object of his affections, which inspire him to worship yet detest her; he projects onto her extraordinary powers, even as he—a poet who already aspires to immortal fame as an author—deliberately castigates her for all time. And although he presents himself abjectly as her mute and languishing victim, still he hordes his hopes and "sweet sighs" and displays them (somewhat disingenuously) as badges of honor testifying to his martyrdom; he wallows in self-abasement as a form of passive-aggressive revenge.

Here, as in the other verses contained in the *Rime sparsi,* Laura serves as a pretext for Petrarch's infinite range of feelings, each couched in brilliant conceits and exquisitely wrought language. Bembo would point to the careful alternation between harsh and sweet consonants: the hard sounds ("crude," "ancidono," "agghiaccia," "aspro scoglio") mimicking the aggressive assault Petrarch here claims to suffer, the soft ones ("belle," "mora amando," "mei dolci sospiri") granting us access to the poet's vulnerability. For most of the duration of the sonnet's fourteen lines Petrarch pursues his complaint into audacious tropes involving both nature (the frozen Rhein) and art (marble statuary). Only in the first stanza and the final line does he offer explicitly his own subjective response. But of course the entire rant takes place within him—both the extravagant perceptions of her cruelty and the confessions of his woundedness. Each reaction both incites its opposite and cancels the other out, leaving the tension at the end more exacerbated than closer to resolution (see Ex. 8).

Willaert's musical setting of this sonnet highlights the warring impulses of the text and their ultimate standoff. He selects for his purposes G-Dorian: a mode that allows for fully developed secondary areas on both fifth (D) and fourth (C) degrees, enabling both acute and passive tendencies to emerge on either side of the battle-torn center (Fig. 22). Dorian also permits strategic use of the flexible sixth degree: oddly enough to our tonal sensibilities, the sixth degree (E♮ in this transposition) is flatted (E♭) in stable diatonic contexts, but raised to its natural scalar position (E♮) when the piece veers into other areas (Fig. 23). And as the most flexible of modal types, Dorian makes available the entire spectrum of possible cadence points; B♭ and F, for instance, both appear in this madrigal, utilized mostly as relatively neutral positions standing on the sidelines of the more antagonistic factions.

Yet, as in Petrarch's sonnet, all possible solutions to the dilemmas posed

FIGURE 22. G-Dorian, with subregions

FIGURE 23. 6̂ in G-Dorian

G-Dorian diapente with E♭   Cadence on D   Cadence on C

are doomed to failure from the outset. If most of Willaert's serious compositions share with this madrigal an unbroken web of contrapuntal interweaving and open-ended cadences, they do not all boast the harsh head-on collisions at moments of anticipated closure that occur throughout "Giunto m'à Amor." The vehemence driving this piece pushes the conflicting trajectories of desire by means of the relentless yet fruitless attempts by each side to dominate the proceedings, with both tendencies occurring simultaneously and concluding ultimately in a standoff.

Arcadelt's strategies tend to make the mode-bearing voice quite obvious except at those moments of deliberate obfuscation, where all parts compete for that role. By contrast, Willaert practices consistently what we now call equal-voice polyphony: all the lines unfold with similar melodic motives (or *soggetti*), and they rarely conform to the functions stereotypical of vertical harmonic thinking in which the bass moves from root to root or the alto fills in whatever pitch seems necessary. Recall that Monteverdi's "Ah, dolente partita" (discussed in Chapter 1) also offers a texture of great motivic saturation, likewise in the service of presenting an internally conflicted interiority. But Monteverdi plays two games at once: most of his motives can double as plausible harmonic bass lines, giving us a sense of (perhaps false) syntactical security, even as he pursues his combinatorial extravagances. Put differently, he wants to maintain some degree of public communication, even as he demonstrates his virtuosity.

But Willaert deliberately eschews in his madrigals the directionality he himself prefers for his villanescas. For purposes of setting Petrarch's dense meditations, he produces something akin to stream-of-consciousness technique, which turns its back on the outside world to dwell exclusively on trains of thought that do not bother with the processes of articulation that make speech intelligible on the outside. His simultaneous and overlapping *soggetti* drift by often on a succession of fifth-related sonorities—but not the circle-of-fifths sequences that produce a sense of inexorable teleological drive in, say, Vivaldi's concertos. If these successions make each new position sound plausible, they say very little with respect to direction. Occasionally a precadential configuration emerges in the mix, as though our persona's mind had suddenly seized onto a solution; but although it might resolve locally, its attempt at definition usually passes disregarded by the other voices, which sweep on unabated to the other side of the dialectic.

Willaert's strategies not only resist ease in listening but also in performance. Although he requires no virtuosic vocal skills of his singers, his madrigals make extraordinary demands on their musicianship and ability to focus intensively on individual parts, unconcerned with the other voices, which compete for attention and contradict one another's meanings. To sing one of these lines from a part book (or even from full score, for that matter) is to experience firsthand the unsettling psychological state of an oddly decorous turmoil; even the motives themselves morph freely, offering only vaguely similar contours to mark their allegiances to a particular idea. The composer offers none of the punctuating features that typically allow ensemble members to keep their places in rehearsal. Within a couple of dozen bars, the music usually grinds to a halt as performers get lost in the ever-consonant superimposition of fiercely independent lines. Even Gesualdo proves easier to sing.

Zarlino's modal theory instructs us still to privilege tenor and canto over the parts that present materials at the distance of a fifth; yet the fact that those other parts in Willaert replicate the same gestures—albeit at a different pitch level—means that all voices simultaneously claim to serve as syntactical guide. Thus the kind of confusion that reigns in "Il bianco e dolce cigno" in the passage leading up to the cadence on D prevails throughout most of Willaert's *Musica nova* compositions. In Willaert, we are always already and inextricably caught between those conflicting currents—or, to return to Petrarch's words, "between lovely, cruel arms."[7]

The opening passage of "Giunto m'à Amor" introduces five voices, each moving similarly with intervals of thirds and fifths. The voice labeled as

---

7. I first engaged with this madrigal in the late 1970s when Donna Cardamone Jackson invited me to explain modal analysis by means of this piece to her seminar. "Giunto m'à Amor" has haunted me ever since.

quinto (rather than the one marked as tenor) works in tandem with the canto, making it—in this section at least—the probable mode-bearing voice. If we follow these coupled voices, we find that they outline the G-Dorian diapente and gradually move as though toward closure on the implied final, G. Yet tenor and bass form another pair and simultaneously register D as a possible modal center. The alto, which remains unpaired, begins like the canto and quinto on G, yet its contour anticipates that of the other couple. Nor does the vertical dimension necessarily assist the listener in deciding whether to consider the center as G or D, for the "chords" that occur in succession usually represent only the consonant but noncommittal pitches generated by entirely linear processes.

There is, however, a way of hearing a kind of teleological progression in these first measures: the gradual descent of the canto/quinto from D to C to B♭ finds support in the vertical collections that coalesce around them ($\hat{5}$ supported by harmonies on G and D, $\hat{4}$ by F and C, $\hat{3}$ by G and B♭). If we perceive this passage according to this outline, then we have something quite close to Petrarch's image of gradual entrapment. Without our knowing quite how, the voices move elegantly, seductively, pulling the ear inexorably toward G.

But before the implied G can materialize, its antagonist suddenly emerges: on the words "che m'ancidono à torto" ("that unjustly kill me") the canto departs from its lulling descent and picks up the opposite strand—namely, the D-centered descent from F already foreshadowed by tenor and bass. Not only does the tessitura of the top voice move into its highest range, thus simulating a shriek (of protest? of assault?), but also the rhythmic quality in all voices becomes far more agitated. If the canto could not manage to descend all the way to the implied final of its first line, this passage knows precisely where it is headed as it moves purposefully twice down to D. The first of these falls in the middle of the sentence, though the bass meets it in an uncharacteristically clear cadential confirmation. The second approach would seem even stronger: the tenor hovers on E♮ ready to descend to D on the downbeat of m. 13, while the quinto's A sounds like a classic dominant preparation.

Yet D turns out to be no more viable in this madrigal than G, for at the moment of truth, the bass enters to harmonize D with G—a deceptive cadence far more wrenching than the more familiar move from V to vi in the bass. Indeed, given the urgency of the expectation, this cadence has the impact of a fist in the gut—a real sucker-punch among harmonic strategies (and, incidentally, one of Willaert's favorite moves). Repercussions from this shock continue to reverberate for some measures as alto and bass strive for a similar cadence on G and quinto and tenor attempt the arrival on D once again. None of these, however, meets with satisfactory confirmation in the rest of the polyphonic complex. Moreover, by the time the bass supplies the long-denied cadence on D in m. 17, the canto is already most of the way through its next *soggetto*—a moaning motive that explains the dilemma ("if I complain, [love] redoubles my torment"). Already by this point in the madrigal the situation is clear: neither passive acceptance nor violent resistance avails; rather passivity gives way to resistance and resistance collapses back into passivity—over and over, at one and the same time, ad infinitum.[8]

Yet Willaert has only begun to unveil the convolutions of this state of mind. Just as Petrarch reveals his central theme in the first two lines and then proceeds to develop it through extravagant analogies, so Willaert explores for another 116 measures the musical impasse delineated in this opening section. The new *soggetto*, "e s' io mi doglio," also occurs on both D and G levels. In canceling out the electrifying E♮ of the D diapente, the E♭ in m. 19 marks a resigned fall back into G—though not a G context that allows for any comfort. Next, a would-be approach to G in the canto in m. 23 stalls on the second degree, for the other voices refuse to coalesce in such a way as to confirm its precadential stance. By the same token, none of the desire-laden trajectories of the other voices reaches satisfactory closure either.

Finally, the poet opts (or so he claims) for silence, and Willaert's voices try to abandon their struggle between G and D by listing toward C. A couple of cadential configurations greet the word "taccia," though the signed-in return of E♭ in m. 36 renders the status of C ambiguous: the secondary area on C ought to have the diatonic E♮, and the flatting of that pitch implies a reorientation toward G (Fig. 24). When the setting of the quatrain finally reaches its conclusion in m. 39, it signals the same kind of standoff witnessed earlier, though now located between G and C: the implied approach to C does not fully materialize and, further, is marred by the equivocation over its mediant, while the G-sonority of m. 39 sounds like a preparation for a cadence on C. And following Petrarch's verbal advice, this

8. I wish to remind the reader once again that the madrigal would need to be *performed* in the ways suggested here for these effects to emerge. I am not here describing an extant recorded interpretation (unfortunately none is available) but am, rather, proposing a reading that can be realized in sound.

FIGURE 24. Versions of C

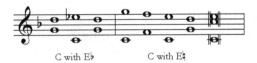

C with E♭   C with E♮

tortured first part comes to a halt, with the voices evaporating one by one. In the face of a no-win situation, the music quite simply shuts up.

Neither poet nor composer truly accepts silence as a solution, however; in both cases, this profession of muteness only incites an outburst of extravagant and violent imagery. Just as Petrarch moves away from his own condition temporarily to conjure up the frozen Rhein, the shattering of rocks, and the arrogant pride of his mistress, so Willaert steps away from the principal tensions sustaining his allegory. Much of the second quatrain centers around B♭: an area that serves to sustain both the fifth degree (D) and the mediant of G (B♭), while casting its lot with none of the opposing forces. And the violence of Petrarch's metaphors inspires a rare instance in Willaert of word painting, as he sets "et rompre ogni aspro scoglio" with an aggressive motive of repeated notes that simulates hacking away at stone (Zarlino praised Willaert's sensitivity to text enunciation, and this *soggetto* achieves a perfect match in both declamation and meaning). Moreover, whereas Petrarch moves on from his image of shattered rocks, Willaert chooses to equate Laura's ability to wreak havoc with the effect of her pride. Accordingly, he maintains for his setting of this line the hammering aggression generated for the one before, thus conveying in music the underlying unity of Petrarch's array of analogies (for it is, after all, his perception of Laura's unyieldingness that produces them all).

Although Willaert moves swiftly through some lines of text, he deliberates over the final statement of the second quatrain: to please others seems to displease her. One by one, the various alternatives presented thus far in the madrigal process by, each met by cruel rejection: thus a potential cadence on B♭ in m. 69 (the principal area of this entire section) receives a deceptive harmonization, a descent toward D recalling "che m'ancidono à torto" meets with the same sucker-punch chord in m. 75, while a possible arrival on G two bars later is prevented from grounding itself because of on-moving lines. The madrigal's *prima parte* concludes with a half cadence: on D—especially with the canto poised stridently on that pitch—but pointing harmonically toward G. We get no satisfaction with respect to the tensions raised thus far, but neither sonnet nor madrigal is yet finished.

I will not go through the *seconda parte* in the same detail (though I cannot resist mentioning the deliciously searing parallel thirds and sixths in mm. 94–95 on "duro"); suffice it to say that the dilemma persists, always with new variations but with no viable outcome other than the now-familiar standoff. Thus the final line presents once again an attempted cadence on D in m. 131—its urgency exacerbated by the extravagant melisma on "sospiri"—but with the same wrenching deceptive harmonization as before. Note that this unexpected harmony actually brings us back to G-Dorian, but it sounds in context like anything but resolution. The madrigal ends inconclusively with yet another fallback position: a halfhearted cadence on G, with the canto joining in at last with a resigned, wistful, noncommittal drop from D to B♮. The bittersweetness of this unrequited mediant continues to resonate on into the silence that follows the performance, even as Petrarch's plaints persist despite his full acknowledgment of their futility.

What Willaert accomplishes in this madrigal is the simulation of a subjective interior torn among a number of impulses, none of which can ever prevail. His modal strategies allow him to present these warring alternatives within a single restless complex; each voice pulls articulately in a particular direction, only to find the others tugging in opposition. The kind of centered speech offered by Arcadelt never even tries to emerge from Willaert's thorny counterpoint in "Giunto m'à Amor"—not because his stylistic proclivities take precedence over his commitment to representation of the Self, but because the model of subjectivity he pursues for this madrigal precludes the possibility of any one voice emerging to speak forthrightly and unambiguously. Through this setting we gain access to the interiority of the divided subject as it experiences this unending tumult of hope, hostility, defeat, and defiance.

I' VIDI IN TERRA ANGELICI COSTUMI

I' vidi in terra angelici costumi
et celesti bellezze al mondo sole,
tal che di rimembrar mi giova et dole
ché quant' io miro par sogni, ombre, et fumi.

Et vidi lagrimar que' duo bei lumi
ch' àn fatto mille volte invidia al sole,

et udi' sospirando dir parole
che farian gire i monti et stare i fiumi.

Amor, senno, valor, pietate, et doglia
facean piangendo un più dolce concento
d'ogni altro che nel mondo udir si soglia;

ed era il cielo a l'armonia sì intento
che non se vedea in ramo mover foglia,
tanta dolcezza avea pien l'aere e 'l vento.

I saw on earth angelic qualities
and heavenly beauties unique in the world,
such that the memory pleases and pains me
for all I see seems dreams, shadows, and smoke.

And I saw shedding tears those two beautiful lights
that have a thousand times made the sun envious;
and I heard words said amid sighs that would make
mountains quake and rivers stand still.

Love, wisdom, valor, piety, and sorrow
made, weeping, a sweeter music
than any other to be heard in the world;

and the heavens were so intent upon the harmony
that no leaf on any branch was seen to move,
so much sweetness filled the air and the wind.

Petrarch's sentiments do not all involve inner strife, however, nor do Willaert's musical strategies all concern themselves with battles between modal polarities. If Willaert restricted himself to this modus operandi, then we would discern formal conventions rather more easily in his work. But just as Petrarch explores a vast range of affective states over the course of the *Rime sparsi,* so Willaert experiments with and expands the expressive capabilities of the modal system he inherited. Each new text suggests yet a different modal type, yet another way of configuring musical time and space.

"I' vidi in terra angelica costumi" resides at the other end of the emotional spectrum from "Giunto m'à Amor": in place of the seething hostility and flaunted masochism of the sonnet considered above, this one offers a condition of unruffled serenity. To be sure, literary critics have long argued that the gesture of elevating the Lady of courtly love to a pedestal, where she acquires the attributes of the Blessed Virgin, represents but the flip side of the psychological coin from resentful aggression and misogyny. While not forgetting the dialectic for which the beatification in "I' vidi in terra" serves as only one dimension, I would like to focus for now on the ways Willaert constructs a sense of timelessness in response to this sonnet (see Ex. 9).

One of the grave dangers of attempting to capture the quality of uneventful bliss suggested by Petrarch in this sonnet is that such states can rapidly become monotonous. Most readers, for instance, greatly prefer the dramatic horrors of Dante's *Inferno* to its symmetrical Other, the *Paradiso*. David Byrne sings, "Heaven is a place where nothing ever happens,"[9] and although we often pretend to long for such a condition, most temporal simulations of it prove empty and tedious—or so they seem, at any rate, to Western ears grown accustomed to teleological processes. Even the relatively free-ranging modal polyphony of Willaert usually involves at least implied cadence points (if only to frustrate them at the last minute) and purposeful melodic trajectories (if only to superimpose them with simultaneous but contradictory impulses): recall, for instance, the dramatic struggle between tendencies toward G and D in "Giunto m'à Amor."

In other words, Willaert has to work against the proclivities of his own style in order to accomplish the otherworldly quality of "I' vidi in terra." The antinomies that structured the previous madrigal find no counterpart here; even the linear diapente descents that made Arcadelt's strategies so lucid rarely materialize in Willaert's response to Petrarch's fantasy of angels and arrested temporality—human desire counts for little in this tableau. In certain ways, the task suits the visual arts more obviously than music. Think, for example, of an Ascension by El Greco or the mandala-shaped illuminations accompanying Hildegard's accounts of her visions. When faced with such paintings the viewer may stand rapt in contemplation for a very long time, rendering temporal a static image that seems somehow to move while remaining constant. By contrast, the modal exigencies of the sixteenth century usually demand some degree of goal orientation in the shaping of time; even sixteenth-century ears tended to perceive the opposite of syntactical direction not as bliss but rather as incoherence. How, then, does Willaert contrive to sustain a moment of suspended animation for the 124 measures it takes to set this poetic text?

First, he eschews for this madrigal the diapente-based activity character-

9. Talking Heads, "Heaven," *Fear of Music* (Sire Records, 1979).

istic of music of this time, though he does offer by way of compensation the gesture of the rising fourth. A glance at the score will reveal this interval stamped virtually all over the polyphonic complex: it appears seven times within the first four measures alone. Moreover, many of the madrigal's *soggetti* feature prominently the rising fourth—not only the first, but also those for "angelici costumi," "tal che di rimembrar," "ché quant' io miro," and especially the beginning of the second quatrain, "Et vidi lagrimar," which resonates poetically and musically with the very beginning. This gesture suggests synaesthetically something like the raising of worshipful eyes as though toward the heavens—or the Lady's pedestal—and its ubiquity throughout the polyphonic texture produces a consistent effect (recall that the unruly eyes in Arcadelt's "O felic' occhi miei" also made use of this hopeful interval).

Yet the rising fourth also suggests a number of different syntactical functions. The canto's filled-in tetrachord at the beginning ascends through the modal diatessaron from the fifth degree to an octave above the final—a readily identifiable figure, yet one without the gravitational inevitability of the diapente descent. Indeed, the ascent to the eighth degree seems to strain against gravity (the second pitch, D, should by all rights return again to the fifth degree, rather than undertaking the leap of faith necessary to get to F), and this quality contributes greatly to the sense of mystical elevation that pervades the madrigal. By contrast, the alto's initial open fourth operates as a harmonic bass, introducing a plagal F / B♭ harmonic move—an Amen, if you will—that also pervades the piece.

When these two implications begin to run through the other voices, however, and in a variety of transposed positions, their original syntactical functions begin to blur. Whereas the bass entrance clearly replicates the alto's gesture in m. 1, the sesto begins as though in direct imitation of the canto, only to fall short in its leap of faith by reaching a chromatically altered E♭. Meanwhile, the tenor accomplishes the move from C to F in a single bound that reaches even farther to A before returning to earth ("in terra"). And the quinto echoes at a quarter-note remove the pitches of bass line—though the fact that it does so near the top of the polyphonic texture instead of in the range of a harmonic bass renders its syncopated series of rising fourths both exuberant and enigmatic. In other words, even within these first four bars, the characteristic fourth operates in a variety of ways with respect to the modal species. It thus maintains a tight sense of motivic unity while pointing to no consistent destination.

This quality of constant rising throughout the motivic fabric also serves to balance what otherwise counts as a remarkably static structure. In contrast with "Giunto m'à Amor," which tosses restlessly between the "lovely and cruel arms" of its two impossible goals, "I' vidi in terra" serenely accepts F-Ionian as its home base. No question ever arises concerning its modal identity, which explains why Willaert selected this type. For compared with tonal major (with which we often confuse it), Ionian—with its ever-present leading tone and incomparably stable final—lends itself to dynamic activity far less readily than any of the other modes: thus its association with the pastoral topos, from here through at least Beethoven's Sixth Symphony.

I want to return for a moment to that failed ascent in the sesto—to the E♭ that converts the expected C-major triad of m. 3 to minor. We might explain that E♭ as the result of part-writing principles: the proximity of B♭ in other voices (or, in the alto's m. 7, the same voice) may suggest that we need this alteration for the sake of avoiding the dissonant tritone. Yet a flagrant A♮ succeeds the sesto's E♭ in m. 3, creating an unapologetic tritone. Unless we want to pursue a daisy-chain of *musica ficta* alterations to produce a covert chromatic fantasy à la Edward Lowinsky (incidentally, for another Willaert composition),[10] we probably should accept the signed-in E♭ as a significant compositional choice.

And what that E♭ accomplishes, beyond its performance of linear shortfall, is to provide ballast, a counterweight to the apparently unimpeded rising fourths that surround it. Without the frequent appearance of the E♭, the rest of the piece might offer the illusion of actual and unproblematic elevation. But that alternative would project a simplistic reading of Petrarch's sonnet, which does not in fact ascend into heaven but rather perceives angelic qualities in earthly beings. The slightly melancholy E♭ reminds us of the terrestrial grounding of the vision; it keeps the piece tethered to some shred of reality. Over and over, throughout the madrigal, Willaert's lines coalesce to form the harmonic sequence F-B♭-c-F, until it almost sounds like an ostinato: the ubiquitous rising fourths encourage us to imagine we may sight celestial beings at any moment, while the passing cloud of the E♭ repeatedly pulls us back to earth.

In contrast to my usual linear orientation, I am here suggesting a kind of vertical thinking on Willaert's part. The short-winded *soggetti* of the opening rarely control more than a few pitches at a time, yet they interact to

10. See Edward Lowinsky, "Adrian Willaert's Chromatic 'Duo' Re-Examined," *Tijdschrift van de Vereniging voor Nederlandse Musiekgeschiedenis* 18.1 (1956): 1–36.

produce a relatively stable series of (mostly) root-position harmonies. But the progression of harmonies does not resemble those characteristic of later tonality; indeed, the madrigal would sound far more "tonal" if Willaert did not throw in those altered E♭s—if, in other words, he allowed it to work within diatonic Ionian. But the very element that blemishes the potential tonal implications of "I' vidi in terra" is also the element that causes it to deviate from standard modal practice; the E♭ operates as a crucial factor in Willaert's overarching allegorical reading of the sonnet.

Despite the deflating E♭s, however, the madrigal sustains Ionian quite un-ambiguously and returns to confirm its grounding on F with great regu-larity. This corresponds to the sonnet itself, which likewise maintains a more or less uniform flow with no reversals or surprises: the poet attempts through his succession of images to bring into focus this vision always nearly (but not quite) within his grasp. Willaert even smudges some of the formal di-visions of the sonnet so as to stress its greater commitment to continuity. Thus the end of the first quatrain (m. 34) simply evaporates, like the dreams, shadows, and smoke presented in the lyrics—on F, but with no sense of finality—and the concluding lines of the first terzet actually overlap with the opening of the second (mm. 96–100).

The madrigal's great *coup de théâtre*, however, occurs between the *prima* and *seconda parte*. Near the end of the first half, with the words describing the arrested motion of the rivers, the harmonic rhythm slows from the half note, to the whole, to the double whole as the *soggetto* restricts itself to a reciting tone. And in contrast to the previously reliable cycling through the fundamental functions of F, the chords devolve from F to c to g to d, stop-ping finally on a mysterious A-major triad, functioning apparently as V/d minor. For a piece so rooted in modal certainty, this odd arrival at such a critical juncture should sound somewhat ominous, as all normal activities—including even the laws of nature governing the behavior of mountains and bodies of water—grind to a halt in preparation for . . . what?

At last, the revelation hinted at since the beginning of the piece ma-terializes. A series of platonic essences—LOVE, WISDOM, VALOR, PIETY, SORROW—file by as though emblazoned in golden letters across the sky. Willaert immortalizes the succession of words with a sequence of chords moving very slowly (as though in ritual ceremony) by means of a circle of fifths through the entire gamut: A-D-G-C-F-B♭-E♭. This is, of course, the reverse of the process that brought us to this point, though with major rather than minor mediants; if the sequence of minor chords helped to disorient the listener at the end of the *prima parte,* their major counterparts bring with them the inevitability of the dominant-to-tonic cadential progression. Yet as each arrival converts into the preparation for the next, a powerful sense of infinite regress also emerges. Far more than Petrarch's words, the irresistible logic of Willaert's setting allows us to glimpse Eternal Truth, with the nouns merely standing in for a much more profound experience.

But this heart-stopping vision cannot last. Gradually the momentum builds, the chords change more rapidly, and suddenly we find ourselves back on terra firma and a more ordinary sense of temporality. The procedures that characterized most of the *prima parte* return: the lyrics attempt to re- cover the mystical insight that appeared so inescapable in the middle of the sonnet, and the musical setting offers again the aspiring fourths and E♭s that Willaert used earlier to produce his condition of hopeful reality.

The sequence of events presented so brilliantly in this madrigal parallels that of various sixteenth-century saints who achieved quietistic or ecstatic states and who then struggled to approximate in words the experience of being lifted up out of time. Willaert gives us both the struggle and (quite against any reasonable expectation) something of the experience itself, in- sofar as it can be simulated within human discourse. Although this ex- plicitly mystical agenda proves relatively uncommon in the madrigal, it will become the basis for an entire repertory based on Divine Union in the first half of the seventeenth century. Willaert's successors in this project— Monteverdi, Alessandro Grandi, Girolamo Frescobaldi, Heinrich Schütz— will invent rather different strategies in keeping with a desire-driven con- ception of transcendence.[11] But Willaert's representation of the Sublime does not hinge on desire. The local goal orientation so prevalent in Arcadelt and even the conflicting, mutually canceling trajectories of "Giunto m'à Amor" do not figure in "I' vidi in terra." Instead, the vague currents of as- piration and melancholy cycle until suddenly the Vision appears, unearned and unheralded, except for the ominous stillness that overwhelms the end of the *prima parte,* only to vanish, just as suddenly, into the mix.

"I' vidi in terra" grants us a version of subjectivity grasping at and then— as though by accident—briefly encountering the Sublime. Willaert's in- sight takes shape, of course, within the options available within sixteenth- century modal practice, and he bends those options brilliantly to produce his complex illusion. But something of this same project emerges on occa-

11. *Power and Desire in Seventeenth-Century Music,* the book for which *Modal Subjectivi- ties* serves as an upbeat or prequel, will deal at length with this later phenomenon.

sion in later repertories. Recall, for instance, the cataclysmic interruption in the finale of Beethoven's Ninth Symphony on the words "vor Gott," where a cadential preparation suddenly swerves to VI♭ before breaking off into utter silence. Or the slow movement of his String Quartet Op. 127, in which the profound experience of a VI♭ variation gradually slips away to be glimpsed again for a moment just before the movement's close.[12] Or virtually everything in late Mahler.

As I write, I am also painfully reminded of the critic's role in the face of art, which repeats at another remove the frustration of KNOWING yet grappling with the inadequacy of language to capture in words what music or painting or poetry accomplishes. My use-worn vocabulary and metaphors can only gesture at the effect of the opening of the *seconda parte;* any verbal description falls short of the mark—especially one that has to rely on stock phrases such as "circles of fifths" or "infinite regress." Yet I cannot accept the alternative, which entails maintaining a respectful silence in the face of a madrigal that lies buried under generations of the respectful silence more accurately termed neglect.

Saint Teresa apologized constantly about the inability of her prose to convey what it felt like to achieve rapture, yet she persisted in her attempts because even those pale verbal reflections might attract converts. Don't take my word for it: that is, do not imagine that I offer in my description a substitute for Willaert's creation. I just want my discussion to lead to performances and recordings, to audiences of listeners who can hear it for themselves—but only if the music becomes audible.

LASSO, CH' I' ARDO

Lasso, ch' i' ardo et altri non mel crede,
sì crede ogni uom se non sola colei
ch' è sovr' ogni altra et ch' i' sola vorrei:
ella non par che 'l creda, et sì sel vede.

Infinita bellezza et poca fede:
non vedete voi 'l cor nelli occhi mei?
Se non fusse mia stella, i' pur devrei
al fonte di pietà trovar mercede.

12. For a discussion of VI♭ excursions, see my "Pitches, Expression, Ideology: An Exercise in Mediation," *Enclitic* 7.1 (Spring 1983): 76–86.

Quest' arder mio di che vi cal sì poco
e i vostri onori in mie rime diffusi
ne porian infiammar fors' ancor mille,

ch' i' veggio nel penser, dolce mio foco,
fredda una lingua et duo belli occhi chiusi
rimaner dopo noi pien di faville.

Alas, I burn and others don't believe me,
rather everyone believes me except for her, who is
above all others and whom alone I wish to convince:
she doesn't seem to believe it, but still she sees it.

Infinite beauty and little faith:
do you not see my heart in my eyes?
If it were not for my star, I should surely
at the fountain of pity find mercy.

This ardor of mine which matters so little to you
and your praises in my well-known rhymes
could perhaps yet inflame thousands,

for I see in my thought, my sweet flame,
a tongue cold in death and two lovely eyes closed
which after us will remain full of embers.

The angelic pedestal cannot last forever, however, and the bill for such adoration eventually comes due. In Sonnet #203 Petrarch unleashes his resentment in no uncertain terms, both castigating his Lady for her cold disregard
and boasting in anticipation of his own posthumous fame, which will ig-
nite generations to come with his ardor and guarantee her everlasting in-
famy. If her beauty seems to prevail during their lives, his immortal lyrics
will continue to radiate heat long after his death while she lies corrupt and
mute in the grave. A nasty sentiment of jeering self-justification if ever there
was one—especially given that Laura possibly did not even know of Petrarch's existence, let alone his widely circulating love/hate fantasies concerning her.

For his setting of this sonnet, Willaert turned to the most extreme of the
modal types available: namely, Hypophrygian—an option that usually lies
dormant within the system but that can be conjured up *de profundis* when
called upon to help spew out particularly harsh affective states or, in the
case of Verdelot's Machiavelli settings, extreme equivocation. The latest and
most concentrated infestation broke out in the late 1980s when some of the

more transgressive genres of heavy metal—including most clearly bands such as Metallica and Megadeth—adopted Phrygian as their modus operandi.[13]

The relationship between mode and affect rarely operates according to a one-to-one correspondence; witness the fact that the three Ionian madrigals discussed thus far (Arcadelt's "Il bianco e dolce cigno" and "Ahime, dov' è 'l bel viso" plus Willaert's "I' vidi in terra") occupy very different expressive terrains. Phrygian, however, possesses certain formal characteristics that render it unsuitable for the vast majority of situations. Principal among these is its second scale degree, which, because it lies a half step above the final, does not allow for strong melodic or harmonic arrivals on the modal tonic. Deprived of the "rational" means of projecting a secure identity, its compositions hover between seeming indecision and stark assertion. It lacks, in a word, credibility, for it does not have the apparatus that could make its meanings clear in conventional terms. Yet it remains true to its fundamental nature, clinging tenaciously to its inflexible propensities. Its procedures fetishize its genetic abnormality and arrange for it to prevail—against all odds—over more likely, less pathological alternatives.

The commitment of tonal composers to dominant/tonic syntax made Phrygian a rare occurrence indeed in music of the eighteenth and nineteenth centuries. Only by warping the very basis of tonal logic could Beethoven suggest the quality of Phrygian (recall, for instance, his E-Minor String Quartet Op. 59, no. 2, or the outer movements of Op. 131), and Bach on occasion took on the challenge of setting a Phrygian chorale tune, which required him to twist his harmonization every which way but loose, often culminating in chromatic meltdowns that simply obscured the fundamental irrationality of the process.[14]

Nor was the Renaissance much more comfortable with the peculiarities of this mode, which tended to accompany expressions of abject grief when it appeared at all. After music theorist Glareanus let his colleagues off the hook by proclaiming a new modal pair on A (the most common shelter for

13. For an examination of modal practice in heavy metal, see Robert Walser, *Running with the Devil: Power, Gender, and Madness in Heavy Metal Music* (Hanover: Wesleyan University Press, 1992). I wish to thank my former student Professor Daniel Goldmark for first bringing this madrigal to my attention.

14. See, for instance, his various harmonizations of the so-called Passion chorale, "O Haupt voll Blut und Wunden," some of which attempt to interpret the last melodic pitch as a mediant but others of which take that pitch as a Phrygian final. See also the settings of "Kyrie, Gott Vater in Ewigkeit" and "Kyrie, Gott heiliger Geist" in the *Clavierübung Part III*.

quasi-Phrygian pieces), music affiliated with Phrygian—true or quasi—almost disappeared. Yet it lurked there in the system, awaiting the chance offered by lyrics such as "Lasso, ch' i' ardo," and Willaert relishes the opportunity to display his intellectual virtuosity for the occasion (see Ex. 10).

At first glance, the madrigal appears simpler than either "Giunto m'à Amor" or "I' vidi in terra," for it has only four voice parts. Moreover, its lines resemble each other far less than is usual in Willaert; much of the time, they even seem to accept a kind of functional division of labor—especially in the passage setting the invective "Infinita bellezza e poca fede" (mm. 38–43), declaimed in clear homophony. Yet this apparent simplicity quickly disappears as one enters the madrigal, whether through score study, performance, or audition.

The first thing that strikes the ear is the dark, growling sound image Willaert has chosen. His highest voice sings in the tenor clef—a good octave lower than the usual canto—and the bass descends regularly to low E. The voices overlap constantly, producing a dense, murky miasma. Not accidentally, Willaert writes the madrigal for an all-male ensemble, with no relief provided by female or falsetto voice types. It belongs with a tradition traceable back to some of the low, almost impenetrable fifteenth-century masses of Ockeghem. If Willaert's favorite female singer, La Pecorina, starred in many of the numbers from *Musica nova*, she would have had to sit this one out.[15]

One could imagine, however, a piece restricted to lower ranges that still projected syntactical clarity: men's choruses do so all the time. What compounds the grungy effect of "Lasso, ch' i' ardo" is its obscure Hypophrygian procedure. In fact, it takes a while for the mode's identity to emerge at all, and it does so not with forthright presentations of its species or characteristic progressions, but rather by indirection and a whole succession of default positions. If tenor and canto both often circle around E and B—the boundary pitches of the Phrygian and Hypophrygian species—they rarely find their implications confirmed by the other voices. A cadence on E does appear in m. 7, but it scarcely qualifies as an anchor: as the tenor holds its E (rather than progressing there), the other voices fall to what might have been a half cadence in A except for the alto's refusal to provide a leading tone. The phrase seems just to congeal around to E, not out of any

15. For more on La Pecorina, see Newcomb, "Editions of Willaert's *Musica nova*," and Feldman, *City Culture.*

rhetorical conviction (E never serves as a desired goal), but just because that's its nature underneath. No other area explored along the way to this moment can qualify as the final, and so we are left with this cynical conclusion.

The bleak outcome of this opening line is exacerbated by its very first sonority on D, which—if only momentarily—holds out the possibility of another modal option; just as the word "lasso" heaves a sigh bidding farewell to disillusion, so the tenor traces in his initial two pitches the F that holds out hope of another universe, only to pull it down as an appoggiatura to E. The rest of the madrigal will do little more than elaborate over and over again those false hopes, invariably punctured by the grim, unnegotiable reality of its Phrygian foundation.

As is the case in most Phrygian-type compositions, "Lasso, ch' i' ardo" often presents much stronger implications of other possible areas—areas capable of dominant/tonic cadences, such as A, C, D, F, or G (in other words, all the other available modal finals). But just as the poet's Lady refuses to believe any of his protestations, so too these musical feints and dodges fail to convince. All would-be cadences on these pitches fall short of the mark, receive incomplete or deceptive harmonizations at the moment of truth. The final phrase of the initial quatrain, "et sì sel vede" ("but still she sees it"), occurs twice, both times implying confirmation of D. The first time, however (m. 31), the canto and tenor find themselves stranded on an open octave, abandoned at the last minute by the other voices; the second time (m. 37), only the canto reaches the destination, while the other voices resort to a harmonization on G. A bad-faith maneuver, if ever there was one.

Which leads directly into the second quatrain and the passage of most concentrated invective: "Infinite beauty and little faith." Willaert sets this venomous line homophonically, starting with the sweetness associated with a C-major sonority, moving first to a guileless full cadence on G, then to a cadence on E, its arrival not even graced by a raised mediant that would mask it as a possible function of A. Like the New Testament parable that describes hypocrites as sepulchers—outwardly white marble, inwardly full of corruption—this phrase offers us an image of purity, then turns it over to reveal a hideous underbelly. (Note, however, that at the moment of that E cadence, Willaert seems to have second thoughts: both tenor and bass sidle off to G after the arrival; he pretends not truly to be saying what he is in fact saying, to ameliorate halfheartedly and too late the viciousness of the attack.)

In contrast to their portrait of the Lady, the protagonist of Petrarch's sonnet and Willaert's setting presents himself as misunderstood. For the arrivals on E (mm. 48 and 52) in the next line—"do you not see my heart in my eyes?"—receive precisely the hopeful G♯ denied the cadence in m. 43. The madrigal will end with this same contrast: when Laura lies cold and mute in her grave (marked with a brutal arrival on E in m. 113), the verses of our persona will continue to glow like embers—with the G♯ that holds out the promise of relief somewhere beyond the confines of this finite madrigal setting.

But like most character assassinations, this one threatens to backfire. The mud cast at the Lady splashes back on the speaker, whose bitterness makes him a most unsympathetic point of identification. If Petrarch's sonnet already produces this unpleasant effect, the Willaert's choice of Hypophrygian only underscores it. Consider that he could have set the sonnet in, say, Dorian, which would have allowed for greater rhetorical range, which could have persuaded us musically of the persona's ambivalent plight. Phrygian, however, achieves something like Bertolt Brecht's "alienation effect," as the self-pitying vindictiveness of this interiority discourages straightforward belief or empathy. Who would want to go around feeling like this madrigal? Or to socialize with someone this devoted to his moroseness?

Yet we have only to return to "I' vidi in terra" to recall the other side—the attitude of worshipful adoration that can produce a sense of sustained elation in the subject, allowing for moments of transcendental bliss. In between extremes of the rapturous experience of Ionian in "I' vidi in terra" and the depressive assaults of Phrygian in "Lasso, ch' i' ardo" resides the relentless inner strife of Dorian in "Giunto m'à Amor." Three very different affective worlds, each giving voice to or performing another facet of subjective psychology—the tip of the iceberg, as a matter of fact—and all without stepping beyond the limits of modal propriety. We must keep this in mind when, in the following chapter, the very system that enables such representations itself becomes the enemy.

FIVE

The Prisonhouse of Mode

Cipriano de Rore

My grave sighs will not fit into rhymes,
My harsh martyrdom vanquishes all style.
PETRARCH
"Mia benigna fortuna"

For all the emotional violence simulated in the *Musica nova* madrigals, Willaert rarely deems it necessary to step outside the neomodal complex that constitutes his base of operation. Indeed, his success in inhabiting so many of its possibilities inspired Zarlino's theoretical explanations, for Zarlino wrote not in order to pass along a dead tradition but rather to celebrate, codify, and propagate for pedagogical purposes the extraordinary intellectual and artistic accomplishment of his own mentor. Willaert did not so much perpetuate a set of transhistorical procedures as reinvent and thoroughly enliven those ancient categories for the sake of a thoroughly contemporary expressive enterprise. Like Mozart, he worked to demonstrate the compatibility between Reason—as defined in Willaert's case by the constraints of the musical system within which he operated—and a vast range of emotional experiences.

But it sometimes seems that the perverse human imagination no sooner witnesses the imminent perfection of a system than it lashes out against the artificial utopia it represents. The more comprehensive and airtight the construct, the more it appears to invite rebellion. In any case, just as Beethoven pushed to the limits and subjected to extreme stress the balanced tonality of Mozart or even of his own earlier works, so Cipriano de Rore proved a restless tenant of Willaert's and Zarlino's neomodality. And for much the same reason: the compelling harmony between social propriety and subjective feeling advocated by aesthetic projects of both the High Renaissance and the Enlightenment came to appear stifling—as wishful thinking at best, deceitful oppression at worst. Whether called Mannerism or Romanticism, violent reactions followed hard on the heels of classic order, even though the great practitioners had made their respective versions of order seem infinitely accommodating in expressive potential.[1]

We know very little of Cipriano's life, save for his early years in the Nether-lands, his move to Italy, his string of professional appointments and pub-lications. His entry by Jessie Ann Owen in *The New Grove Dictionary of Music and Musicians* considers carefully every shard of biographical evidence that survives, but those shards shed little light on his personal inclinations. Martha Feldman has read his transgressions in view of Pietro Bembo's the-oretical distinction between the style of Petrarch and that of Dante, aligned by Feldman respectively with Willaert and Cipriano.[2] Like Willaert, with whom he shared many of the same Florentine exiles as patrons, he was re-ferred to often as "the Divine," indicating that his music met with the ap-proval of his contemporaries. No controversies of the sort that surrounded Nicola Vicentino or Gesualdo or even Monteverdi attached to him; Monte-verdi will even appeal to his prestige as a way of justifying his own practices.[3]

Music historians such as Owen and Harold Powers have wrestled with the question of whether modal categories remain viable in Cipriano's more experimental music, which explicitly signals the inadequacy of Willaert's procedures for his own agenda.[4] Indeed, Cipriano himself had celebrated the codification of neomodality in his *Primo libro* of 1542, which adopted

1. For more on the latter phenomenon, see Chapter 4 of my *Conventional Wisdom: The Content of Musical Form* (Berkeley and Los Angeles: University of California Press, 2000).

2. Martha Feldman, "Rore's 'selva selvaggia': The *Primo libro* of 1542," *Journal of the Amer-ican Musicological Society* 42 (1989): 547–603, and *City Culture and the Madrigal at Venice* (Berkeley and Los Angeles: University of California Press, 1995).

3. See the gloss by Giulio Cesare Monteverdi of his brother's *seconda prattica* polemic, pub-lished in Claudio's *Scherzi musicali* in 1607. I will examine this debate at greater length in Chapter 8.

4. Harold Powers, "Tonal Types and Modal Categories in Renaissance Polyphony," *Jour-nal of the American Musicological Society* 34 (1981): 428–70; Jessie Ann Owen, "Mode in the Madrigals of Cipriano de Rore," *Altro polo: Essays on Italian Music of the Cinquecento*, ed. Richard Charteris (Sydney, 1990), 1–15. Powers's concept of "tonal types," which has been adopted by many who study the music of this era, bothers me not because it is his own late twentieth-century creation but because it aspires to unambiguous classification rather than offering a way of understanding the internal strategies of compositions. See Chapter 9, *"I modi,"* for a more extensive discussion.

those categories as a means of systematic organization; he started out, in other words, as a mode-abiding citizen. And his powerful grasp of mode as a method of structuring no doubt allowed him to subject its very premises to the pressures his later allegories bring to bear.

But Cipriano's rebellion against formal propriety occurred at the same time and for similar reasons as the resistance of Mannerist painters and sculptors to the perfect proportions embodied by work such as that of Leonardo da Vinci. The implications of these violations of established convention touch on matters that must lead us far afield from the block of marble, the canvas, or the score to consider the increasingly conflicted world of sixteenth-century culture and political life.[5] The lines at the top of this chapter, although borrowed by Cipriano from Petrarch's then two-hundred-year-old sestina "Mia benigna fortuna," could stand as his motto, as well as that of Michelangelo, the later Beethoven, or Schoenberg.

All of these moments present the critic with a dilemma. Should we accept an artist's frustration with his/her immediate conventions and eschew them ourselves in our attempts at interpretation? Or do those conventions still stand as the necessary context up against which the rebellion makes sense? Ought we to measure the excesses of Beethoven's *Große Fuge* or Schoenberg's *Erwartung* up against the tonality they resist? Or should we likewise throw away that orienting grid and grapple directly with what we hear? Does any critical approach that proceeds from the violated paradigm always serve to haul the transgressive artwork, kicking and screaming, back inside the strictures it strives so desperately to escape?

I take very seriously the problems just outlined, even though I nearly always advocate making use of available conventions in the reading of resistant works. As Nietzsche stated: "We must cease to think unless we do so within the prisonhouse of language." Yet bringing existing models to bear does not necessarily mean denying the fact of rebellion, nor does it have to imply that the work in question still operates neatly within whatever system the previous generation prized. Put differently, explaining need not entail explaining *away.*

Some scholars who champion Cipriano's break with modality do so because they wish to see musicians begin to acknowledge as no longer viable

---

5. The classic treatment of Mannerism in musicology remains Maria Rika Maniates, *Mannerism in Italian Music and Culture, 1530–1630* (Chapel Hill: University of North Carolina Press, 1979). Note that Maniates begins her study of Mannerism in 1530, which corresponds with my sense that the madrigal is always already Mannerist.

their tradition-bound system, which (or so the story goes) must give way to prepare the way for the advent of tonality. But surely Cipriano's transgressions take us much further away from anything recognizable as tonality; they do not contribute, in other words, to a linear development of the system for which we've all been supposedly waiting. Nor does the labeling of this extreme style as "atonal" help very much, except as it suggests an affinity between this moment of crisis and the one that occurred in the early twentieth century. Consequently, I will examine Cipriano's work itself as I seek to understand both why he resisted the procedures he and his mentor had brought to a kind of perfection and also how to make sense of the compositional choices he made.

DA LE BELLE CONTRADE D'ORIENTE

I will start with a madrigal that establishes itself complacently within an orthodox modal framework before it begins to act out against it. A late work, "Da le belle contrade d'oriente" appeared in the Fifth Book of Madrigals of 1566. Its text operates within the generic bounds not only of the Petrarchan sonnet, but also of the *auba:* a dialogue between lovers for whom dawn announces the dreaded moment of separation.

Da le belle contrade d'oriente
chiara e lieta s'ergea Ciprigna et io
fruiva in braccio al divin idol mio
quel piacer che non cape humana mente,

quando sentii dopo un sospir ardente:
"Speranza del mio cor, dolce desio,
te 'n vai, haime, sola mi lasci, adio.
Che sarà qui di me scura e dolente?

Ahi crudo Amor, ben son dubiose e corte
le tue dolcezze, poi ch' ancor ti godi
che l'estremo piacer finisca in pianto."

Nè potendo dir più cinseme forte
iterando gl'amplessi in tanti nodi
che giamai ne fer più l'edra o l'acanto.

From the fair region of the East
bright and joyful arose the Morning Star, and I

in the arms of my divine idol enjoyed
that pleasure that defies human understanding,

when I heard, after an ardent sigh:
"Hope of my heart, sweet desire,
you go, alas! You leave me alone! Farewell!
What will become of me here, gloomy and sad?

Ah, cruel Love, how false and brief
are your delights, for while I yet enjoy you,
the extreme pleasure ends in tears."

Unable to say more, she squeezed me tightly
repeating her embraces in so many knots
that never made more ivy or acanthus.

The poet divides the dialogue against the grain of the sonnet's characteristic four-part structure: lines 1–5 belong to the speaker, who also delivers the concluding terzet, while lines 6–11 convey the utterances of his lover.
(Note that once again, the sonnet's Italian pronouns avoid assigning gendered identities to these voices, and some may wish to maintain the possibility of indeterminate sexualities in the madrigal. Yet the reigning conventions of the time would seem to mark the speaker as male, the lover as
female; moreover, Cipriano's compositional choices appear to draw on recognizable clichés of sexual difference, even as they put them into music—
perhaps for the first time. I will proceed in this reading with this gendered
difference assumed, for reasons I hope to make clear, but the madrigal lends
itself to other vantage points as well.)

In truth, all fourteen lines actually proceed from the speaker's subject position: his frame (lines 1–5, 12–14) does not address his mistress in the heat
of passion but rather recalls at a later moment the scene—complete with
the ostensibly direct quotation that testifies to his lover's travail—for un-
specified auditors (who, of course, include us). In keeping with that fundamental difference, the framing voice indulges at its leisure in long, syntactically complex sentences, classical references, and extended metaphors;
by contrast, his mistress's gasping phrases resemble the involuntary exclamations of lovemaking (line 7 alone, for instance, contains four quite distinct impulses), and if the first terzet all coheres as a single continuous
thought, the effort ultimately melts down in the bodily secretions associated with "the little death."

At worst, the sonnet offers us a sixteenth-century version of locker-room braggadocio, as a man recounts to others the graphic details of an intimate encounter. He speaks in the present moment in past tense, while the woman speaks in present tense in the past; he offers the responses of his partner with simulated immediacy, as though conveying his listeners to the site itself, but he wraps evidence of his own impassioned contributions to the scene in the flowery language of rational decorum. We have already examined the struggle between discursive reason and surrender to ecstasy in Arcadelt's "Il bianco e dolce cigno"; in "Da le belle contrade d'oriente," however, the two impulses do not battle within a single persona, for the poet aligns reason and rhetorical sophistication with the male speaker, ecstasy and interiority with the mistress. The anxieties of losing control in lovemaking are thus alleviated: the secure ego boundaries of male subjectivity can prevail, even while we are still given access to the excesses of female sexuality—albeit at a safe distance.

Viewed in this way, the sonnet becomes slightly pornographic in both form and content. Yet it may also be read as a sincere memory of mutual love, for the speaker does confess to having tasted "that pleasure that defies human understanding." Still, he refuses to document his own moments of slippage from the bounds of reason with audiotapes or snapshots. (If he interspersed his own exclamations—"Oh my God! Not yet! Yes, now!"— along with hers, we would have rather a different dynamic. Note that such a scenario is not an anachronistic projection onto the Renaissance: the exceedingly popular text of "Tirsi morir volea," discussed in the next chapter, presents precisely this dialogic give-and-take, with a neutral narrator introducing the two equally engaged lovers.)

Whatever the intentions of the poet, however, the sonnet offers Cipriano an extraordinary opportunity for exploring and challenging the limits of his inherited musical language. His compositional choices reveal much about his notions of modality and its relationship to avant-garde experimentation. Yet although he sets two discursive options in opposition to each other in this madrigal, he does so not only for the sake of pushing the boundaries of accepted musical practice, but also (and more important for our present purposes) as the means of configuring particular models of human subjectivity (see Ex. 11).

Just as the sonnet's author employed a lofty register of speech for the male persona who addresses us directly, so Cipriano presents those lines within a musical style that would have met with the approval of even the most conservative Venetian arbiters of taste. The framing sections of the madrigal operate within a resolutely diatonic F-Ionian. Moreover, they match the speaker's complex syntax with studied, equal-voiced counterpoint.

Of course, this display of polyphonic dexterity need not signal a preference for academic values over expression: both Arcadelt and Willaert used such textures to construct analogues of interiority, and Cipriano too draws on that tradition of representation in "Da le belle contrade d'oriente." Thus his lavish treatment of each line lends weight to its meaning and underscores its sincerity; his persona exhibits the depth of his feeling in exquisite detail. Moreover, much of the counterpoint also responds directly to the content of the lyrics: for instance, the opening section matches the poem's references to the morning star and to the defiance of human understanding with spectacular images of tumescent, rising scales (the alto voice in both passages ascends from its rightful register to merge with the pitch of the canto), while the final section strives to simulate the intertwining limbs and ecstatic union of the two lovers.

Recall, however, that Arcadelt's persona in "Il bianco e dolce cigno" clings to homophonic speech patterns in an attempt at postponing his swooning dissolve into the ragged entrances and discontinuous declamation of his polyphonic passages. By contrast, Cipriano moves gradually from the elegant contrapuntal web of the opening, to increasingly uniform declamation (beginning already in m. 10), to the erratic quasi-monody of the woman's quoted pleas,[6] and back abruptly to an even more intricate contrapuntal web for the conclusion. He thereby presents two very different phenomenological states: on the one hand, the urgency of the conjured bedroom scenario and, on the other, the autoerotic contemplation of that experience from the vantage point of temporal and spatial distance. He associates intellectual and aesthetic control with counterpoint, the illusion of cinematic immediacy—what we are to hear as the direct transmission of spontaneous, unrehearsed utterances—with homophony.

With respect to his modal syntax, Cipriano could not have made his choices in the contrapuntal sections clearer. His *soggetti* all unfold within the principal modal species, emphasizing the boundary pitches F and C repeatedly,

---

6. Claude Palisca discusses another Cipriano madrigal, "O sonno," as lending itself to performances with solo voice plus accompaniment. See his *Baroque Music,* 3rd ed. (Englewood Cliffs, NJ: Prentice Hall, 1991), 12–16. I had the opportunity to perform "O sonno" in this fashion with the late Nino Pirrotta in the 1970s. I have also performed "Da le belle contrade" with a full five-voice ensemble rendering the outer parts and a monodic performance (i.e., solo voice with continuo) of the woman's section.

pausing only occasionally on D or B♭ for minimal contrast. Despite the melodic mobility and contrapuntal complexity (or perhaps to counterbalance them), the cadence in m. 9 occurs complacently on F. As the next line prepares the dramatic flashback of the madrigal's center section, it produces a slight ruffling of the serenity that otherwise prevails throughout the opening part: twice—on "et io" and "mio," both of which call attention to the speaker per se—the voices converge and halt briefly on a D-minor sonority, and m. 14 indulges in a single Arcadeltian E♭ *frisson* on the words "divin idol." But these slight inflections quickly give way again to diatonic certainty, and another complacent cadence on F in m. 21 seals off the opening quatrain.

Thus far, the madrigal has given no indication that it might be harboring radical tendencies. The opening of the second quatrain, however, ushers in the flashback with a brief, destabilizing transitional phrase. Within a mere four-bar span of speechlike homophony, the harmonies travel rapidly from their established point of reference to a half cadence that points toward the region on the second degree, G—a gesture that manages both to simulate the actual sound of the ardent sigh and also to parallel the grammatical effect of the colon that conveys us forward to the woman's speech. And with no more warning than that, Cipriano hurls us across the threshold into another musical world.

Whereas the opening section managed to sustain a single mode for twenty-one measures, the next thirty measures suggest (depending on one's criteria) at least ten or eleven distinctly different key orientations. Even these statistics fail to capture the degree of chaos conveyed by the passage between m. 26 and m. 56, for many of the possibilities assert themselves repeatedly over the course of those thirty measures. Suffice it to say that we rarely get more than a couple of harmonies in a row that point to the same mode.

We are meant to understand this section of the madrigal, of course, as a musical analogue to the irrationality called for by the attendant lyrics, and we could write off the entire passage simply as "word painting." Yet the fact that Cipriano implicitly grounds his departure from normative practice in the excesses of the text does not really let the analyst off the hook. A casual listener can make perfectly good cultural sense of this series of discontinuous fits and starts by hearing them through the scenario that seems to have provoked this extraordinary musical display. But can serious critics of this repertory afford to cordon off a passage of this length and obvious significance as musically unintelligible? Are there ways of accounting for the specificity of Cipriano's choices? What do we want to understand about his procedures, and how can we go about finding about them?

Clearly, an orthodox modal approach will not take us very far. If Cipriano achieves nothing else here, he at least frustrates any attempt at analysis through a unified theoretical system. Yet despite their deliberate assault on conventional rules of order, his choices do not reduce to arbitrary cacophony. Rather, he delineates a sequence of feelings in minute detail, and if we cannot explain the passage through a consistent external theory, we nonetheless have the tools necessary for following his tracks through this theoretically uncharted terrain.

First, Cipriano continues to make extensive use of those units of cadential syntax that announce impending closure—even though he deflects these cause-and-effect mechanisms more often than not before they reach their implied goals. By means of these elements carried over from standard modal practice, he maintains signals that indicate directionality and varying degrees of energy, expectation, and interruption. Second, Cipriano's various motivic fragments continue to align themselves with modal species, even if he harmonizes them in ways that strain against their primary connotations. (As we will see in Chapter 7, Gesualdo too often produces his effects by means of outrageous harmonizations of otherwise intelligible melodies.)

Finally, Cipriano relies on the experiences of the performer and listener as embodied beings to translate the resulting patterns into meaningful gestures. That is, those degrees of energy that rise only to break off suddenly, that sink inexorably into unplumbed depths, that accelerate or hover in suspension map onto the body by way of metaphor.[7] The music yearns and despairs, heaves and thrashes like a body in the throes of extreme stress (think, for instance, of Michelangelo's sculptures of bound slaves). And as Zarlino himself teaches us, such kinetic patterns not only represent the physical activity but also serve as keys to the inner emotional landscape.[8] Zarlino, of course, intends to codify only the more socially acceptable affects. But once he admits the relationship between musical shapes and emotional types, the gate swings open to the articulation of illicit and hitherto unimagined passions. Cipriano consequently can break all the rules of syntax, thereby grant-

7. See George Lakoff and Mark Johnson, *Metaphors We Live By* (Chicago: University of Chicago Press, 1980), for the classic presentation of this way of regarding metaphor. My former student Lawrence M. Zbikowski has recently published a new model for music theory based on Lakoff and Johnson: *Conceptualizing Music: Cognitive Structure, Theory, and Analysis* (Oxford and New York: Oxford University Press, 2002).

8. Gioseffo Zarlino, *Istitutioni harmoniche* (Venice 1573; facsimile ed., Gregg Press, 1966), pt. 4, chap. 32.

ing us access to feelings we never knew existed, and yet remain (to some degree, at any rate) intelligible: he rings his changes on our bodies.

The woman's speech begins in the key implied by her lover's introduction, answering his dominant to G with its logical consequent. Yet she inhabits G fitfully: the canto strains upward ("Speranza del mio cor") through her lover's diapente, with a B♮ to intensify an arrival on C, only to fall back a measure later with a B♭ on "dolce" and a return to G. Yet at the moment of the anticipated cadence (m. 30), the canto's melodic G receives a deceptive harmonization with C (the F-Ionian fifth degree) in the bass. Some of these moves accompany words that would seem to clarify their meanings (the rising energy of hope as she reaches out for her lover, the "sweetness" of the soft hexachord's characteristic B♭ in m. 28, the melisma of "desio"). But Cipriano is not just following the dictates of the verbal surface, punning off each word in turn. For already in the first five measures of the woman's speech we have a vivid image of her fevered physicality as she alternately rises and swoons.

Her distracted mental condition inspires the texture of the next line, with "te 'n vai, haime" rippling as though haphazardly through the voices. And although this deliberately incoherent phrase ends by pointing to D, the implied resolution never occurs. Instead, the canto emerges as an isolated voice ("sola mi lasci") that levitates despite all the forces of gravity (the B♭ should return to A) to break off stranded on an unexplained B♮. Although direct chromaticism no longer causes listeners to flinch, such a stark violation of hexachordal propriety would have stunned Cipriano's audiences. This B♮ resonates, of course, with the one in m. 26, and the other voices enter to "rationalize" this hysterical outburst after the fact by leading it on as before to C and a quick cadence ("adio") on F, her lover's final. But the erratic quality already discernible in the opening phrase now shows signs of escaping the modicum of reason it had barely maintained. That tiny, apparently resigned "adio" (a mere hiccup acknowledging the madrigal's reigning mode) does not end the diatribe but only registers a slight gesture toward self-silencing before the recriminations begin in earnest.

Immediately, the F gives way to an E-major triad—eventually functioning as a secondary dominant to A, but in the meantime raising exponentially the level of disorientation. In contrast to the previous phrase, which featured antiphonal, discontinuous declamation, the passage on "Che sarà qui di me scura e dolente?" marshals all four voices in a concerted effort, bearing down insistently on that irrational chord for two full measures. When movement resumes, the canto, alto, and quinto all continue to hover around A, the F-Ionian mediant. But the harmonies trace a quick succession of triads that spirals with dizzying speed through implicit tonicizations of A, F, and G, concluding with a massive rhetorical preparation for D.

But when only a grand pause (m. 41) responds to that buildup, all hell breaks loose. In place of the D-minor sonority we had every right to expect, the woman lashes out with a C-minor triad, which seems to bear no relation to anything that has preceded it. Yet the canto is actually tracing an Ionian descent from C to A, throwing back in his face her lover's complacent identity, even though her statement is rendered bitterly ironic ("Ahi, crudo Amor") by the tenor's E♭. Pursuing the inexorable logic opened up by the E♭, the passage penetrates deeper and deeper into the dark region on the flat side, until it halts on an enigmatic D♭ major triad.[9] Those false and brief delights appear here as the nadirest of nadirs: the site furthest from the discursive clarity of the male lover's social realm, that mysterious locus of female pleasure. Time stands still for a moment of unfathomable bliss. Then, gradually, Cipriano retraces the process that brought us to this eventuality, surfacing finally on a dominant of D for the conclusion of the speech; the woman's music thus ends with familiar a rhetorical gesture, just as she complains of the inevitable weeping (of parting, but also of ejaculation) that signals the end of all lovemaking.

Only that D♭ remains as unknowable as it was when it occurred. Cipriano has taken us into modality's dark continent and has proposed a tentative answer to the age-old question: "What does Woman want?" Woman's *jouissance* resides (or so he suggests) on the same VI♭ that becomes the standard Never-Never Land of Schubert and Mahler.

The woman's concluding dominant to D goes unanswered. Another musical ellipsis . . . and we find ourselves back in the male lover's time, place, and mode.[10] The flashback completed, he continues to narrate his erotic

9. Note that the bass moves down through the tetrachord from F to C, thus still holding the Ionian species boundaries firm and providing a tight logic to back up this apparent aberration. But Cipriano's substitution of the minor form of the tetrachord for the Ionian diatessaron still qualifies as highly irregular. His decision to halt on the position of greatest urgency and vulnerability, the flatted sixth degree, reveals how well he understood both the melodic tendencies of the species and the passions he wanted to simulate.

10. In fact, Cipriano prepares the return to the Ionian mediant during the woman's last phrase, as he harmonizes A with A, D, V/D, then F in mm. 54–57. The quinto even retains the same pitch between the end of the middle section and the beginning of the conclusion. The overwhelming effect, however, is that of disorientation and disruption.

adventure—in the past tense, with himself once again in the picture—to his rapt audience. The exquisite counterpoint that prevails from m. 57 to the end in m. 81 admits not a single chromatic alteration—not even for a secondary dominant. F-Ionian serves as the sufficient terrain for the depiction of the embraces, and although an occasional extravagant melisma ("nodi" in m. 66, "acanto" in mm. 72–75) can also be heard as registering the speaker's passion, he resists indulging in the unbridled ecstasy of his mistress. He operates always in the public domain, within the strictures of musical decorum shared by his peers.

And what about Cipriano, the composer who stands behind all the musical details we witness? Clearly the D♭ is as much a product of his imagination as is the elaborate counterpoint of the final section. No woman actually speaks here—let alone grants us access to her most secret recesses where she experiences that brief, false delight as a pause on D♭. Like the persona who relates the sonnet, Cipriano maintains his grounding in the realm of reason while purporting to reveal directly the nonrational feelings that attend female *jouissance.* Yet it is for the middle section of the madrigal—the woman's speech—that Cipriano wants to be remembered; this radical experimentation constitutes his bid for the status of genius. Any of his competent contemporaries might have composed the opening and closing sections of "Da le belle contrade d'oriente," for they stick resolutely to the conventional musical language of common practice. But in order to inscribe the interiority of the Other—she who by definition evades conventional language—he must venture outside the bounds of accepted (male) discourse. Here be dragons.

I have already analyzed this formal strategy in an essay concerning musical representations of madwomen: whether in Monteverdi's "Lamento della Ninfa" or Donizetti's mad scene from *Lucia di Lammermoor,* a male-performed frame of diatonic rationality introduces to but also contains the female dementia that is the main exhibit.[11] I know of no earlier pieces that attempt to distinguish masculine and feminine manners of discourse within music, and I find it fascinating that this paradigm of excess and frame should

---

11. Chapter 4 of my *Feminine Endings: Music, Gender, and Sexuality* (Minneapolis: University of Minnesota Press, 1991). Many seventeenth-century operas defy this principle, however, and allow women to evade the frame that would contain them. I will address these in *Power and Desire in Seventeenth-Century Music.*

emerge as an obvious way of representing gendered subjectivities right from the beginning.[12]

But, of course, Cipriano did not invent his transgressive style in response to the demands of this particular sonnet, for he had long since been trafficking in musical irrationality—and usually in the context of texts not concerned with envoicing women. I began with "Da le belle contrade d'oriente" because the diatonic framing device helps to clarify his conceptual and representational apparatus—the ways in which he understands mode, chromaticism, reason, and unreason. What happens, however, when he locates all these forces within a single persona who happens to be male?

MIA BENIGNA FORTUNA

Mia benigna fortuna e 'l viver lieto,
i chiari giorni et le tranquille notti
e i soavi sospiri, e 'l dolce stile
che solea resonare in versi e 'n rime,
vòlti subitamente in doglia e 'n pianto
odiar vita mi fanno et bramar morte.

Crudele, acerba, inesorabil Morte,
cagion mi dài di mai non esser lieto
ma di menar tutta mia vita in pianto
e i giorni oscuri et le dogliose notti;
i mei gravi sospir non vanno in rime,
e 'l mio duro martir vince ogni stile.

My benign fortune and happy life,
bright days and tranquil nights

---

12. See Thomas Morley, who explicitly affiliates diatonicism with masculinity, chromaticism with the feminine: "The natural motions are those which are naturally made betwixt the notes of the scale without the mixture of any accidental sign or chord, be it either flat or sharp, and these motions be more masculine, causing in the song more virility than those accidental chords which are marked with the sharp and the flat, which be indeed accidental and make the song, as it were, more effeminate and languishing than the other motions which make the song rude and sounding. So that those natural motions may serve to express those effects of cruelty, tyranny, bitterness, and such others, and those accidental motions may fitly express the passions of grief, weeping, sighs, sorrows, sobs, and such like." *A Plaine and Easie Introduction to Practicall Musicke* (London, 1597), 177–78. As presented in Piero Weiss and Richard Taruskin, eds., *Music in the Western World: A History in Documents* (New York: Schirmer Books, 1984), 144–45.

and gentle sighs and the sweet style
that used to resound in verses and rhymes,
turned suddenly to grief and weeping,
making me hate life and long for death.

Cruel, bitter, inexorable Death,
you give me reason never to be happy
but to live my life in weeping
with dark days and sorrowful nights;
my grave sighs will not fit into rhymes,
and my harsh martyrdom vanquishes all style.

"Mia benigna fortuna" appears close to the end of Petrarch's *Rime sparse* (item 332 in a sequence of 366 numbered poems), well into the section that purports to document the poet's reactions to news of Laura's death. The most celebrated of nine sestinas composed by Petrarch, "Mia benigna fortuna" labors formally through a schema that requires the endless recycling of the same six words (in this instance: "lieto," "notti," "stile," "rime," "pianto," "morte") that must serve as line terminations for all stanzas.

In the introduction to his definitive translation of the *Rime sparse*, Robert Durling explores the symbolic significance to Petrarch and his contemporaries of the number *6*, associated with the days of Creation. Concerning the cultural implications of this demanding formal schema he explains that

[t]he sestina is a particularly clear example of a cyclical form expressing the embeddedness of human experience in time. . . . In Petrarch's sestinas the recurrence of the six rhyme-words expresses the soul's obsession with its inability to transcend time. The rhyme-words recur cyclically but with changing meanings, and the form reflects the nature of the mutable world, governed by cycles in which all things change but recur.[13]

Petrarch's sestina unfolds through twelve (6 × 2) complete stanzas. But no matter how many times he tries, he cannot produce a harmonious world by means of the words "happy," "nights," "style," "rhymes," "weeping," and "death." At the end, he adds a final stanza of three (6 ÷ 2) lines in which the obsessive words occur not only at ends but also at midpoints: a *mise-*

13. Robert Durling, Preface to *Petrarch's Lyric Poems: The* Rime sparse *and Other Lyrics,* ed. Durling (Cambridge: Harvard University Press, 1976), 16–18.

en-abîme strategy that condenses—but never resolves—the irreconcilable sentiments of the end rhymes fate has dealt him.[14]

Cipriano chose to compose music for only the first two stanzas of the sestina (Book II, 1557). Perhaps he stopped there for considerations of length, though he had previously (1548) dared to set the entire "Vergine bella" cycle that concludes the *Rime sparse*. Or he may have guessed that listeners would not tolerate immersion in this musical nightmare for more than its present duration. Moreover, ending with the second stanza highlights the two lines that stand as the epigraph to this chapter: the passage that focuses on the incompatibility of conventional style and feeling, the aesthetic justification for what Monteverdi later calls the *seconda prattica*. Whatever his reasons for stopping after two stanzas, Cipriano gave us with "Mia benigna fortuna" one of the masterpieces of musical art (see Ex. 12).

As we might anticipate from Petrarch's lyrics, the madrigal opens with an affect so benign that it borders on the bland: as the canto slowly rises by step from the final of D-Aeolian to the mediant, the harmonies lend support in the most straightforward way imaginable. Following a leisurely melisma in the canto in m. 4, all voices cadence complacently on F. Like many Aeolian-mode compositions, this madrigal exhibits a strong gravitational pull toward the area on the fourth degree, with G (in this case) serving as an alternative divisor of the D octave. But this tendency has a rather more ominous tinge in "Mia benigna fortuna," for the very key signature hardwires it in: Cipriano notates the basso with two flats, in contrast to the single flat in the other three voices.

Of course, mixed signatures had a long and honorable pedigree; many fifteenth-century scores display the same apparent conflict. Most of these predecessors, however, featured the extra flat in the bottom part for pure convenience: because of the exigencies of part writing, the lowest voice within Dorian had a much greater statistical probability of needing the chromatically lowered sixth degree. But it is not the sixth degree that finds itself altered in the bottom part here, for within Aeolian (as opposed to Dorian), the sixth degree already occupies the pitch a half step above $\hat{5}$ in all

---

14. Far mi po *lieto* in una o 'n poche *notti*,
e 'n aspro *stile* e 'n angosciose *rime*
prego che 'l *pianto* mio finisca *Morte*.

She can make me happy in one or two nights,
And in harsh style and anguished rhymes
I pray that my weeping may be ended by Death.

voices. No, the extra flat in "Mia benigna fortuna" affects the *second* degree, potentially undermining the ability of the piece to secure its final.

For purposes of this opening section, however, even the potentially sinister side of this split identity behaves innocuously: in m. 6 the alto swivels simultaneously into a frottola-like dance rhythm and into a formulaic descent through the G-Dorian diapente, harmonized in such a way as to tonicize B♭ twice over. A happy life, indeed! And we continue into the bright days with carefree melismas embellishing an easy elaboration of the G diapente, halting just before the implied cadence. The tranquil nights receive a somewhat darker coloring, with a chromatically altered E♭ in the alto in mm. 11–13; yet we might well be inclined to write this off as a local "word-painting" effect, for the canto moves serenely down by step to E♮ in preparation for cadential confirmation of the final, D.

And so it goes for the setting of the next two lines; the lines list back and forth between D and G orientations—matching musical declamation to both diction and meaning (e.g., "sospiri," "dolce")—without the slightest hint of affective trouble, of the serpent that lies hidden amidst the flowers of this fool's paradise. Even the very last moments of innocence—"Che solea resonare in versi e 'n rime"—continue in a similar vein, with only an accelerated rate of motion present to mark the enthusiasm of its attendant words.

All this time, however, the alert listener might have wondered about the delayed verb. For despite all the activities depicted so lovingly in the opening twenty-three measures, they comprise but a very long string of nouns—the compound subject clause of a sentence that seeks to delay as long as possible its inevitable predicate. And the sudden turnaround ("vòlti subitamente") emerges out of nowhere. Just as the voices settle down unsuspectingly into yet one more half cadence, the basso jumps the gun with the disastrous news: the passive quality of its move from B♭ to A in m. 23 converts to percussive assault with the second A, which marks the beginning of an aggressive motive and ushers in a post-Edenic world.

The fissures already noted in the opening passages—the latent incompatibility of flat and natural versions of pitches, of D and G orientations—now break wide open. The basso loses its E♭ mooring as it traces ahead of the canto a descent through E♮ to D, while tenor and alto join forces to stomp decisively down through the G diapente; the two modal tendencies that had simply alternated throughout the first twenty-three measures now appear at loggerheads. But not even this prepares the wail emitted by the canto in m. 26.

A word of explanation here. Our postmodern ears can discern without too much historicizing the points at which Cipriano acts up with chromatic deviations. But tonally based melodies have inured us to the leap of a major sixth; in our beginning theory classes, we teach students to think of this interval as the opening of "My Bonnie Lies Over the Ocean"—a jump from fifth degree up to the mediant over a tonic harmony. No big deal. But in a musical grammar that depends on the linear functions of the modal species, this interval makes no sense because it exceeds the limits of the diapente. That the composer intends for us to hear this interval as a cry of anguish becomes increasingly clearer as he compounds it over the course of the next twenty bars. Thus we may have to adjust our semiotic habits if we want to understand the full brunt of Cipriano's strategies, and performers will need to find ways of molding their sound in ways that make these major sixths audible as howls of the damned.

In its first appearance (canto, m. 26), the major sixth conforms quickly to the D diapente that had functioned as the designated mode up until this point, and the melody moves down by step to a position prepared to cadence on D. Although the words speak of sorrow and weeping, the line carries itself stoically after its initial outburst, with subdued, unremarkable harmonies—all of which just serves to lull us again into a sense of false security. For we do not get the anticipated D, but rather an isolated, wrenching F♯ in the alto, which alone has persisted in its G orientation. This lone pitch seems to goad the piece forward, past the moment that might have accepted within the bounds decorum the tears of grief, on to the unhinged and irreparable madness the sestina's formal design itself forecasts.

Whereas during the opening section the flat and natural sides of the spectrum simply took turns, now the entire complex swerves from one extreme to the other. In m. 29 the tenor initiates a point of imitation on the canto's earlier major sixth, but Cipriano places it now on a scale degree that requires the violation of the signed-in B♭ (and, two beats later, the violation of E♭ in the basso's response); the motive not only exceeds the bounds of the modal diapente, but it also revolts against the pitch system implied by the key signatures. But by the time the phrase has concluded in m. 34 it has devolved down through E♭ and even A♭, to a Phrygian cadence on G. The searing vehemence of hatred (with the B♮ pushing up beyond the sharp side of the long-standing duality) converts rapidly to the dark semblance of death (as the A♭ sinks below the normative span of the flat side). In other words, what had begun as a struggle between the constitutive E♭ and E♮ of the two signed-in systems now expands pathologically in each direction, spawning B♮ against the previously unchallenged B♭ and A♭ against the hitherto-undisputed A♮. To make sure we actually heard this extraordinary process, Cipriano repeats it note for note, thus bringing to an end the madrigal's *prima parte*.

A glance at the beginning of the *seconda parte* reveals that the split consciousness of the first part has become even further exacerbated, for now the alto too sports an extra flat in its signature: the persona is now permanently divided from within. Moreover, rather than devising a new *soggetto* to fit the next line of text (the practice in virtually every other madrigal in the repertory), Cipriano starts his *seconda parte* with yet another point of imitation on the lamenting major-sixth motive—just as Petrarch starts his second stanza by locking horns again with the still-unresolved last word of the first verse: Death. And just as Petrarch proceeds to recast the remaining five end words in funereal attire, so Cipriano produces a kind of mirror image of his *prima parte:* what before was bright, tranquil, or benign now turns into its affective opposite, as we gaze back at the scraps of former happiness through eyes permanently clouded over with despair.

As already mentioned, the madrigal does not follow the sestina's obsessive cycling through thirteen stanzas. Instead, Cipriano builds his own structure of futility: a symmetrical—even quasi-palindromic—formal plan rigorously self-contained and tyrannically complete from which there seems to be no exit. Indeed, by the end, the various possible avenues of rational closure (requiring a second degree a whole step above the final) have been systematically sealed shut: A♮ often appears deformed into A♭, even in the canto, and E♮ loses its privileged position to E♭. All that was lovely turns to ashes.

But all these observations come from a synchronic viewing of the score; they may capture the essence of the madrigal's allegorical strategy, but they do not begin to account for the ways Cipriano produces the experience over time of self-division. The naked cry of anguish in the canto stretches upward toward C, then D (m. 45) before collapsing down the octave to murmur "death." By the time the canto reaches C, the alto has arrived on an E♭ that compels the canto to B♭, but the tenor soon enters to push the suit of B♮, once again through that bereaved major sixth. In other words, the opening phrase twists uncomfortably between B♭ and B♮ before it ends inconclusively on what might be a dominant of D—except that the canto fails at the last moment to contribute the C♯ that might lend some hope to the proceedings. Of course, the singer of the phrase might well inflect that delayed pitch in m. 50 as a leading tone according to the principles of *mu-*

sica ficta, but the high chromatic content of this madrigal has led Cipriano to notate quite precisely the notes he has in mind. The fact that the canto holds out its suspension in the classic precadential formation before drooping to C♮ makes the moment all the more dispiriting.

On the other side of the pause, the ensemble does take up in a perfectly diatonic D-mode, briefly reflecting "cagion" (reason) before its negation: the A♮ that had served as a reminder of former lucidity crunches down in the canto to A♭ on "mai"—"never." Nor does this A♭ lead to a realm (e.g., C-Aeolian) in which it might establish an alternative system; rather it fashions itself as a kind of Neapolitan to arrive on a bitterly ironic cadence on G: "lieto" ("happy"). But the flat side doesn't stick either, for the canto picks up again and traces a straightforward, completely rational statement in D for the phrase "but to live my life in weeping." This line actually wrenches the alto and basso out of their flat-oriented domain for a painful support of the canto's sentiment. Despite the fact that the alto in mm. 58–60 transposes the canto's *soggetto* to the G diapente (thus preserving some measure of the reigning modal split), this passage of direct acknowledgment counts as the only moment of undivided truth we will get in the madrigal. Immediately after the hollow, open intervals that conclude this statement in m. 60, the flats return with a vengeance for "oscuri" ("dark"), the hard hexachord's E♮ for "dogliose" ("sorrowful"), and the Neapolitan cadence for "non vanno in rime" ("will not fit into rhymes").

Petrarch's final line—"and my harsh martyrdom vanquishes all style"— receives the most lavish treatment of all, nothing less than a summation of what we have witnessed over the course of the madrigal: a sequence of direct cadential diapente descents—from D to G, A to D—but with the second degree mutilated into its Neapolitan version. Parallel cadences on G and D do in fact occur, but with that bitter inflection that vanquishes style— violates irreparably the cosmic laws guaranteeing musical convention. To ensure that the point has been conveyed adequately, the entire final complex repeats, systematically refusing reasoned recourse. In the aftermath of the cadence on D in m. 85—the point of structural arrival—the lower voices continue, most obviously as a means of draining away excess energy. But they also open up all the wounds yet again, for they halt on what can be heard equally as a triad on the D final *or* as a dominant preparation for G: a standoff that not only has failed to resolve the internal division but has managed to destroy all sense of grammatical efficacy along the way.

I have referred consistently to the words Cipriano sets as I have proceeded through "Mia benigna fortuna," for many of his musical choices operate in tandem with Petrarch's sestina. Some of them even respond to surface images, especially in the opening section that matches "happy life" with dance rhythms, "nights" with darkened tones, "sighs" with abrupt rests that result in actual gasping. He does this deliberately, of course; even as he pursues something like what film theorists will denigrate later as Mickey-Mousing, he produces a higher-level effect of naïveté: a world of innocence in which one does just skip along smelling each of the roses in turn. Yet even these relatively simple instances of text/music correspondences draw on very different realms of experience: if "sospiri" strives to map the word onto the sounds to which it refers, the dance rhythms rely on the social associations of a music genre. Our ability to perceive those E♭s on "tranquille notti" as somber requires that we have already internalized a grid of cultural metaphors that link sharps with hardness and brightness, flats with softness and darkness. In other words, none of these word paintings—not even the most obvious—is transparent.

Yet for all their cleverness, these images only set up the more consequential aspects of "Mia benigna fortuna." Far more significant is the complex rendering after m. 24 of a self in anguish. To be sure, the initial justification for the excesses in the madrigal from there to the end come from Petrarch. But Cipriano is not just responding to the poetic surface here: he produces a multilayered representation of suffering. Not "suffering" as a word waiting there for a pat musical painting, but an experience of extended suffering choreographed in extravagant phenomenological detail. Among the components of this representation are the elements already discussed above: the irrational major sixth, the trespassing of modal limits in both sharp and flat directions, the recalcitrant dualities already embedded in modal identity. These do not relate to particular words, but rather combine to produce a particularly obsessive, self-divided form of interiority: one that lashes out in anger, howls in pain, and collapses in resignation—often in quick succession, sometimes simultaneously. If Petrarch's lyrics indicate the emotional ballpark within which Cipriano is operating, they do not prepare us for the psychological intensity, the depth of insight in this devastating madrigal.

As in the woman's speech in "Da le belle contrade d'oriente," Cipriano here acquires coherence through analogues to the body. If we have no way of communicating our sense of inwardness, we do share experiences of physicality and can observe others as they reach for something beyond their grasp, as they writhe in anguish, as they shriek involuntarily in response to injury, as they slump over with despondency. And these external phenomena get transferred inside to make up the vocabulary of the invisible internal world of feeling. Without those common notions of somatic response we would have no tools for unpacking Cipriano's imagery. We can rely on the body, however, as our Rosetta Stone.

And also as in the woman's speech in "Da le belle contrade d'oriente," Cipriano achieves musical intelligibility in "Mia benigna fortuna" by working systematically from patterns already familiar from modal practice—even if he pushes their tendencies far past established boundaries. Put differently, he does not abandon shared discursive practices to set up shop in an imaginary zone often simply dismissed as "no longer modal, not yet tonal," nor does he perform these outrages just for the sake of formalist experimentation. In response to the challenge posed by Petrarch's sestina, "What would it feel like to be this distraught?" Cipriano in effect responds: "Imagine that you were inhabiting two modes at the same time, and instead of gradually moving toward reconciliation they pulled you in opposite directions to the brink of insanity."

More significant than any other aspect of Cipriano's later work is his tireless interrogation of the very premises of his musical language. His preference for lyrics *in extremis* reveals his own agenda, which goes far beyond the mere setting of whatever text comes his way. In his reading of Petrarch's "Mia benigna fortuna," he presents a Self alienated not only from happy times but also from Reason itself, understood as a function of external, socially constituted order. In the words of Jim Morrison of The Doors, he seeks to "break on through to the other side," except that there is no other side waiting there—nothing but a shattered mirror. As an artist, he had ceased being at home in the world, but he had no alternatives other than his marks of defiance against cultural authority.

Yet far from abandoning the premises of mode as archaic, Cipriano de Rore takes it very seriously indeed. If anything, he is obsessed—even more so than composers such as Arcadelt and Willaert, who developed and built their musical and subjective worlds within it—about how to do things with modality. He knows better than anyone that he cannot speak outside this prisonhouse, which shackles him, to be sure, but simultaneously grants him subjective voice. His violations always display method in their madness.

SIX

A Coney Island of the Madrigal

Wert and Marenzio

The madrigalists examined thus far—Verdelot, Arcadelt, Willaert, Rore—differ considerably from one another in their priorities, but they share a commitment to conceptual unity. That is, they read their chosen lyrics in ways that allow for a consistent point of view from beginning to end, and although they may respond at times to the particularities of succeeding lines of text, they subsume these responses to the exigencies of their larger allegorical schemata. In this they resemble their much later successors of the nineteenth century who attended to what aestheticians understood in terms of organic metaphors, though in other respects (motivic organization, modulatory patterns) they operate according to a very different set of practices. Still, this commitment to conceptual unity aligns them with the classic figures of the High Renaissance (say, Leonardo), who produce images of a centered subjectivity; even Rore, who pushes the envelope in allowing his individuated logic to wreak havoc on standard modal principles, balances his excesses with his rigorous attention to motives and structural symmetries. Consequently, their music (and also that of Monteverdi, who follows them in this tendency to work within overarching allegorical schemata) proves easier to justify to those who still assume organic unity as an essential criterion of artistry. We can forgive their occasional flirtations with text-inspired images by concentrating instead on the manifestations of formal integrity in their compositions.

And then there were the guys who gave the genre a bad name: their purported abuses, which came to be called "madrigalisms," came under critical attack even during the sixteenth century. Vincenzo Galilei, for instance, wrote scathingly about the ways certain composers translated the words of their lyrics into literal musical equivalents, thus overwhelming the rhetorical thrust or obscuring the expressive meaning of their texts.[1] Today we delight in giving our students examples of such pieces, in part because they can discern so readily in them the close correspondences between words and music. Too often, however, a simplistic grasp of such pieces colors not only our assessment of the composers given to extravagant imagery but also of the madrigal repertory as a whole.

For although text informs both the surface imagery and formal structure of madrigals, it does not *determine* them—not even in styles famous (read: infamous) for self-conscious translations of words into musical equivalents. We frequently act as though a one-to-one relationship obtains between words and corresponding imagery—a habit left over, I suspect, from the days when we restricted the discussion of meanings to those instances we could verify in keeping with positivist criteria. If we can reduce an extravagant musical passage back to the words that provoked it, then we can end the discussion and also (not coincidentally) demonstrate yet again the primitive conception of signification underlying madrigal composition. When we label such correspondences "madrigalisms," we trivialize the cultural work performed by both the practice and the repertory.

I hope already in the preceding chapters to have destabilized some of this reductive notion of both the madrigal and word painting: Verdelot's simulations of Machiavelli's dark moral equivocations, Arcadelt's analogues between musical patterns and subjective experience, Willaert's Petrarchan settings, and Rore's individualistic resistance against normative practices all depend upon relationships to texts, but they do so in ways that differ profoundly from one another. These composers hold a certain prestige within Renaissance musicology, in part because they maintain a commitment to

---

1. Vincenzo Galilei, *Dialogo della musica antica, et della moderna* (1581); see the excerpt translated in Oliver Strunk, *Source Readings in Music History,* rev. ed. (New York: Norton, 1998), 463–67. Galilei also ranted about what he regarded as overindulgence in counterpoint, which he claimed also destroyed rhetorical communication and even intelligibility. As Zarlino's student, he clearly had been instructed in these skills, though his own music does not display much evidence of his training. Still, because he advocated monody in place of complex polyphony, Galilei has often been embraced as the only theorist at the time who saw which way the wind was blowing. If his predictions turned out to anticipate a principal shift in the seventeenth century, he does not necessarily offer the best means of understanding the sixteenth-century madrigal.

purely musical integrity that holds their responses to texts tastefully in check. The intellectual complexity of allegory and the political resonances of avant-garde violations win respect for artists whose reliance on words serves such higher-level interests. But what of those who shamelessly reveled in outrageous displays of word painting?

Until quite recently, literary critics similarly recoiled in distaste from the extravagant imagery of the so-called metaphysical poets, who liked to take a conceit and then push it in all directions, many of them purposely grotesque. The metaphysical poets, like the madrigalists discussed in this chapter, pursued *maniera,* or mannerisms, which gave its name to Mannerism: an aesthetic characterized by deliberate exaggerations and an emphasis on the artist's seemingly arbitrary—even forced—connections between one item and another. They insisted that one perceive the world through the distorting lenses of their far-fetched metaphors. But although an earlier generation of scholars held to unbending standards of classic balance and thus spurned such poetry, a later one recognized its own transgressive preferences in these writers and used them to produce a radical shift in literary theory. Today the work of John Donne and Richard Crashaw enjoys considerable prestige in the academy, despite—or even *because* of—the excess and deliberate "tastelessness" in which they indulge on a regular basis. Their latter-day descendents, such as the Surrealist painters or Beat poet Lawrence Ferlinghetti, to whose *A Coney Island of the Mind* I allude in my title, likewise seek to stretch the limits of consciousness; by drawing on dreams or drug-induced states, such artists suggest ways of being resistant to the conformity demanded in the public sphere.

The madrigalism problem might be profitably compared to a similar debate of more recent times. I have referred already to the organicist assumptions of those steeped in the "absolute music" ideology of the nineteenth century. Their nemeses—the composers of program music—allowed extraneous items such as literary models to shape their formal procedures. As I have argued elsewhere, the nineteenth-century absolutists also invested in narrative strategies, though they did so within the schema of sonata, thus reinscribing a particular cultural version of centered subjective *Bildung.* Music—that most ineffable of media—could consequently present its "purely musical" arguments as though with no "extramusical" interventions. Not infrequently, critics and listeners ascribed some kind of metaphysical essence to symphonies or quartets. Artists on the programmatic side, on the other hand, happily admitted to the constructedness of their music; indeed, they announced in advance the *contingency* of their forms on something other than strictly musical convention. But although their detractors accused them of playing down for untutored audiences who needed such guides to help them make sense of their music, composers such as Berlioz, Liszt, and Richard Strauss used programs to explore other structural possibilities and also to suggest other potential ways of being than those traced in the sonata: they bent "the music itself" to other agendas, thereby destabilizing what the absolutists want to position as universal truth.

When Vincenzo Galilei attacks the pictorialisms found in certain madrigals, his arguments betray a strong desire to prioritize speech. For he not only expressed his disapproval of word painting but also of polyphonic counterpoint—anything, in other words, that would seem to call attention to musical ingenuity at the expense of verbal clarity and communicative transparency. As his own compositional experiments reveal, he preferred— very much like Saint Augustine or John Calvin—to shackle music to his texts, relegating it to the status of supporting role. But composers such as Giaches de Wert and Luca Marenzio mine their texts for unusual images, which (when taken literally) suggest a vast range of nearly psychedelic inner experiences. If the words serve as points of departure, they quickly become demoted to the status of mere signposts identifying the outrageous musical patterns they help to instigate.

So long as composers relate their music to lyrics in ways that do not call attention to the musical imagination per se, they apparently pass aesthetic muster.[2] Wert and Marenzio, however, make music go places it had never gone before (or since, for that matter). In taking the text "at its word" and literalizing its often bizarre tropes, they produce virtual realities that invite the listener to imagine the Self as infinitely malleable. I can demonstrate this best by undertaking a comparison between settings by Wert and Marenzio of a couple of particular texts.

SOLO E PENSOSO (WERT)

Few of Petrarch's *rime* provoke extreme reactions in composers quite so readily as "Solo e pensoso." As Martha Feldman has demonstrated, the influential sixteenth-century literary critic Pietro Bembo argued for the superiority of

---

2. Similar debates erupt with considerable frequency in popular music. Witness, for instance, the backlash against the musical virtuosity of late 1980s heavy metal and the emergence of "alternative," or the valorization in punk of a "do-it-yourself" crudeness, which is exalted by fans as "authentic."

Petrarch's verse over that of Dante because of its greater elegance, its avoidance of violent or excessive imagery.[3] But "Solo e pensoso" indulges extravagantly in Dante-esque tropes in its bid for depicting the utter violence seething inside the poet's serene, formally controlled exterior. Not only does Petrarch here describe vividly his inward feelings (and his paranoid terror that they can be discerned from the outside), but he casts about through an assortment of wild landscapes in his search for parallels to the savagery of his interiority. In other words, the sonnet extends an engraved invitation to composers who might be inclined to employ Mannerist strategies in their musical settings.

Solo e pensoso i più deserti campi
vo mesurando a passi tardi e lenti,
e gli occhi porto per fuggire intenti
ove vestigio uman la rena stampi.

Altro schermo non trovo che mi scampi
dal manifesto accorger de le genti,
perché negli atti d'allegrezza spenti
di fuor si legge com' io dentro avampi.

Sì ch' io mi credo omai che monti et piagge
et fiumi et selve sappian di che tempre
sia la mia vita, ch' è celata altrui;

ma pur sì aspre vie né sì selvagge
cercar non so ch' Amor non venga sempre
ragionando con meco, et io con lui.

Alone and pensive, the most deserted fields
I go measuring with slow, hesitant steps,
and I keep my eyes alert, so as to flee from
where human footprint marks the sand.

No other means I find to shield myself
from the curiosity manifested by people,
for in my actions, bereft of joy,
from without all can read how I burn inside.

3. Martha Feldman, "Rore's 'selva selvaggia': The *Primo libro* of 1542, " *Journal of the American Musicological Society* 42 (1989): 547–603, and *City Culture and the Madrigal at Venice* (Berkeley and Los Angeles: University of California Press, 1995).

Indeed, I believe that mountains and fields
and rivers and woods know the temper
of my life, which is concealed from others;

but so harsh and wild a path
I cannot find, but Love will always appear
discoursing with me, and I with him.

As in so many of the Petrarch sonnets discussed in previous chapters, "Solo e pensoso" presents a binary opposition between inside and outside. But it goes far beyond the apparent simplicity of this model, as inside becomes conflated with outside, outside becomes inside. Finally, the last line of the sonnet indicates that the problem does not really lie with the tensions of public and private at all, but rather with the needling irritant of Love, which the sonnet's persona carries like a parasite within himself at all times. A later, somewhat less subtle lyricist will write: "I attempt from Love's sickness to fly in vain, since I am myself my own fever"; Petrarch creates a text in which all of human society and even mute nature seem to hound him, forcing him to pursue an increasingly centrifugal (literally, fleeing the center) trajectory. But at the end he acknowledges that the real opposition is rooted at the core of his very being. Here we find a return to the beginning—"alone and pensive"—except that "alone" never truly can mean solitary; it always involves the internalized dialogue between Love and the Self ("con meco, et io con lui") (see Ex. 13).

Wert's setting of "Solo e pensoso" begins, as one might expect, with a solo voice in response to Petrarch's initial word. What one could not anticipate, however, is the path taken by that voice: a *soggetto* comprising two consecutive falling fifths—D to G to C—outlining not the mandatory modal octave but a ninth. Now, if any law of platonic order had seemed beyond violation, it was surely the limits set by the diapason of the basic musical terrain. Of course, composers often flirted with competing ways of dividing the modal octave, yet their strife usually occurred within the boundaries of the diapason. In Wert's extraordinary opening gesture, however, each successive note requires that listeners reorient their ears and conceptual frameworks with respect to implied mode. If the first pitch, D, could belong to Dorian or Mixolydian, the G seems to consolidate G as final (with D as cofinal); but the subsequent C throws all these attempts at calculating one's probable position into utter confusion. C will turn out to serve as the mostly unambiguous center in this C-Ionian madrigal, yet that D continues to resonate unresolved as a source of unease throughout.

Needless to say, the text made him do it. But Wert's reading of the text is not quite so obvious as it might seem initially. The bass makes its way down in free fall through the open spaces of those consecutive fifths, navigating erratically "the most deserted fields." But that deserted landscape presents itself as already beyond the control of civilization in its flagrant overreaching of the octave. And the composer who could conceive and perform such a transgression of fundamental cultural (and, by extension, mathematical and metaphysical) norms also implicitly sets himself outside all known terrain. Label him a genius or a madman, but he refuses (quite literally) to color inside the lines. And so far, he has given us three notes.

Wert compounds the initial offense by running his *soggetto* through imitative counterpoint, whereby the tenor and canto likewise reproduce the consecutive falling diapente at the interval of a fifth: G to C to F. If these answering voices at least situate G at the top of the tessitura, they also add F to the list of pitches vying for attention, expanding further the potentially endless expanse of those "deserti campi." Moreover, once the other voices enter, the bass begins to thrash about in all directions, contributing harmonic support but through multiple leaps of sixths (C to A, B to G, G to E), often crossing the tenor, who, in turn, commences presenting awkward sequences of sixths. In my discussion of Rore's "Mia benigna fortuna," I mentioned the outlaw status of the major sixth as a melodic pitch; Wert's ricocheting sixths disorient the ear almost as much as the falling fifths. The five voices enter tethered by no greater law than adherence to this bizarre *soggetto* and its equally bizarre countersubject. Together they produce the effect of echoes bouncing randomly off the walls of an empty canyon, both marking the expanse of wilderness and mocking the narrator's solitude by throwing his utterance back at him like a mob of jeering individuals—his greatest fear, as we shall see. Also in the manner of echoes, the rebounded replies begin to contract temporally: thus the quinto and alto present their versions in syncopation. Eventually, in m. 8, the bass grounds itself on C, thereby providing some grounding for the wildly careening voices above it. They too gradually consolidate (though by way of outlandishly large melodic leaps) around a C-major triad: the echo finally dies away, though its effects linger on even after the last entry falls below the threshold of audibility.

This opening gambit asserts its virtuosity in two principal ways. First, as the discussion above suggests, Wert finds more and more ways of representing the idea of solitude and deserted landscapes: solo voice, falling and open fifths, the transgression of fundamental codes regulating civilized behavior, the excessive interval of the ninth, the ricocheting figures composed of sixths, the syncopation of echoes, the open triad within which voices continue to rebound, the gradual fading away of sound. And I haven't even mentioned the way the bass in m. 7 extends the scope to B♭ as a means of harmonizing the generative F but also as yet another violation of the rules and a symmetrical counterbalance to the A just presented in the quinto. The open field now stretches out on either side of the final thus: b♭-f-C-g-d-a.

Second, these images allow Wert to play with all kinds of unexplored and even illicit musical relationships *yet while always maintaining intelligibility.* A critic still wedded to the criteria of later instrumental music might object that we couldn't, in fact, make sense of this passage without the text. True enough (though this objection also pertains to Schoenberg's *Erwartung*), but Wert knew that the text would be there to justify him. And it permits him to press the limits of his received musical language in extraordinary new directions. If *maniera* are meant to provoke wonder, this passage sizzles.

A few words on harmony before we proceed to the setting of line 2. One could undertake a chordal analysis of this opening section without much difficulty (G-C-F-d-G⁶-G-C, etc.). It is not clear, however, what such information *means.* The chords do not line up in ways that suggest goal-oriented tonal progressions, and a reduction of this sort loses sight of the manipulations and their implications that go together to produce that series of vertical collections. Yet from another point of view, the harmonies matter enormously, for the consonant coincidences among the various lines allow for the extreme disjunction in the individual melodies themselves. Wert pulls us into a circular logic whereby the melodic *soggetti* generate the principal meanings, then suggest a number of possible harmonizations within which the other voices happen to insert themselves without friction, though also without a sense of teleological progression. This circularity contributes to the effect of steady though never predictable movement through a wilderness of constantly changing vistas.

Petrarch takes up this very image—that of measured, slow, hesitant steps—in line 2, and again Wert responds with a dazzling musical analogue: the slow, stepwise ascent in each of the staggered voices through a C or G scale. In great contrast to the chaotic activity of the previous passage, this one proceeds with caution, methodically placing one foot in front of the other. In retrospect, the whole opening section converts to a portrait of the deserted fields, while the second introduces the physical gestures of the narrator. But, as we've seen, it's never that simple, for the wilderness rages also within the narrator. The distance between the seething excess of the first section and the attempt at imposing strict control over his behavior and/or feelings in the second marks out the affective extremes of the madrigal.

Yet just as in Monteverdi's "Ah, dolente partita," the parallel presentation of the same materials on different pitch levels does not necessarily spell security or order. Which voice is really in charge? Which decides on cadence points? The bass certainly serves as anchor for the first several measures, as it mounts up through the C-Ionian scale. The alto, which had started off in this same guise, loses its bid as leader as it melts in downward cascading ornaments. At this point, the quinto—which has sounded like a mere filler—pushes its way upward past its own octave goal of G to A in m. 17, pressing even the bass into its service for an elided cadence on G. In the meantime, the canto has started its own long-delayed ascent, with even longer durations. Underneath that slow, hesitant climb, the lower voices begin hopping about in a quasi-ostinato pattern that keeps repeating (intensified by close syncopation), as though stuck in an obsessive loop. If the canto finally attains the peak of the scalar ascent through those measured steps, it does so despite the obstructions and distractions that now manifest themselves underneath that controlled exterior. The canto leads to the madrigal's first strong cadence in m. 27—a brief tonicization of D, the still-unresolved pitch that began the piece—but the struggle of rising above and subduing those inward disturbances is palpable: this scarcely counts as a moment of reconciliation.

To allay the reader's fears, I promise that I will not go through each line of text in this kind of detail. I think it necessary to do so for the first two passage, however, for a couple of reasons. First, they count as among the very most spectacular in the literature, and they reward close scrutiny; I cannot even claim to have exhausted their complexities in the course of these pages. Second, and more important, they illustrate the problem of reducing musical passages too quickly back to the words that inspired them. Wert's settings may start out as literal "paintings" of corresponding lines of text, but as they unfold through their musical elaboration, they reveal many different levels of meaning not explicitly stated in the poetry. Granted, the idea of matching the measured steps with ascending scales may appear obvious and almost trivial in its Mickey-Mousing. But as Wert layers in ambiguities, inner conflicts, indecision concerning harmonic goal, and obsessive cycling, we come to realize the psychological depth of his reading. He accomplishes all this, moreover, in a mere sixteen bars.

Wert had an inexhaustible arsenal with which he created musical images to match those of the poetry he set, and I would be remiss if I did not at least mention a few of the other marvels that occur within this particular madrigal. "E gli occhi porto" (m. 27) receives a jerky motive (introduced in the very high—might one say hysterical?—range of the tenor) to match the paranoid surveillance confessed in the text; "ove vestigio uman" (m. 31) recalls in far less heroic terms the stepwise footsteps of "vo mesurando"; "altro schermo non trovo" (m. 42) brandishes an insistent repeated-note *soggetto* as if to ward off all glances; "dal manifesto accorger de le genti" (m. 49), which is set homophonically, both illustrates the solidarity of this invasive mob of curious people and also presents a nudging or maybe even a peeping gesture on the first syllable of "GEN-ti"; this casual prurience gives way (m. 53) to a brief portrait of the poet's inward state of collapse—especially marked in the second iteration in which the voices combine to simulate a failed attempt (on the second syllable of "at-TI") at wresting himself from the melancholy in which he is mired; and the devastating last line, which admits that everyone sees straight through him despite his self-protective strategies, offers a gleeful skipping motive (m. 61), as though all his anguish serves as but a source of not-quite-so-innocent merriment. In contrast to all the previous lines, many of which receive extended, lavish treatment, this line appears only once. It concludes the *prima parte* with the cruelty of children mocking a weakling in the schoolyard, and it requires no second hearing to create its impact.

This humiliating invasion and rejection by his fellow creatures compels the narrator into the *seconda parte,* in which he seeks refuge in empathetic nature, and here Wert pulls out all the stops. The extravagances of the *prima parte* fade quickly, almost as if they had functioned primarily as antecedent to this remarkable consequent. As if to recover lost dignity, the *seconda parte* opens with a steely recitation tone in three voices, outlining the C-Ionian species boundaries—what should have happened at the outset of the madrigal. A soft caress on B♭ marking "piagge" (m. 64) gives way, however, to a stunning simulation of rivers: swirling sixteenth-note melismas in three voices in parallel *fauxbourdon.* The most spectacular pictorialization thus far, this setting of "fiumi" also matches the wildness of the speaker's interiority, for he claims that only such natural phenomena can comprehend his condition. The recitation tone returns in the canto, and although the poet continues to communicate on the outside, we witness the flood raging within, and it even sweeps the canto along in its torrential wake. After offering this shockingly candid glimpse into the narrator's "true state,"

Wert pulls back as though in embarrassment to a more subdued, muttering conversational style (m. 70).

But he does so only to unleash the most bizarre image of the entire madrigal. On "ma pur sì aspre vie né sì selvagge / cercar non so," the three upper voices burst out in a jagged melody, reminiscent of the sixth-laden countersubject of the madrigal's very first passage. Although it has no chromatic pitches, the angularity of this *soggetto* makes it almost as difficult to execute vocally as a song by Anton Webern. As though in an attempt at fleeing civilization, the motive leaps from rugged peak to valley, around hairpin curves, but finds rest in neither extreme. To compound the effect, Wert sets this ungainly tune in three parallel, *fauxbourdon* voices, both heightening the sense of peril and the impossibility of breaking loose from those shadow figures that persist in following, regardless of the terrain. Most of all, however, he delivers an image of interiority so distraught that it seems to be trying to shed its own skin. If Wert produces a Coney Island of the mind, this passage would qualify as the roller-coaster.

Despite the violence of this image, the last line returns us to rigid recitation, as ubiquitous Love whispers unfailingly in his ear. The two final images continue in superimposition until the very last four measures, when the murmuring psalm-tone at last usurps all the voices. Throughout this concluding page, the gapped melody tries to shake off that obsessive reminder—or at least to drown out its monotonous drone—but to no avail. The struggle ends in defeat. Note too that Wert refuses to give us cadential confirmation of this eventuality. Instead, the piece seals itself off with the other bookend from the one that marked the beginning: in place of the overexpansive D-G-C, Wert now give us the symmetrical contraction in the bass of B♭-F-C. The madrigal folds up like a fan, no closer to a solution than at the beginning, though free, perhaps, of the futile illusions that generated both poem and madrigal.

In the works discussed in previous chapters, the centered Self served as a kind of anchor. Even when Rore sought to dismantle the eternal verities of diatonic pitches and modal propriety, he did so because his notions of identity bridled at external regulation—somewhat like Schoenberg throwing off the chains of tonality for the sake of truer self-expression. By contrast, Wert does not concern himself here with overriding allegories or with modal structure per se; although he does produce that brilliant gesture of consecutive fifths to tie off (while not at all resolving) the opening *soggetto*, most of the madrigal's motives and cadences confirm the C-Ionian species boundaries. Mode serves, in other words, primarily as a relatively stable backdrop for the special effects of the surface, among which one would have to count the opening gesture.

But if Rore opened the gates for the representation of the alienated Self, Wert follows with his constructions of centrifugal subjectivities. His madrigals subject us to stunning sequences of rapidly changing images; he aims to surprise, shock, startle, amaze. Even if Petrarch's sonnet suggested this sequence of vivid ideas, Wert's literalization and surreal expansion of them takes us to an entirely new level. Just imagine feeling inwardly like the musical passage setting the line "ma pur sì aspre vie"! No one could have anticipated a musical setting of this sort, compared to which Petrarch's initially outrageous metaphor appears quite tame.

Despite their eccentricities, Wert's compositional strategies still pay homage to matters of artistic economy. In retrospect, one finds that these ever-shifting images make use continually of a small reservoir of shapes: monotonal recitation, orderly stepwise ascents, melodies that thrash about through wide intervals. The final page of the madrigal brings the most important of these into direct confrontation with one another, thus reversing the centrifugal proliferation of imagery in "Solo e pensoso" to a centripetal bid for unity. In other words, Wert calculates his excesses from his sophisticated knowledge of norms.

But something else manifests itself in Wert's setting of "Solo e pensoso"— something not necessarily intended as part of the message but crucial nonetheless. The composers discussed in previous chapters designed their madrigals for participatory performance: the singers also served as the target auditors. And although others often listened to the resulting music, their pleasure qualified as vicarious compared to that of the executants, whose voices interacted to produce the experiences of interiority heard from the outside. Accordingly, Arcadelt makes few technical demands on his singers; even Willaert—whose fiercely independent lines require the highest degree of concentration—avoids anything that would ordinarily count as virtuosic, such as rapid ornaments, disjunct contours, or high pitches. Castiglione himself testifies to the music-making skills expected of courtiers. They provided themselves with their own entertainment and at the same time displayed (as though casually) the grace and cultural discernment they had worked to develop.

Wert's madrigals, however, bear witness to a new phase of music's social history. He composed increasingly for professional musicians, who rehearsed until they had polished their scores to a high state of perfection, then performed them proscenium-style before a passive audience. Anthony Newcomb has investigated in detail these shifts, which occurred first at the d'Este court at Ferrara,[4] and Wert absorbed these new practices at Ferrara before he brought them back to Mantua, the court where this Flemish composer produced most of his music.[5] But even if we did not know from external sources about these shifts, they make themselves felt in pieces of this sort. Few amateur musicians could negotiate the illicit fifths of Wert's opening *soggetto,* and even the best sight-singers would make a mess of the images on "fiumi" or "ma pur sì aspre vie"—scarcely the effect Wert had in mind! Something similar happens with the entry of jazz into the painstaking arrangements of Fletcher Henderson and Don Redman. Listen, for example, to "Wrappin' It Up" (1934), in which the reeds play dazzlingly fast diminutions in parallel motion—remarkably like those that occur in the *seconda parte* of Wert's madrigal. Henderson's and Redman's commitment to ensemble-oriented precision sets a new (and very different) standard for jazz performance and had the effect of marginalizing improvisation during the Swing Era. In like manner, Wert's score warns: "Don't try this at home!"

This shift in the madrigal had profound effects on conceptions of subjectivity. If Willaert immersed his performer/auditors in the structuring of interiority from the inside—actually making each singer experience the conflicts between his/her line and those that battled for supremacy around it—Wert positions his listeners as spectators who watch the process unfold in pyrotechnics from the outside. Participation gives way to the gaze, dense interaction to awe-inspiring surface. In view of this change, Wert's setting of Petrarch's line "di fuor si legge com' io dentro avampi" ("from without all can read how I burn inside") takes on new shades of meaning. But, of course, Petrarch's project itself strove for the most public circulation of his own purportedly intimate confessions, always already intended for the gaze.

SOLO E PENSOSO (MARENZIO)

In the hothouse environment of the Renaissance Italian courts, ideas quickly spawned imitations and flagrant instances of one-upmanship, ev-

---

4. Anthony Newcomb, *The Madrigal at Ferrara, 1579–1597* (Princeton: Princeton University Press, 1980).

5. Carol MacClintock remains the principal musicologist to focus on Wert. See her *Giaches de Wert (1535–1596), Life and Works* (n.p.: American Institute of Musicology, 1966). MacClintock shares my concern with mode in her analyses.

idence of both homage and competition. Not infrequently a composer would seize a particularly striking image from another and ring changes on it to show that its originator had failed to realize or (at least) to exhaust its potential. Wert's younger contemporary Luca Marenzio—incidentally, the first native-born Italian composer we have discussed thus far—responded to the former's setting of "Solo e pensoso" in a way that threw down the Mannerist gauntlet. A northern Italian, Marenzio entered the service of Cardinal Luigi d'Este and thus had strong connections with the court of Ferrara and its musical establishment, even though he lived and worked principally in Rome. With respect to the influence on Marenzio of Wert's music, James Chater writes: "Wert's *VII a 5* . . . is therefore something of a time bomb where Marenzio is concerned: its full impact only becomes apparent more than a decade later."[6] Marenzio works, of course, from the same specificities of Petrarch's sonnet that previously had inspired Wert, but he also has Wert's setting in front of him as he composes (see Ex. 14).

The idea that seeds Marenzio's "Solo e pensoso" is Wert's setting of the line "vo mesurando"—in particular, the presentation in the canto in mm. 18–27, which mounts slowly by step the scale from G to G, then descends partway for a cadence on D. Instead of Wert's diatonic ascent, however, Marenzio has his canto rise through a chromatic scale from G to G—and then (in a hair-raising extension of the original) on through G♯ to A before reversing direction and moving by half steps down to that same D that had served as Wert's arrival point. Direct chromaticism of this sort rarely occurred in music of the time: it still counted as irrational or beyond the grasp of standard theory. Of all the modes, only Dorian had the innate capacity for direct chromaticism (as we have seen, it had access to both versions of sixth and seventh degrees), and few composers exploited that capability except for extreme circumstances. Marenzio's canto does not even pretend to derive its pitches from within a set mode (actually Mixolydian, as it turns out); it simply measures by orderly (but fundamentally and scandalously irrational) half step the entire gamut from G to G.

Wert produced this image for the second line of Petrarch's sonnet; he had already presented his dazzling setting of the first on the basis of an entirely different metaphor. Again in an attempt to do Wert one better, Marenzio combines the first two lines. Not only does the canto sing directly through

6. James Chater, *Luca Marenzio and the Italian Madrigal 1577–93* (Ann Arbor: UMI, 1981), vol. 1, 123.

the first two lines in the course of the ascent, but it does so all alone ("solo"): whereas Wert's measured steps triggered a point of imitation involving all voices, only Marenzio's canto sings this *soggetto*. But the modally distorted outline of Wert's opening gambit also makes its appearance at the beginning of the Marenzio. Whereas Wert gave us two consecutive fifths, outlining a ninth, Marenzio produces a countersubject to the canto made up of falling thirds, embracing sometimes a seventh and sometimes a ninth. Like Wert, Marenzio wants his image to signify in several different ways: this unruly motive, which jumps about wildly, occurs in imitation, thus compounding the mischief. It calls to mind explicitly the jagged countersubject at the beginning of the Wert as well as the cycling, syncopated motive underneath the canto's "vo mesurando," thus condensing two of Wert's concepts into one.

Finally, unlike Wert, who did not make his distinction between inside and outside on the basis of voice parts, Marenzio casts the canto alone as the alienated subject, struggling on its methodical path over the rugged landscape and against the busy social chattering that goes on around it. This latter effect comes through particularly well because the canto begins the ascent at a lower pitch level than the alto's countersubject, and its very slow motion (one quarter the rate of the other voices) makes it relatively inconspicuous at first. To be sure, each successive chromatic pitch serves to generate the harmonies to which the other voices must accommodate themselves. But the logic of its astonishing trajectory becomes apparent to the ear only around m. 7 or so. Suddenly its defiant climb commands the attention, and one can listen to little else as it attains the octave, then exceeds it. It literally separates itself from the crowd in its lonely, heroic quest, oblivious to the mundane bustle that surrounds it.

Gradually the canto pulls the other voices into its orbit—or (depending on your interpretation of this shift) the other voices likewise take up lines of slow, measured scales when they too reach the words "vo mesurando." The latter reading seems more self-evident: the text changes and so does the musical imagery. But given the overarching gesture in the canto, which joins the two sections together into one, we might well hear the decreased rhythmic clamor and the austere chromatic harmonic moves in mm. 15–21 as the successful emergence into those "più deserti campi" mentioned at the outset. If most of the lines take on the methodical quality of the canto, the bass throws in one more reference to the wildness of the landscape in m. 22, when it jumps a ninth (a direct ninth, in contrast to Wert's successive fifths) in preparation for the cadence on G in m. 24. And in response to "lenti"—the last word in Petrarch's line—the motion slows and finally halts with an exaggeratedly articulated arrival. All the voices participate except the canto, who remains aloof, still holding that D that also served (though with different harmonization) as its end point in Wert's passage.

Rather than scrolling this very rich madrigal, I will fast-forward to the conclusion of the *seconda parte*—the setting of the last terzet, which inspired Wert's most extraordinary set of images. Marenzio had already alluded to two of the devices that made Wert's parting shot so extraordinary: Wert's jagged melodic profile that seeks to throw off all traces in "ma pur sì aspre vie" occurs in Marenzio's settings of the lines "dal manifesto accorger de le genti" (m. 56) and "di fuor si legge" (m. 71), and his virtuosic *fauxbourdon* shows up in Marenzio's "perché negli atti d'allegrezza spenti" (m. 63).

Consequently, he pursues a somewhat different tack for the concluding collision between wild searching and the inevitability of Love's reason. Marenzio's passage includes in bass and quinto voices the wide leaps that had appeared in Wert at this point, but Marenzio's wilderness is chromatic—referring back to his starting gesture, but now not even holding onto the tenuous rope bridge that made the canto's opening gambit at least methodical. In a series of glacially slow interlocking shifts that recall Willaert, Marenzio begins at one end of his available spectrum—at E, confirmed with F♯—through to the far-flat side to E♭. One could trace this sequence of changes to the fundamental tension between B/B♭, which the canto's opening line prepares. The first several harmonies pivot around B, and it is the canto's unexpected collapse to B♭ in m. 116 ("aspre") that brings forth the other extreme. Marenzio's Self, in other words, can grasp onto either side of the chromatic divide and quickly scan through all possible options.

And yet, all this internal wrestling avails nothing. With the line "ch' Amor non venga sempre / ragionando con meco," Marenzio presents a straight, unadorned scalar descent in the canto from G to G. This is, of course, the same terrain traced by the canto's arduous chromatic climb at the very beginning; like Sisyphus's boulder, the weight shoved with so much strenuous labor up the Mixolydian scale just bounces effortlessly back down. As Robert Palmer would say, "Might as well face it, you're addicted to Love." A cadential motive for "et io con lui" flickers through the contrapuntal fabric, conceding the futility of all those gnarly avoidance strategies. *No lo contendere.*

In Chapter 2 we examined Verdelot's enigmatic musical response to Machiavelli's "O dolce notte." Although Machiavelli's play qualifies generically as a comic play, its dark resonances and cynicism situate it closer to the other end of the spectrum from comedy, and much of the play's moral ambivalence condenses around this particular canzona, under the oblique cover of which the actual liaison takes place. Verdelot set this verse in praise of night and obscurity with a sonority that might be either Phrygian with a raised mediant or a desire-saturated precadential harmony, the leading tone of which lends urgency to the situation but does not (at least not within the boundaries of the canzona itself) reach fulfillment. When the curtain rises on the final act of *La Mandragola,* we discover that Callimaco's scheme worked beyond the scope of his wildest dreams. But Verdelot's music withholds that knowledge, instead holding the spectator in a state of reverberant suspense.

I want to return to that ambiguous configuration that opens Verdelot's setting of "O dolce notte," though if it played the first time as something akin to ethical tragedy, it functions in its later context unequivocally as farce. Moreover, my reading of Verdelot's strategy, which may have seemed an overinterpretation to those skeptical of such sophistication in early madrigalists, here reaches confirmation, for Marenzio's celebrated "Tirsi morir volea" depends for its ribald effects on precisely the same modal complex. In his setting of Guarini's sexually graphic madrigal verse, Marenzio strives to make his intentions perfectly clear; as we shall see, so do Peter Philips (who arranged Marenzio's three-part sequence for virginal) and Wert (who sets Guarini's text as a quasi-theatrical dialogue).

Many of Arcadelt's madrigals that trade on the equation of "death" with sexual climax do so in ways that resonate with the Divine Love sought after by mystics. Not so Guarini, whose madrigal reduces the conventional double entendre to something that truly does count as little more than a protracted dirty joke.[7]

Tirsi morir volea,
gli occhi mirando di colei ch' adora;

---

7. Laura Macy deals briefly with these and other settings of "Tirsi morir volea" in her "Speaking of Sex: Metaphor and Performance in the Italian Madrigal," *Journal of Musicology* 14.1 (Winter 1996): 1–34. According to her calculations (p. 19), at least twenty-seven composers set this text over the course of the sixteenth and seventeenth centuries.

ond' ella, che di lui non meno ardea,
gli disse: "Ohimè, ben mio,
deh, non morir ancora,
ché teco bramo di morir anch' io."

Frenò Tirsi il desio
ch' havea di pur sua vita all' hor finire,
et sentìa morte e non potea morire.
Et mentre fisso il guardo pur tenea
ne' begli occhi divini
et nettare amoroso indi bevea,
la bella Ninfa sua, che già vicini
sentìa i messi d'Amore,
disse con occhi languidi e tremanti:
"Mori, cor mio, ch' io moro."
Le rispose il Pastore:
"Et io, mia vita, moro."

Così morirno i fortunati amanti
di morte sì soave e sì gradita,
che per anco morir tornaro in vita.

Tirsi wanted to die,
his eyes gazing on her whom he adored;
she, who burned no less than he,
said to him: "Alas, my love,
do not die yet,
for I too wish to die with you."

Tirsi checked the desire
he felt to end his life immediately,
And felt death but could not die.
And while he held his gaze fixed
on the beautiful, divine eyes
and there drank of amorous nectars,
his lovely nymph, who now close by
felt the messengers of Love,
said, with languid, trembling eyes:
"Die, my heart, for I am dying."
The shepherd answered her:
"And I, my life, am dying."

Thus died the fortunate lovers
a death so sweet and so welcome,
that to die again they returned to live.

Whatever Guarini's verse lacks in subtlety, however, gets added back in with the religiosity of Marenzio's setting (see Ex. 15). The solemn fall of an open fifth at the beginning sounds like the lugubrious "Aus tiefer Noth" (the Protestant chorale version of "Out of the depths have I cried unto you, O Lord!") or Victoria's "O magnum mysterium." After the canto sustains its naked B for a full tactus, the other voices come in to harmonize it with an E-major triad. The canto plummets to its would-be point of rest, E; but its partner voices merely sustain their sonority, then cadence in their own right (with the bass falling the open fifth) on A, leaving the canto and alto to circle impotently around E for a Phrygian conclusion in m. 6. Leading tones—those producers of musical desire—work overtime in this short sequence, as G# intensifies a desire for A, C# for D. But alas, the voices do not coordinate properly, the energy drains away, and we end on an E circumscribed on top by F♮.

In Marenzio's reading of "Tirsi morir volea," that starting configuration of the E-major triad will stand for the urgent wish to die, expressed by both Tirsi and his inamorata, but they will not manage to get their act together for a cadence on A until the conclusion of the *seconda parte.* Numbers one and three of the sequence end up stranded on that yearning E-major triad— the first as Tirsi's Beloved begs him to wait for her, the third as they decide to rev up again for another go at it. The E-major triad, their emblem of resurrection, would qualify as the key note, if statistical frequency matters; but the three-part madrigal probably belongs not with the E modes, despite its strongly Phrygian proclivities, but with A-Aeolian. Indeed, Marenzio defines A as the desired point of arrival throughout. Clori dwells mostly in D, with its attendant B♭, first to indicate how very far she still is from Tirsi's imminent climax on A, eventually to stake it out as the terrain for her own *jouissance.* At the outset of the *seconda parte,* "Frenò," Tirsi himself has to mark time in D as he tries to avoid cadencing prematurely. But after the resounding convergence of D and E species on A at the end of the *seconda parte,* the narrator returns us to the newly aroused E-major triad of the beginning, its B natural on top yearning for resolution, exacerbated by the already-tumescent G# in the harmony.

As in Monteverdi's "Ah, dolente partita" (see Chapter 1), A-Aeolian with all its standard internal tensions provides the mechanism that drives "Tirsi morir volea." Like Monteverdi, Marenzio knows how to harness those tensions, how to map them onto a text to create a powerful, apparently self-generated allegory. To be sure, the Guarini verses Monteverdi chooses differ significantly from those that inspire Marenzio's sequence. Yet diatonic Aeolian manages to accommodate both situations; neither composer even has to depart from the rules.

So secure are the grammatical implications of Marenzio's madrigal that its allegorical jokes survive intact in Peter Philips's keyboard arrangement, which appears in the *Fitzwilliam Virginal Book*. Musicologists usually emphasize the abstract patterning that the English virginalists—especially Philips and William Byrd—bring to their arrangements of contemporary songs, and this preference emerges very clearly in pieces such as "Walsingham," in which a short popular tune serves as the basis for a series of increasingly dazzling variations. But Philips often set entire through-composed vocal pieces that had been smuggled into Protestant England from the Catholic continent: in addition to the Marenzio's "Tirsi" cycle, he also arranged French chansons by Lasso and even Giulio Caccini's celebrated monody "Amarilli, mia bella." He apparently assumed the familiarity of some of his listeners with the vocal versions of these pieces, and this seems particularly the case in the arrangement of the Marenzio, some of whose madrigals Philips himself had edited for English circulation.

One can, of course, enjoy the *Fitzwilliams* "Tirsi" without knowing Guarini's pastoral poem or Marenzio's original five-voice madrigal: its dynamic pacing, extravagant variety, and technical virtuosity more than hold the attention. Indeed, when Frescobaldi later instructs performers to perform his free-form toccatas as though they were madrigals, he must have had in mind practices such as the one conveniently written out for us by Philips. It sounds quite simply like a Froberger toccata or a Louis Couperin unmeasured prélude, neither of which relies on hidden texts. If one knows how Marenzio's music dramatizes Guarini's ribald dialogue, however, the Philips becomes downright hilarious, for he enhances to the breaking point Marenzio's jokes concerning delayed gratification.

The opening gambit of Marenzio's pseudomotet, for instance, receives from Philips a setting of great pathos: each of the two pitches of the canto's fifth on "Tirsi" gets enunciated with a trill, which will become a sign of urgency. Passage work in both hands drives the energy forward to the A sonority that will stand for gratification, only to have the supporting voices suddenly dry up. The right hand, now completely alone, twists and turns before devolving onto a dissatisfied (and sadly trilled) E. Philips marks his repetition of the phrase with even greater agitation, especially (if one is clocking his intabulation against the Marenzio, which he follows measure for measure) on the word "volea": Tirsi really, REALLY wants to die! When the dialogue turns to the quotation from Tirsi's Beloved (m. 25), Philips presents her melodramatic languishing in a rhythmically displaced right-hand part that leans heavily and repeatedly on a dissonant F ($\hat{6}$ in A but a Phrygian $\hat{2}$ against the E in the bass). Yet the flurried action stops abruptly with her demand: "ché teco bramo," three A-major triads, each jangling with trills, each held for the duration of a half note—and this after a frenetic series of thirty-second notes.

As in the Marenzio, however, it is the middle madrigal, "Frenò," that really turns up the heat, as Tirsi refrains from cadencing using any and all deceptive devices available to him. Note in the passage where he feels death yet cannot die: the preparatory E-major triad of m. 71 (matched with "non") pushes all its pent-up energy instead onto D ("potea"), whence it continues to churn away to reach at last in m. 74 a brief cadence on A (what "morire" will finally be). This evaporates immediately, however, giving way to yet another holding pattern that plunges ahead seeking some kind of relief. When our attention turns again to the Beloved ("La bella Ninfa," m. 84), a mechanical figure enters, virtually marking time (whether this represents Tirsi doing multiplication tables to keep from spilling or his nymph's apparent impassivity, we cannot tell). But at last, she announces her arrival, which Philips marks in m. 105 with trills in both hands. And for nearly the first time in this madrigal, the diminutions stop, as we hear Tirsi's valediction and the simultaneous release of both parties.

Of the return to life in Philips's *terza parte,* I will point only to the excessively grand arrival on C to mark the words "i fortunati amanti"—by far the most stable cadence in the entire piece and a moment that flies by without much articulation in Marenzio. But the point of this last section is to return us to the agitation and erotic frenzy that seems to have dissipated in m. 124, and so the *passaggi* begin to swirl again, leading impulsively forward to the ever-so-fraught final sonority, the return to opening position, where Tirsi once again wants desperately to die.

In his intabulation of Marenzio's "Tirsi morir volea" cycle, Peter Philips produces a tone poem: an instrumental composition that maps out a sexual encounter in graphic detail. To be sure, one needs to know the "program" to follow all the details, and the performer needs to be in on the joke to make it aurally effective; its ability to communicate its full meaning is contingent on something that resides "outside" the music itself. But this entry in the *Fitzwilliam Virginal Book* differs from all the others in its determination to enact in vivid musical gesture a narrative scenario. It stands as a kind of missing link between the verbally confirmed signification of the madrigal and the wordless flamboyance of the seventeenth-century keyboard toccata.

TIRSI MORIR VOLEA (WERT)

Marenzio's setting of "Tirsi morir volea" had acquired such fame that it could even serve as a touchstone for the beleaguered English-Catholic community. When Giaches de Wert published his setting of the same Guarini text in 1581, the year after Marenzio's, he took an entirely different tack; in place of Marenzio's ostensibly somber pseudomotet, Wert composed what he classified as a *Dialogo* for seven voices, the bottom four for the narrator and Tirsi, the top three for the nymph. The increasing popularity of the dramatic idiom in the court of Ferrara—where Tasso and Guarini produced their celebrated pastoral plays—encouraged Wert to start honing his musical skills for purposes of theatrical declamation. Although his multivoiced setting does not offer the realistic representation of single individuals speaking their own lines in monody, it does anticipate many of the temporal and syntactical solutions eventually ascribed to Jacopo Peri in his opera *Euridice* of 1600 (see Ex. 16).

To preserve a sense of speech and dynamic propulsion, Wert maintains only occasionally ruffled homophonic declamation throughout. As a result, the leisurely unfolding of Marenzio's three-madrigal series gets compressed into a short, fast-paced recitation: Wert reaches the word "Frenò" (the beginning of Marenzio's *seconda parte*), for instance, in m. 15 and "Così morirno" (Marenzio's *terza parte*) in m. 39; it's over before you can sneeze. Wert also seems to realize that he has to alter radically his harmonic rhythm—his temporal sense—in order to satisfy his new criteria. Thus, although the voices all move at more or less the same time, each recites the same pitches for the most part until ready to move to the next syntactic unit.

He also eschews for this *dialogo* the allegorical twists and turns that Marenzio carries to such heights in his setting. Wert's Tirsi, his breathless narrator, and even the nymph all drive forward with single-minded zeal; they take time out for a single cadence on the fifth degree, and never traffic at all with more obfuscatory tactics. Contributing to the utter transparency of this scenario is Wert's reliance throughout on the most familiar formula for improvised recitation and instrumental jamming: the G-Hypodorian diapente, harmonized in its most fundamental ways (including B♭ as one of the most stable supports of $\hat{5}$). This impulse to capture the drive of spoken dialogue, the model of Guarini's pastorals (rather than Greek tragedy, as backers of the Florentine Camarata will later claim), and even the stripped-down syntax upon which Wert relies will result in the cluster of musical practices that condense around monody a couple of decades later.

Within his setting of Guarini's text, Wert directs the listener's attention primarily to his jagged rhythms, rife with anticipations that constantly threaten to jump the gun and leap for immediate satisfaction. The contrast between tense, simultaneous declamation and moments of imitative counterpoint that marked the distinction in Arcadelt between speech and passion-rattled interiority obtain throughout this *dialogo*. Even the narrator comes apart slightly at the seams with the first mention of the nymph in m. 5, which provokes—over the static harmonies that hold us in place—a point of imitation on an extravagant *soggetto*. When the nymph herself enters (sounding quite like the Supremes singing and gesticulating through "Stop in the Name of Love"), she issues her demand with the clearest of grammar, halting only over a sustained and strained E♭ in the lowest voice to offer a two-voice simulation of what her intertwining with Tirsi might sound like. (The top three voices were no doubt designed for the fabled *concerto di donne,* the Ladies of Ferrara whose high-voice virtuosity—as featured in compositions by Wert and Luzzasco Luzzaschi—pushed the envelope of the madrigal almost beyond recognition and led to many of the generic transformations that make seventeenth-century Italian music so radically different from that of the sixteenth.)[8]

Tirsi now casts around for ways of delaying the inevitable. He moves to B♭ (m. 17), to a prepared then voided cadence on G in m. 18, to a suggestion of D in m. 19, to a melodically disappointed arrival on G in m. 21. Finally the narrator hunkers down like a sportscaster at an especially critical moment in a game. Beginning in a stage whisper low in their ranges in m. 21, the four bottom voices trace the incremental rise of erotic excitement from B♭ to V/G to D, to V/C, and finally in m. 32 to a ludicrous depiction of the nymph's trembling eyes over V/G. Wasting no more time, the nymph enters with her long-awaited announcement: "Die, my heart, for I am dying," set in the most direct possible terms as $\hat{2}$-$\hat{3}$-$\hat{4}$-$\hat{3}$-$\hat{2}$-$\hat{1}$, to which invitation Tirsi responds in kind. The two characters echo back and forth anti-

8. See my "Fetisch Stimme: Professionelle Sänger im Italien der frühen Neuzeit," in *Zwischen Rauschen und Offenbarung: Zur Kultur- und Mediengeschichte der Stimme,* ed. Friedrich Kittler, Thomas Macho, and Sigrid Weigel (Berlin: Akademie Verlag, 2002), 199–214.

phonally at closer and closer time intervals and finally come together—all seven voices at once for the first time in the piece—for a powerful G-Hypodorian cadence in mm. 37–38.

Wert instructs the singers to abandon their last pitches abruptly on a weak beat. Although the grand pause that ensues lasts only half a measure, the frenetic pace of the *dialogo* up until that point causes this gap to sound like an energy vacuum, and it rarely fails to draw guffaws from audiences. On the other side of the grand pause, the entire ensemble enters with mock solemnity (nearly as hilarious as the silence itself) to explain the lovers' need to return to life. And rather than simply report their desire to die again ("di mille mort' il di," as Arcadelt would say), the seven voices split once again into their roles to present yet another simulation of mounting friction to heat and simultaneous ejaculation.

If Marenzio presented the encounter between Tirsi and his Beloved as pseudoreligious ecstatic transcendence, Wert offers it up as a Sid Caesar routine from *Your Show of Shows;* Marenzio pulls Guarini's ribald text back to parody the elevated world of Willaert's Petrarchan madrigals, while Wert matches the playwright's sly humor stroke for stroke and with the rapid-fire temporality theatre requires. The comic timing he displays here should make us regret all the more the fact that Wert died before he could try his hand at opera. The genre might have developed in entirely different directions— or at least we would arrived much earlier at the sex farces of Cavalli's Venetian stage without having to wade through the cardboard shepherds of opera's first decade.[9]

But Wert's experiments in dramatic declamation point forward to the concerns of my next book.[10] And these will have to wait, for we have not yet finished with the classic madrigal. Indeed, some of its greatest triumphs appear in the years following Wert's *dialogo.* If Wert moves in "Tirsi morir volea" in the direction of surface rhetoric, one of his sometime colleagues in Ferrara will plunge into a vision of interiority unparalleled in its dark intensity. Although he documents in detail affective realms many of us might not care to know about, Carlo Gesualdo, Prince of Venosa, also demands a hearing.

9. See my "Gender Ambiguities and Erotic Excess in Seventeenth-Century Venetian Opera," in *Acting on the Past: Historical Performance across the Disciplines,* ed. Mark Franko and Anne Richards (Hanover, NH: Wesleyan University Press, 2000), 177–200.

10. See my *Power and Desire in Seventeenth-Century Music.*

SEVEN

The Luxury of Solipsism

Gesualdo

In 1995 German cinematic auteur Werner Herzog released *Gesualdo: Death in Five Voices,* a documentary of sorts on the composer's life and music.[1] Rarely has an artist found so ideal a biographer: the filmmaker who gave us *Aguirre, the Wrath of God; Fitzcarraldo;* and *Nosferatu* here adds yet another mad genius to his gallery of eccentrics. If he had opted for a narrative approach, Herzog would no doubt have cast someone like the late Klaus Kinski in the leading role. Instead, he interviews a wide range of unlikely people: the caretaker of Gesualdo's ruined castle (truly worthy of a Dracula movie); a bagpiper who has assumed the task of performing weekly exorcisms on the castle; an elderly cook who reflects on the mind-boggling menu recorded for Gesualdo's wedding (plus the cook's wife, who simply shrieks "Gesualdo—il diavolo!" over and over in the background); the director of a local asylum, who reports having not one but *two* delusional patients who think they are Gesualdo's reincarnation; a parking-ramp attendant for the building in Naples where Gesualdo murdered his wife and her lover; a lurid account of the composer's indulgence in flagellation; and so forth. To be sure, Herzog's documentary also includes exquisite full-length performances

---

1. Werner Herzog, *Gesualdo: Death in Five Voices* (1995; available on DVD through MMI Image Entertainments).

of several madrigals, as well as musicological commentaries from the directors of the featured ensembles: Gerald Place with the Gesualdo Consort of London and Alan Curtis with Il Complesso Barocco. But this hilarious film clearly means to concentrate on the macabre, on the impact of the composer's bizarre life on its most glorious side product: the music described repeatedly as having more to do with Schoenberg's Expressionism or with Stravinsky than with its own time.

That Gesualdo's own unorthodox proclivities influenced his aesthetic choices seems undeniable.[2] Nevertheless, too many have tried to explain Gesualdo's work exclusively through the prism of his violent predisposition, as though his psychological quirks and pathological behaviors made their way onto the page without cultural or technical mediation. Yet his compositions all adhere to a considerable extent to the extenuated polyphonic and modal conventions of late sixteenth-century Mannerist style and also to the subjective formations already put in circulation by musicians—indeed, those examined in previous chapters—whose sanity has never been seriously questioned.

Carlo Gesualdo, Prince of Venosa, ought never to have put himself in the subject position of composer. By birth and privilege he belonged to the class of patrons; like his peers, he ought to have sought out innovative artists and commissioned works from them that would reflect on his taste and glory. For all the honor they received, Renaissance artists occupied a much lower class status; often they saw artistic endeavors as the means for rapid upward mobility in a world still locked in a stratified hierarchy.[3] Of course, members of the nobility learned to dabble (as Castiglione reminds us) in music, poetry, and philosophy: dukes frequently strove to pass themselves off as well-rounded humanists, and Henry VIII is even credited with having composed "Greensleeves," though this tune counts as only the most familiar surviving instance of the Romanesca pattern. But no highly ranked person of the era other than Gesualdo concentrated his energies on artistic creativity or aspired to be taken seriously as a composer by other musicians and connoisseurs.

2. For a balanced account that avoids prurience as much as possible, see Glenn Watkins, *Gesualdo: The Man and His Music*, 2nd ed. (Oxford: Clarendon Press, 1991). Watkins's analyses in his book rely heavily on harmonic configurations and differ considerably from mine.

3. For an examination of the relationships between the ruling élite and artists, see Lauro Martines, *Power and Imagination: City-States in Renaissance Italy* (Baltimore: Johns Hopkins University Press, 1988).

If a court musician had written the madrigals of Gesualdo's Book VI, we might excuse the composer, tracing the concentrated violence of the works to the patron who fostered them or explaining them as a means of meeting the demands of a public market that fancied such artifacts. In point of fact, however, Gesualdo answered to no one but wrote increasingly for himself, thus justifying to some extent those who would view him as anticipating a Romantic vision of "self-expression." The madrigals examined thus far in *Modal Subjectivities* might present images of Selfhood, but rarely do those interiorities invite us to hear them as belonging to the composer per se. Gesualdo's do.

Nonetheless, to have written his madrigals Gesualdo not only had to have had the economic security that allowed him to pursue his own fantasies so single-mindedly but also needed to absorb enormous amounts of highly technical information. He acquired his insider knowledge of avant-garde compositional practices at the court of Ferrara, where he interacted (however uneasily) with Luzzasco Luzzaschi, Giaches de Wert, and others employed as professional musicians within that extraordinarily vibrant scene. He published his first four books of madrigals in Ferrara, and he set lyrics of Ferrarese poets, as did the other musicians at court. Around 1597 he returned to his estate near Naples, where he continued to compose—for himself and his immediate cohort. His last two books of madrigals both appeared in print in 1611, and these books contain the idiosyncratic compositions for which the Prince of Venosa has maintained his reputation and his curious position within the official canon.

This chapter will treat the Gesualdo of the first four books as a Ferrarese composer—one who shared with Luzzasco an enthusiasm for their predecessor Nicola Vicentino's arcicembalo and theories of chromatic and enharmonic genres, along with a penchant for lyrics that mined a rich vein of feelings located at the intersection of pleasure and pain. For the more esoteric later madrigals, I will explore the ways an economically independent artist of this stripe extended the experiments already familiar to anyone who knew Cipriano's opus. As tempting as it may be to resort to explanations grounded in Gesualdo's own erotic preferences and mental deviance (or, indeed, to reduce the music to his literally murderous rage), such approaches never get us closer to understanding how these pieces operate discursively; they always just stand as freak-show exhibits. Judging from contemporary testimony, Gesualdo may well have been a nut case, but he was an exceptionally talented artist as well—one capable of producing searing beauty and astute psychological insight in his music. It is this Gesualdo I seek to illuminate.

The enigmatic chromatic extremes of Gesualdo's compositional palette have attracted most of the attention from modern scholars. Yet just as characteristic of his modus operandi—and, I would argue, of his conception of subjectivity—are the rapid changes in rates of declamation that occur not only in the late pieces but throughout his entire opus. He did not invent this *maniera,* of course: Rore's "Mia benigna fortuna" often surprises us with sudden jolts, and Wert's "Solo e pensoso" also features erratic flurries of fast-motion activity when Petrarch's sonnet invites them. But Gesualdo appears to identify alternations of speed—between exaggeratedly slow-motion harmonic changes and quicksilver motivic exchange—as fundamental elements of interiority. Phenomenologically speaking, he has his personae either stretched out spread-eagle on the wheel or falling apart into gibbering points of imitation. Not too surprisingly, the rapid-fire sections behave in accordance with diatonic dissonance treatment (otherwise they would lose even the most tenuous claim for intelligibility), while the elongated passages of suspended animation eventually play host to the strategies of harmonic intensification for which we celebrate Gesualdo. A twentieth-century doctor might have prescribed lithium for the bipolar disturbances traced in these madrigals—and we would have missed out on these attempts at simulating radical mood swings through the cultural medium of sixteenth-century modality.

I will begin my discussion with a madrigal in Gesualdo's Book IV (published in 1596 during his Ferrarese period): "Luci serene e chiare," which includes some harmonic experimentation but which produces most of its effects without recourse to modal transgression. It functions for my purposes as a kind of paradigm, for it presents the bipolar alternations of tempi and a touch of innovative chromatic bending in the service of a text by a leading Ferrarese poet, Ridolfo Arlotti. Arlotti's pleasure/pain paradox (also ubiquitous, for that matter, in Guarini's epigrammatic lyrics and in the madrigal tradition from its very inception) becomes so congenial to Gesualdo that he gradually finds that he can make do without actual poets; he later comes to manufacture his own poems that concentrate even more intensively on these same contradictions.

Luci serene e chiare,
voi m'incendete, voi, ma prova il core
nell'incendio diletto, non dolore.
Dolci parole e care,
voi mi ferite, voi, ma prova il petto
non dolor nella piaga, ma diletto.
O miracol d'amore!
Alma che è tutta foco e tutta sangue
si strugge e non si duol, more e non langue.

Serene, clear eyes,
you inflame me, but my heart feels
delight in the flames, not pain.
Sweet, dear words,
you wound me, but my heart feels
not pain in the wound, but delight.
O miracle of love!
The soul that is all fire and blood
is consumed without pain, dies without languishing.

Despite the chromaticism that marks the conclusion of this madrigal, the principal axis on which "Luci serene" turns consists of an entirely diatonic tension: the sixth degree, which hovers just above $\hat{5}$. Indeed, so domestic is this pitch within a serene F-Ionian that the listener may not even notice it as semiotically marked, as an irritant capable of generating the composition. Yet Arlotti's lyrics likewise point to unlikely dissonances: "serene, clear eyes" (and, later, "dear words"), which nonetheless produce the speaker's inner conflagration (see Ex. 17).

Gesualdo does not conceal his device; like Poe's purloined letter, it sits right out on the surface: it unfolds extravagantly over the course of the opening passage, as the canto moves from C to a D made more emphatic by an ornamental arch up to F and back. The harmonies traced—F, d, B♭—do not call particular attention to themselves, though they will recur throughout the madrigal as the chief points of articulation and reference. They present boldly the displacement of the stable modal boundaries by D and its associated verticalities (a third harmonization, G, will appear later on and with much less prominence).

But Gesualdo accomplishes a good deal more in his initial phrase in terms of its response to the text. Its outwardly placid demeanor may suggest the serene eyes themselves, yet these eyes have already been filtered through the subjective gaze of the lover (the same rising-fourth figure that depicts Arcadelt's "felic' occhi" or Willaert's vision of angels on earth), and I suggest that we hear those as reflected reactions rather than as the Beloved's eyes themselves. For despite a pervasive sense of calm, the first line presents simultaneously an image of a quite different sort: as the spatial configuration of voices expands in slow motion from a relatively closed position to the luxuriant open sonority on "chiare," they deliver an erotic gesture altogether worthy of Michelangelo's *Dying Slave*. Even as the canto reaches up achingly to linger on F, the tenor—who for now holds the responsibility of spelling out the modal coordinates—jumps up the octave, to its own high F. Counterpoised against these extenuated voices, the bass and alto both move down (in slight rhythmic displacement) by third from F to D to B♭. And although at the moment they appear to function as mere harmonic support, these two voices contribute another crucial part of the puzzle, for this triadic shape will turn out, paradoxically, to suture the wound inflicted in the canto's opening gambit. Taken together, these apparently innocuous and completely diatonic progressions delineate the sweet torture of the rack, not yet bloodied by recourse to more extreme measures.

The exquisite suspension offered in this first image abruptly gives way to a radically different affect. As the lyrics indicate, the Beloved's serene eyes serve causally to incite the opposite effect—that of flames that rage inside the lover. On the simplest level, Gesualdo's rapid point of imitation counts as a representation of spreading fire as its jagged motive leaps unchecked from voice to voice. Taking into account the alternation of these two qualities of motion throughout the madrigal, we might also hear the release from the rack as producing not relief so much as muscle spasms. Moreover, the clear homophonic declamation of the opening line, which resembles communicative speech, suddenly dissolves into what can only be a simulation of conflicted interiority with all its contradictory impulses dutifully registered.

Throughout this jumbled passage, most of the motivic pitches fall well below the level of the half-note value that marks the rate of actual motion. The shorter pitches contribute greatly to the sense of chaos that prevails here—without them, no conflagration. But a glance at the principal pulses of the passage reveals a consistent struggle between sonorities featuring D (including B♭ and its associated E♭) and those affiliated with C. The desire introduced with the sixth degree, D, in the opening line disrupts the ability of the modal final to maintain control over the proceedings.

Yet if the invasive D threatens identity, Gesualdo's musical persona seems even more ambivalent about this fate than Arlotti's verse would indicate. On the words "nell'incendio diletto," the voices come together to deliver in m. 9 a makeshift cadence of sorts on F: "pleasure" equals regained identity— or so it would seem initially. Arlotti's poem continues in a brief denial of pain, but although Gesualdo faithfully renders the two words "non dolore," he does so in such a way as to belie their original implication. No longer the throwaway opposite of "diletto," "non dolore" puts us back on the rack to twist and turn in slow motion—still wrestling between C and D, but with D getting the palm for a final cadence in m. 12 on D minor.

Following the rather provisional and highly fraught cadence on D minor on "non dolore," the voices resume with an exact duplication of the opening phrase, though "dear words" now substitute for "serene eyes." The section does not recur note for note, however, even if it means to register as a parallel with the first; the incendiary motive reappears (now associated with "wounding"), but with a different ordering of voice entrances. When the voices come together this time, their makeshift cadence—on "piaga"—articulates D minor. Arlotti's verse holds to a severe symmetry: line 3 states "diletto, non dolore," and line 6 responds with "non dolor, ma diletto." If Gesualdo jumped on "non dolore" like a duck after a june bug, he has little interest in its corresponding "ma diletto," which he sets quickly in a passage leading to a relatively perfunctory cadence in m. 25 on F. He thereby restores modal order, but with a distinct absence of affective investment. (Note, however, that he does reverse the canto's opening gesture here, leading from F back through D to C, indicating a tendency to draw on materials already introduced, thus reinforcing their continued significance.)

This arrival back on the modal final halfway through the madrigal proves too easy: mechanically reversing the terms of the binarism only leaves them intact. Indeed, the concluding tercet of Arlotti's poem only condenses the cliché—a cliché familiar to the madrigal genre at least since Arcadelt's wish to die a thousand times a day—rather than taking it somewhere new, and a more conventional musical reading of his text would do more or less the same. To be sure, Gesualdo still relies on Arlotti's text to render intelligible the devices he introduces during the second half of his madrigal; yet his interpretation of that text offers a considerably more subtle way of construing the "miracle of love."

The line "O miracol d'amore!" presents the D side of the C/D dichotomy in its most concentrated form, with implied arrivals on D minor, G minor, and Bb major (the three available harmonizations of D) within the brief span of five pulses. This apostrophe to Love changes color from moment to moment, yet it remains always focused on the locus that stands for desire within this madrigal. If the modal boundaries represent stable identity, then this passage qualifies as an out-of-body experience—a mystical vision of the Other that expunges all consciousness of Self. Arlotti simply calls upon Love rhetorically before proceeding, whereas Gesualdo immerses us in a simulation of that condition marked by both intense pleasure and abjection.

As Arlotti continues, he spells out his paradox: a self-immolation that does not cause pain, a death that does not require languishing. Standard stuff. And as Gesualdo returns to his fire imagery, with its alternations of C and D, he seems to be taking the poem at face value. But the burden of Arlotti's last two lines stresses the affirmative—the absence of pain and languishing. Not too surprisingly, Gesualdo prefers to dwell on the negated terms. The phrase "e tutta sangue" begins in m. 33 with the reestablishment of the modal boundaries, but it quickly veers again—significantly, with the mention of blood—toward D.

And here for the first time we get a foretaste of the pitch manipulations that will dominate the composer's later period. The canto in mm. 33–34 moves straightforwardly to tonicize D, even as the tenor and alto strive to hold onto the tenets of F-Ionian. Caught in the conflict between the implications of these potentially mode-bearing voices, the bass waffles, offering first an Eb that might emphasize a temporary G (the tenor intends for its G to sound like $\hat{2}$, but the bass undermines that principal implication). The canto's C♯, however, appears to pull the bass into its orbit and to force it up a half step to E♮, as in preparation for a cadential expansion to D octaves, and for the first time in the composition, a tension between Eb and E♮ seems to present itself. At the last moment, the bass simply falls silent, refusing or unable to confirm D, and the quinto also holds firm to its G instead of conforming to the canto's dictates. After its silence, the bass takes up the canto's motive and attempts to cadence on D; but by now, the canto has become convinced of the need to return to F with a cadence—on "e non si duol"—that dutifully resolves out all dissonances. Except that the tenor has taken up another cause and produces a delicious suspension in m. 36 against the canto's would-be conclusion. Taken together, the voices twist and writhe, unable to arrive at any agreed-upon goal—either the continuation of desire or the reconsolidation of identity—thereby canceling each other out.

Gesualdo reserves his most unusual *coup-de-théâtre*, however, for the last line: how does one die without languishing? He could, of course, simply run roughshod over Arlotti's negative, as he did with the previous line in which he would not budge from pain, despite the contrary claims of the text. Here Gesualdo recalls the opening phrase of his madrigal, the falling thirds in the bass that produced the ravishing expanse for "Luci serene e chiare," the fetish that incited all the turmoil in the first place. The canto has just tried to "correct" its opening phrase, which had moved from C up through D to F before falling back to D—the preference for desire over secure identity that has driven the whole madrigal. But the prepared cadence on F, as we have seen, did not stick. Along with all the other voices, the canto resorts to the opposite strategy and passes down through a triad. But even though all voices linger significantly on C (thus seeming to reestablish the modal fifth degree that has been so beleaguered), the bass halts its descent on A. The quinto hangs on to F until the last minute, as though to presage the bass's expected arrival on F. When that does not occur, the quinto opts for a highly irregular drop not to the anticipated C but, through a diminished fourth, to C♯.

Together the voices conclude this first statement of Arlotti's last tercet with a cadence on A—a pitch theorists cite as available for cadences within F-Ionian (largely to make its description parallel to those of the other modes) but not common in practice. Moreover, within the economy of this particular madrigal, a structurally weighted arrival on A qualifies as exceedingly bizarre, for it lies outside the oppositions that seemed to drive the allegory. And with the appearance of the C♯, the cadence even perverts the boundary pitch C that had always seemed to be within reach (on one level the C♯ qualifies as a conventional Picardy adjustment of what would otherwise be a minor-triad conclusion, but this explanation overlooks the efforts Gesualdo has made toward marking C as a site of modal and subjective identity). In fact, this is a cadence (a death) that does not concede to either Self or Other: it hovers in a new space of palpable mystery.

Part of the mystery is clarified on the other side of the grand pause that follows. The A-major sonority turns out to serve as dominant preparation for D minor, the fraught C♯ acting as leading tone, to bring us back to "O miracol d'amore" and Gesualdo's second iteration of Arlotti's final tercet. In choosing to set the last block of text twice, he changes the formal dynamic of Arlotti's poem from AA' B to produce a musical structure of AA' BB'.

More so than most madrigalists, Gesualdo tends to shape his pieces through lengthy repeating segments. In the case of the first half of "Luci serene e chiare," the composer has simply followed the structural model suggested by the poet, who creates a rhetorical parallel between his first and second quatrains.[4] But Gesualdo will pursue such repetitions, even when it means reiterating an entire section of text, as in the case of this madrigal's second half.

Put differently, if Gesualdo often relinquishes normative practices at the surface level, he also balances his apparent transgressions with a nearly geometrical conception of large-scale architecture. The materials themselves may challenge accepted notions of reason, but they find themselves tethered within rigid, symmetrical forms. Theodor Adorno would have described this tension between the erratic subject and its reined-in, mechanical unfolding as reification, and he would thus direct us back to issues of psychopathology.[5] I would not want to rule out entirely the possibility of a psychoanalytic diagnosis—one that would treat this devotion to redundancy as a symptom of an obsessive-compulsive disorder. Gesualdo's madrigals draw incessantly on that tension, with its implications of being stuck within processes beyond the control of the linear (i.e., rational) progression of the words: a strategy especially noteworthy given the preponderance of through-composed madrigals in the repertory. At the very least, I want to argue that these redundancies count as aspects of Gesualdo's expressive apparatus—whether we understand them as elements of rhetorical design or as manifestations of a drive he cannot suppress—and not as purely formal devices.

In "Luci serene e chiare" Gesualdo repeats his setting of the final terzet exactly until he returns to the final image. Once again it appears in m. 52 that the canto might freeze on A, giving us yet another cadence in the "wrong" place. And here Gesualdo confronts one of the great dilemmas faced by composers who would flaunt modal or tonal structural demands. For it's one thing to introduce dissonances and misplaced arrivals over the course of a composition, but quite another to carry the dilemma through to the conclusion: the rules require a return to the final or tonic at the end. Yet how does one make that requisite return sound like something other

---

4. See the discussion on structural repetitions in Watkins, *Gesualdo,* 120–23. Watkins finds the repetition of music for the two tercets in this madrigal strange, given the differences in rhyme schemes. His discussion starts, however, with the model of *formes fixes* and canzone rather than with rhetorical shaping.

5. This principle underlies Adorno's readings of Beethoven, with his resistance at moments of recapitulation (the largest-scale repetitions in sonata procedure), and of Schubert, whose compulsion to repetition Adorno compares with the facets of nonorganic crystal. Adorno's notorious condemnations of Stravinsky and jazz interpret repetition in psychoanalytic terms.

than concession to convention? To return again to Adorno, many a piece that seems to carve out new possibilities has its free will suddenly revoked in the face of externally enforced definitions of closure, and any kind of truly challenging paradox collapses with it.[6]

Gesualdo does in fact deliver a final cadence on an F-major triad, yet the harmonic contortions that devolve onto F at this most crucial moment qualify as the strangest in the entire composition. Thus far, the madrigal has not indulged in illicit chromatic pitches; all alterations have operated fully within the mode and the system of pitches available for secondary cadences. During the final phrase of the piece, however, E♭ becomes the prevailing mediant of the dominant function on C, coupled (to avoid tritones) with A♭: surely a languishing meltdown if ever there was one. Yet Gesualdo has prepared us for this in the first setting of this phrase. If what started out in the initial statement as a diatonic arrival on F ends up instead on A, then all he has to do is transpose the materials—or so his strategy implies. Moving mysteriously all the way, the various voices find their way to pitches confirming . . . F minor! The canto deploys the motive of the falling triad to pick up its still-unresolved highest pitch of G and bringing it down by thirds through E♭ to C. At last, the voices coalesce for closure, with F and C secure as modal boundaries, but with a languorous A♭ as mediant—until the very last moment when the tenor completes its drop to A♮.

But this A♮, however native to the mode—indeed, however *necessary to modal identity*—sounds in context like a mere Picardy third, the automatic adjustment upward of minor-mode mediants at cadences. In order to resolve the primary tension of the madrigal without simply switching from D- to C-oriented sonorities (the strategy in the first half), Gesualdo chooses to warp almost beyond recognition the essence of his modal home base. Whereas Arlotti clears up his paradox with a well-worn cliché, Gesualdo takes his deep into the very fabric of the Self. Given this experience of love, subjectivity can never return to ground zero: it has changed irrevocably, indelibly marked by its encounter with desire, with those serene eyes and dear words. It no longer bears direct traces of the miracle of love that produced this mutation—D departs from circulation before this final realization. But the subject can never regain its former transparent confidence and autonomy. Or, to put it differently, it *eschews* conventional notions of

6. Adorno takes Brahms in particular to task for his failure to follow through on his own challenges.

the carefully bordered Self, undergoing permanent mutation in exchange for that sublime experience: the transfiguration that constitutes the miracle of love.

Anyone inclined to take such passages as symptoms of the composer's unbalanced psyche must also come to terms with the sophisticated method in their madness. For Gesualdo does not grasp at this sudden chromaticism merely for the sake of shock, nor does he take refuge in the lyrics to justify his trampling of modal norms. Rather he produces this ending by means of a scrupulous internal logic over the course of the piece. In his later works, the same kind of inner integrity continues to prevail, except that he no longer bothers to spell out (as he does in "Luci serene e chiare") the steps linking the various passages. Like Beethoven in the *Große Fuge,* Gesualdo turns to exploring the back alleys of his system, leaving it to those who care to do so to retrace his steps. If both Beethoven and Gesualdo in their middle periods build gradually to their moments of greatest experimentation, they will eventually dare to start right off with their affronts to normative behavior.

"MERCÈ," GRIDO PIANGENDO

A gap of fifteen years lies between the publications of Gesualdo's fourth and fifth books—the first four books hit the press within a three-year period (1594–96), and the last two appeared in a single clump in 1611. Presumably he composed these later pieces over the course of that hiatus of a decade and a half, but the chronology is difficult to reconstruct. In any case, when the new set emerges, it does so with a style that has evolved considerably since Book IV.

"'Mercè,' grido piangendo" begins *in medias res* as a scream for relief. If "Luci serene e chiare" arrived at its climactic moment of strangeness only at the end of the entire composition, this madrigal plunges right in with a level of violence and chromatic enigma unmatched in the earlier collections. Confined to an extended expression of torment and ignored by the one who holds the power to deliver release, our persona cries, weeps, feigns a fainting spell, threatens to fall silent, howls for pity—then condenses it all for the paroxysm of the punch line: the desire only to have the beloved dominatrix hear the groveling sufferer utter "I die" before at last succumbing.

In contrast to Arlotti's carefully balanced lyrics in the previous madrigal, this anonymous poem, with its jagged compilation of seven- and eleven-syllable lines, packs as many extreme images as possible into its two tercets.

The madrigal collapses the distance between speaker and addressee that allowed the elegant buildup of tensions and graceful symmetries in "Luci serene e chiare"; here Gesualdo opts for immediacy of experience, an unprepared assault on the sensibilities of the unsuspecting listener, who is thrown without warning into a sadomasochistic scenario. If (as is reportedly the case with such scenarios) the masochist actually controls the activities in a manipulative alternation of passivity and aggression, then our persona drags us too as voyeurs (auditeurs?) into a compressed drama of deliberate and eroticized pain infliction.

> "Mercè," grido piangendo,
> ma chi m'ascolta? Ahi lasso, io vengo meno;
> morrò dunque tacendo.
> Deh, per pietade almeno,
> dolce del cor tesoro,
> potessi dirti pria ch' io mora: "Io moro!"

> "Mercy," I cry weeping,
> but who hears me? Alas, I faint;
> I shall die, then, in silence.
> Ah, at least for pity's sake,
> sweet treasure of my heart,
> if I could tell you before I die: "I die!"

The mythology surrounding Gesualdo has predisposed us to take such lyrics and their settings as direct evidence of psychopathology. In this madrigal, however, Gesualdo sends up as parody his own favorite palette of affective devices. The poem itself, with its self-referential beginning and ending, already produces a kind of nonidentity between the "I" that speaks and the one that quotes itself speaking. Gesualdo's musical response offers a high degree of Self consciousness, making this madrigal an extremely valuable source of information concerning the composer's constructions of subjectivity (see Ex. 18).

In keeping with the requisite affect of unrelieved anguish, Gesualdo chooses Phrygian for this madrigal—not the pseudo-Phrygian that prevailed before Glareanus and Zarlino formulated the twelve-mode system, but a genuine exploration of the Phrygian problem, with desperate, illicit stabs at F♯ that reach out for cadential confirmation and its normative, disheartening F♮ that slithers unconvincingly to closure. That plea for mercy that starts the piece erupts on a B-major triad: the dominant that E would need to ground itself as a conventional final but that the Phrygian condition customarily forbids. All other modal finals have fully legitimate access to this function through *musica ficta* alterations; but although *musica ficta* can provide leading tones without disturbing modal process, it cannot manufacture with theoretical impunity a "real" (i.e., nonfictive) diapente pitch—the second degree required for a cadential dominant. Gesualdo thereby matches the violent scream of the text's first word with a violation of modal propriety, albeit a violation that comparisons with other modal types renders intelligible as an insistent dominant urgently poised on the very cusp of cadence (= death—as always, in both senses).

That first word, however, turns out to be a self-quotation: a theatricalized performance exaggerated for the sake of effect. And the modal transgression, too, operates under erasure. As the line continues, first with a reinforced statement of "mercè," then with a shriek simulating authentic pain (the canto's A, leapt to and away from), the bass follows the contours of a pure Phrygian diapente, quietly determining the events of this passage despite its apparent role as harmonic support. By the time the bass's F♯ has descended to E, the speaker has backed passively into E, where it weeps (or reports itself doing so); the quinto produces an even greater image of pushiness turned contrite, as it mounts to C♯, then dribbles away through C♮ back to the B with which it started—now accepting its status as mere fifth degree rather than asserting itself as a potential final backed up (as it was in the first sonority) by its root. Within a very short span of time, the aggression of the opening gambit has metamorphosed with all those defeated half-step descents into mere self-pity and concession to modal correctness.

After the ostentatious outburst of the beginning, the lyrics proceed to question its efficacy: does anyone actually hear these screams? With these words, Gesualdo could have chosen to heighten the level of dissonance in protest or to retreat inward for an even more anguished rendering of subjectivity fearing abandonment. Instead, he sets up a distinction between the speaking Self who addresses another and the Self who carries on an inner monologue, monitoring the apparent impact of the extroverted statements. For this odd "voice-over" effect, Gesualdo needs a musical equivalent of a neutral zone, related closely to the modal center but not engaged with the tensions that underwrite its lavish portrayal of suffering. And in this madrigal, he deploys as his neutral position G: a sonority that sustains both fifth degree (B) and mediant (G) of Phrygian and that even has legitimate claim to the otherwise off-limits F♯ as its leading tone.

On the line "ma chi m'ascolta?" this neutral area appears, an entirely uninflected block of G, introduced by its dominant and attendant F♯. Although the canto rises back up into the tessitura that had produced the shriek in the first line, it no longer has the grinding dissonance underneath that lent it such urgency. Indeed, none of the earlier signs of distress—the illicitly positioned F♯, the unlikely harmonies thrown up against the inexorably descending bass line—occur here at all. When no answer ensues, the phrase repeats, again evidently to no avail. One of the most emphatic statements in the madrigal (all five voices singing together in notes of long duration and on relatively high pitches) falls on deaf ears. Stripped of its enactments of musical violence and of its struggle against the exigencies of Phrygian within which it finds itself bound, the madrigal seems to lose its ability to communicate: the line unwinds twice without any friction, as though hurled down a long, empty hallway or into space.

Gesualdo's strategy of pitting neutral speech against stylized histrionics of anguish resonates with Judith Butler's notions of "performance" or subjectivity as masquerade.[7] For beginning with its very first word, this madrigal revels in ambiguities of Selfhood. Does the "Self" reside in those dramatic gestures of agony made audible in the more outrageous section of the piece or in the reasonable voice that speaks so blandly here on G? Recall that Cipriano cast away diatonic security for the sake of an "authentic" presentation of the subject, and one might interpret Gesualdo's "Luci serene e chiare" in this light as well. But " 'Mercè,' grido piangendo" hinges on a kind of metacritique of that now-standard binary opposition. Even its poem places its evidence of most direct expression in quotation marks, putting them self-consciously at one remove. Thus when the music responds with contortions that signify unmediated pain, these representations simultaneously deny and reveal their mediatedness. They deliberately present both the mask and the slippage of the mask.

Following this sustained moment of G, the performative Self reappears, groaning lugubriously with imitative entries that sigh in despair ("Ahi lasso"), then rise briefly in energy level ("io vengo") only to swoon away ("meno"). Most of the voices seem keyed to approach E in some way or other. Yet they either fall short of the goal, or make use of the illicit F♯, or sag into E without the kind of harmonic support that would make the arrival sound truly confirmed. Eventually, the voices collapse by half steps into the sonor-

7. Judith Butler, *Gender Trouble: Feminism and the Subversion of Identity* (New York and London: Routledge, 1990).

ity with which they started: a B-major triad, now more clearly implying the dominant of E that cannot really operate within this system. This cadence in m. 11 sounds like a last-ditch effort, not only because it stops before the resolution to its final but also because it grasps at straws.

Having broken the prohibition against F♯, however, Gesualdo decides to push forward into that territory. Like a child threatening to hold its breath until it turns blue, our persona asserts death as the only solution, and the harsh F♯ major that sets the word "morrò" obliterates temporarily all traces of the Phrygian Self.[8] Death, however, is not really the goal of this game, but rather manipulation of the Beloved. All voices retract suddenly by half step to a genuine Phrygian cadence in m. 14 on E: the "silent" site of subjectivity. Gesualdo repeats this line, resurrecting and sustaining the F♯ (now as V of B), and when the retraction occurs this time, it ends up concomitantly on a Phrygian arrival on A—a pitch that usually figures heavily in E-mode pieces, though not with its own Phrygian (i.e., B♭) inflection. The shouted moves to the sharp side find their response in a systematic flatting, and the protests fall mute ("tacendo"), though not before they have led us at the end of the first tercet to a place no longer truly within the mode. It will remain for the second tercet to return us to the scene of the opening and to reestablish the principal modal boundaries.

Most of Gesualdo's setting of the second half of the poem relies on plain, direct communication, as it attempts to reason with the Beloved—or as the persona once again drops the mask and merely mutters to himself. After all the hypertense F♯s of the previous section, the opening of the madrigal's continuation on F♮ sounds profoundly calm; it also restores the F♮ necessary to modal identity, though not within a context that points back to the quagmire of the Phrygian dilemma. The appeal to pity in the text cranks the pitch level up from F to G, but G (as we have seen) constitutes the neutral zone of choice within this Phrygian composition. Nearly all the second half occupies the G-major terrain—drawn out with homophonic emphasis for the words "potessi dirti."

The intrusion of rapid-fire declamation, so fundamental to "Luci serene e chiare," happens only once in this piece, on the quite unlikely text "sweet treasure of my heart." An odd choice: any girl would tell you that this line,

---

8. Giovanni Battista Doni classifies this moment as a transposition of C-Lydian (he named the modes in yet a different way) to C♯-Lydian. In other words, he labels particular passages as modal entities rather than interpreting them within the context of the whole composition. Doni, *Trattato della musica scenica* (1635), as quoted in Watkins, *Gesualdo*, 198–99, n. 49.

above all the others, needs rhetorical stress if its profession is to be taken seriously. Instead, we get a jabbering, decentered quality, as though the words were accompanied with a grin and a soft-shoe shuffle. Clearly, the Beloved isn't really the point of this madrigal (if the subject's self-quotations and passive-aggressive strategies have not already revealed as much). The cessation of hyperactivity with "potessi dirti" focuses all attention in preparation for the madrigal's punch line: the distinction between the impending death caused by the Beloved and the self-referential "I am dying."

Not surprisingly, Gesualdo pulls out the stops for this moment, all the more highlighted by the relatively diatonic processes of the rest of this second half. We've been waiting for the other shoe to drop, and drop it does. At first the prolonged G-sonority in mm. 27–29 appears simply to presage a consigned cadence on E, as the quinto descends through F♯ to E, the canto down to B. This would be a relatively unremarkable "death"—which in itself would be remarkable for a Gesualdo conclusion. Then, at the last instant, the E-minor configuration (which only needs the drop of G in the tenor down to E for closure) gets cranked up to G♯ major.

Modern synthesizers often have a pitch adjuster—a wheel to the side of the keyboard that allows the performer to take whatever sonority is sounding and queer it upward or downward by a half step. Gesualdo produces precisely this effect: an arrogant override of rational modulatory procedure that just lifts the entire floor. I am not even committing a flagrant anachronism with this comparison, for much of Gesualdo's experimentation descends through Luzzasco from Vicentino and his arcicembalo, which was designed to allow the performer to move chromatically and enharmonically up and down through a stack of connected keyboards.

Within the symbolic economy of this madrigal, the G♯ arrival interprets "death" as the annihilation of Self, just as occurred before with F♯ (which, however, at least had the benefit of stressing one of the mode's sore pitches). It also sounds as though the spasmodic conclusion is (like Macbeth's nemesis) untimely ripped. If we pursue the sexual connotations of madrigalian death, this represents a premature ejaculation: one brought about by the partner without the consent of the Self. And a second approach in m. 32 similarly ends abruptly with a most unsatisfactory twist, this time up to C♯ at the last minute.

But our subject begs to die in his own sweet time and in his own sweet way. Accordingly, the madrigal concludes with a lavish series of chromatic motives that crawl their way in slow motion to languorous closure on E. The F♯ that had seemed necessary for cadence earlier in the piece appears in this final passage, but always as a part of a chromatic line that either corrects itself back to F♮ (canto) or continues to creep upward to the mediant and raised mediant. *This* (it seems to say) is death! But if death it is, it exists on another discursive level than the music leading up to it. When Gesualdo give us "death" in quotation marks, he sets it off ironically and thereby offers us a key to much of his musical language.[9] And he simultaneously calls into question the authenticity of such representations in his music, wherever they occur. To be sure we caught all that, he demands a rehearing of the entire second half by means of a repeat sign.

MORO, LASSO, AL MIO DUOLO

One can scarcely write an account of Gesualdo's madrigals without addressing "Moro, lasso, al mio duolo," his most frequently anthologized composition. Gesualdo published his madrigals in score to make his innovations immediately visible to the eye, to invite study and analysis—perhaps even admiration. But already in the eighteenth century, "Moro, lasso, al mio duolo" had brought down the wrath of analysts. In his celebrated *A General History of Music,* Charles Burney writes:

> ["Moro, lasso"] is presented to the musical reader as a specimen of his style, and harsh, crude, and licentious modulation; in which, the beginning a composition in A minor, with the chord of C sharp, with a sharp third, is neither consonant to the present laws of *modulation,* nor to those of the ecclesiastical tones; to which, as keys were not settled and determined on the fixed principles of major and minor, in the time of Venosa, composers chiefly adhered. But a more offensive licence is taken in the second chord of this madrigal than in the first; for it is not only repugnant to every rule of transition at present established, but extremely shocking and disgusting to the ear, to go from one chord to another in which there is no *relation,* real or imaginary; and which is composed of sounds wholly extraneous and foreign to any key to which the first chord belongs.[10]

Rising to the challenge of this madrigal, Schenkerian analysts have brought their skills of linear reduction to bear on this piece, and Stravinsky stood

9. For an amusing and insightful discussion of this kind of ironic self-consciousness in language, see Marjorie Garber, *Quotation Marks* (New York and London: Routledge, 2003), especially chap. 1.

10. Charles Burney, *A General History of Music* (London, 1776–89; Dover reprint), 222.

in awe of a complex that appeared to him to anticipate twentieth-century atonality.[11] But "Moro, lasso" yields to the bass/canto orientation of Schenker's method only with considerable difficulty, and despite its superficial similarities to the harmonic experimentation three hundred years later, it predates the precepts of tonal organization that served as the target motivating Stravinsky and his contemporaries.

As before. I will approach this madrigal as a modal composition, albeit one that pushes its own inherited precepts close to the breaking point. For it turns out that the vestige of a rational subject lurks beneath the tortured surface of "Moro, lasso." But as with so many of the pieces examined in this book, the argument frequently resides in the tenor: buried perhaps beneath a thicket of misharmonizations and distortions, but present nonetheless. As we have seen, sixteenth-century theorists most often identify the tenor as the usual mode-bearing voice, though modern scholars have proved all too eager to throw that advice aside in favor of their own ways of hearing. In doing so, they frequently throw away the key to otherwise inexplicable passages.

Like Gesualdo's earlier madrigals, "Moro, lasso" (Book VI, 1611) revels in the bipolar opposition between morbidly slow decay and manic displays of hyperactivity, mapped here as elsewhere onto a contrast in the text between death and life. The lyrics eschew anything that might get in the way of this obsession; in the five lines of the anonymous text, the poet rocks back and forth between the two stark extremes, hardly even bothering to dress up the tension with double meanings.

> Moro, lasso, al mio duolo,
> e chi mi può dar vita?
> Ahi, che m'ancide e non vuol darmi aita!
> O dolorosa sorte,
> chi dar vita mi può, ahi, mi dà morte!

> I die, alas, in my sorrow,
> and who can give me life?
> Alas, the one who kills me will give me no help!
> O sorrowful fate,
> The one who could give me life, alas, gives me death.

---

11. See Stravinsky's "Gesualdo di Venosa: New Perspectives," preface to Watkins, *Gesualdo,* v–xi.

A glance at the formal divisions of "Moro, lasso" offers some assistance with respect to orientation (see Ex. 19). Cadences occur on A, C (the area linked with "life" throughout the madrigal), D, and E, with the illicit dominant of E occasionally appearing to direct the ear forward. In other words, the formal landmarks all point toward Aeolian. Like Bruckner, who liked to obscure the fundamentally conventional background structures of his symphonies with chromatic harmonies, Gesualdo operates here within a familiar framework. But whereas Monteverdi introduces the complexities of Aeolian only step by step in "Ah, dolente partita," Gesualdo assaults us with the most extreme of his gestures in the very first sonority: a C#-major triad (C#, E#, G#), which would seem to have no possible connection to any recognizable mode.

If one covers all the voices except the tenor, however, a perfectly clear shape emerges: the mode-bearing voice starts on the Aeolian leading tone—not the most common of beginnings but one we have encountered in several of the Phrygian-tinged Aeolian pieces we have already examined, from Verdelot's "O dolce notte" to Marenzio's "Tirsi morir volea." But in these other madrigals, the other voices match the leading tone with harmonies that make explicit its intention; by contrast, Gesualdo allows the leading tone to generate an outrageous cluster of pitches, in which G# serves as implied fifth degree for a bass note, C#, which even sports its own raised third, an E# tending, one assumes, toward F#. Of course, a C#-major triad on an equal-tempered piano sounds just as good as the one a half step lower, on C. But the keyboards of Gesualdo's day (with the exception of Vicentino's fabled arcicembalo, with its stack of differently tuned possibilities) would have jangled horribly with such an arrangement, the wolf tones howling inconsolably. Even though a vocal ensemble can tune without reference to keyboards, the very pitches would have signified in particular ways to the singers' eyes: C# could only be a leading tone to D, G# only a leading tone to A, and E# . . . ? If sung as though it were F (a function far on the flat side), it would produce an interval with the other voices absolutely intolerable to the ear. But a leading tone to F#?

Put your hand over the other voices again. The tenor leaves its initial G#, where it seems poised to resolve to A, jumps down to E (Aeolian's fifth degree), then up an inflected diatessaron to $\hat{2}$ (B), before resolving sweetly to A for a cadence. On occasion, the other voices even confirm those meanings in the tenor: the second sonority presents the first A-minor chord in the piece (albeit with mediant in the bass), and the harmonies warp around to consolidate a move from V/A to A in m. 3.

But if some modicum of logic threads its way through this still-shocking passage, it does not explain anything away. What we principally hear are the chromatic meltdowns in the outer voices—the voices on which most modern analysts will pin their hopes and which do indeed take on the quality of an inexorable trajectory quite apart from the far less evident tenor; one could argue, in fact, that their greater prominence even sounds as though they force the tenor in m. 2 to F♯ and G♮, whence it must struggle to right itself for the cadence. And although it might be tempting to read the cadential A in the bass in m. 3 as the goal of the opening descent, its B in m. 2 served as V/E, which did not manage to resolve properly owing to the D that appears in place of E in the alto; and once G major takes hold as a sonority, the bass jumps up through that cluster to arrive at G. Only with the quinto's cry of agony on "mio duolo"—set with an excruciating tritone descent—does the bass along with everyone else suddenly convert to an A orientation.

All in the service of simulating pain, of course. But what sort of pain? Except for the passing tones at the end of m. 2 in the inner voices, the harmonies comprise only consonances (leaving tuning problems aside for the moment). Yet the integrity of the tenor's modal line suffers extraordinary stress, as though tied to some instrument of torture worked by means of a slowly turning crank. Each moment of its relatively coherent plea gets pulled and distorted until it can scarcely be recognized. This process gets transferred without mediation to the experience of the singers themselves, who must decide for each of these moves which voice to use for tuning purposes. If the bass seems the likely choice for its first three pitches, even it must participate in this cat's-cradle maneuvering when it leaps for G in m. 3. Whatever counts as the Self here cannot move without engendering even greater distress because of the ways it is trussed up.

But suddenly all tensions evaporate with the words "e chi mi può dar vita." The top two voices flip into an untroubled C major, moving at several times the rate of the opening passage and with carefree, giddy ornamentation. The glee spreads like infectious hilarity through the other voices to produce an extended point of imitation. OK, so this is "life," up against the death and sorrow of the beginning, the two extremes presented as stark opposites as in Maxwell's Demon. Obviously this grotesque parody of joy will not serve as a viable solution to the problem already encountered, even though it provides some temporary relief.

I am reminded of the affective horror in a scene in Fellini's *Satyricon,* in which a terrified man with his hand on the chopping block is distracted momentarily by a comic scene enacted for his benefit; his involuntarily laughter is met by the crunch of the axe and his incredulous gaze at his mutilated limb. For no sooner does the listener succumb to the gaiety of the proceedings in "Moro, lasso" than Gesualdo lowers the boom. The tenor finds himself abruptly abandoned on the C cadence everyone had colluded in preparing; and although he maintains his modal orientation through to the conclusion of the section (over and over again he traces a cadential B to A), he also confronts once again the refusal of the other voices to respond with anything but the most perverse harmonies. His G♯ leading tone in m. 12 once again receives the C♯-major treatment with which we started, and direct chromaticism crops up again to suggest its own trajectories. Indeed, the impotent cadential gestures in the tenor attract less attention and seem less relevant to the unfolding of the passage than any other voice. His last whimper in m. 15 on A, the Aeolian final, serves in context as fifth degree in a D-major triad that evidently points beyond itself as V/G.

As we have seen earlier in this chapter, Gesualdo tends to balance his surface complexities with the repetition of structural blocks. Now he treats us to another presentation of the bewildering events we have just experienced, transposed up a fourth to the D level (with F as the "life" key). Once again, the structural predispositions of Aeolian appear here—but with the initial C♯ leading tone to D in the alto (temporarily taking over the task of mode bearer) in m.16 harmonized as part of an F♯-major chord. A completely faithful repetition would have us end on G, but a few sleights of hand occur to redirect the last section. Note, for instance, that the tenor's isolated C in m. 24 gets met this time not with a minor third but rather with a minor second, which makes the voices veer off in new channels. And the tenor's cry for help can no longer offer tight cadential formulas as it did previously. Now it arpeggiates up through the Aeolian triad, overshooting to the yearning sixth degree before settling back to E—harmonized, to be sure, with C and battling a cross-relation between the canto's C♯ and its own C♮, but now at least with a standard Aeolian support of $\hat{5}$.

The verse's penultimate line, "O dolorosa sorte," receives what counts (for this madrigal anyway) as a straightforward setting. The bass *soggetto* arches up to a sustained F ($\hat{6}$) before resolving back to $\hat{5}$. As is usual for Gesualdo, the sustained bass pitch invites some chromatic twists, even in the tenor, before the voices consolidate on V/A. After subjecting us to the experience of torment, a caricature of happiness, and a cry for help, the persona now accepts what fate has doled out. But if Arcadelt alternates between inside as polyphonically inflected and speech as homophonic, Gesualdo gives us this one moment of lucid communication with the non-identical declamation that more typically marks interiority. Although the syntax becomes relatively clear in this passage, it does feature the searing quality of *fauxbourdon* as well as tinges of chromatic pain reminding us of (and preparing us for) the surrounding context. A short reworking of the same passage culminates on V/E—an extreme position for Aeolian in general, with its nonfictive (thus illicit) F♯, but a remarkably clear signpost for "Moro, lasso." Its open voicing causes it to point forward like a colon in verbal punctuation—"O sorrowful fate: . . . "

After a quick gulp for air, the other side of the colon arrives—" . . . : The one who could give me life, alas, gives me death." And Gesualdo begins this final section in the same lucid manner as the preceding transition; indeed, it even consolidates into homophonic declamation, all pointing for a while toward A. As before, the bass sustains F and descends to E—a sure sign of cadential preparation. The canto, however, cannot yet accept closure, and on "può" (m. 35) this voice moves not to the E the counterpoint would demand (for an expansion of the sixth with the bass to the octave) but to G, as a desperate effort to escape the clutches of fate. (The tenor is primed to follow the bass down by third to G♯, but it has to skip awkwardly up to E to find a place at all, given the canto's dramatic unhinging and to avoid duplicating the quinto.)

The canto then unleashes the madrigal's final series of tortured convulsions. To be sure, the last section of "Moro, lasso" boasts more clearly oriented segments of Aeolian DNA than it might: at all times, at least one voice or other is presenting a cadential formula in A. But the enterprise already familiar from earlier sections of the madrigal takes over again, as perverse harmonic choices flourish, distracting the ear from the thread that could offer some solace. The convolutions reach their moment of greatest complexity in mm. 40–41, where any kind of guiding line seems at best to be divided up into individual pitches, tossed randomly through the mix, each attracting grotesque harmonizations that spawn bizarre twists and turns. (I would suggest a diapente descent starting with E in the alto in m. 40, D in the tenor, C in the alto and then the tenor, which completes the linear resolution to A.)

Gesualdo then repeats this concluding passage (mechanically so, by means of a repeat sign) to allow its utter strangeness to sink in. In the end, the madrigal's persona bows to the dictates of fate—and eventually even cadences on the pitch suggested as the final at the outset of this last part in m. 34. This dimension of fully rational resignation matters for the piece: I am not presenting grammatical paths through the labyrinth just to push this extreme composition back into some semblance of modal convention but rather trying to show the ingenuity of the composer in nailing down the rational side of a very difficult dialectic. Of course, the other side—the tortured strategies of resistance—makes itself much more audible. But arbitrary transgression would scarcely serve Gesualdo's purpose, any more than Michelangelo's Laurentian staircase would be honored if it had fallen in a heap because of its violations of physical laws; the stairwell can (and does) defy architectural convention, but it must rely on a supreme knowledge of weights and balances in order to succeed.

In contrast to the laws of physics, however, the ground rules of musical order change over time. Schenkerian theorists have guessed that some order must underlie Gesualdo's aberrant structures, but they have sought it in the place where later musicians would drive their piles and lay their foundations: in the bass. But as radical as Gesualdo unquestionably is, his experiments do not gravitate toward a greater tonal sensibility. In most ways, he continues to depend—far more heavily than did most of his forebears—on the tenor-oriented linear logic of neoclassic mode.

"Moro, lasso" represents the end point of our narrative with respect to chronology (1611) and technical extravagance. Although madrigals continued to appear in print in the decades following Gesualdo's death (the *real* one, that is), and some of them—those by Sigismondo d'India, for instance—exploit many of the chromatic excesses associated with his predecessor, other genres were starting to push them to the cultural margins. Although the madrigal was inseparable from the exploration of neomodality, Gesualdo holds onto that core ideal with only the most tenuous and ambivalent of threads.

But I don't want to stop here with the genre on its knees begging for the release of death. I opened this book with a madrigal taken out of chronological order: Monteverdi's "Ah, dolente partita," published in 1604 but written in the final decade of the sixteenth century. In fact, Monteverdi integrates many of the strands—conservative as well as radical—examined over the course of this book, making him the perfect subject for my last cluster of case studies.

EIGHT

The Mirtillo/Amarilli Controversy

Monteverdi

I abandoned Guarini's Mirtillo at the end of Chapter 1 as he bewailed his separation from his would-be beloved, Amarilli. Indeed, even when I dealt with his travail in the opening chapter, I treated it as the mere pretext for an introductory illustration of modal construction. At last, after six full chapters of neglect, I want to return to him now and examine his plaints—and Amarilli's responses—in greater depth.

Monteverdi happened to choose the principal moments in the quarrel between these two characters from *Il pastor fido* as texts for some of his most famous madrigals—madrigals that owe much of their notoriety to the attacks they provoked from Giovanni Maria Artusi, a music theorist who had arrogated to himself the task of enforcing pythagorean verities. Artusi's challenge sparked a response from Monteverdi, published at the beginning of his Book V, a collection that led off with the offending madrigals.[1] One of the most celebrated debates in European music history, the Monteverdi/Artusi exchange articulates the collision between vastly different worldviews:

---

1. Giovanni Maria Artusi, *L'Artusi overo delle imperfettioni della moderna musica* (Venice, 1600), excerpted in Oliver Strunk, *Source Readings in Music History* (New York: Norton, 1950; rev. ed., 1998). Monteverdi responded in a short statement prefacing his Book V in 1605. An expanded gloss of this statement appeared in Monteverdi's *Scherzi musicali* (1607); it was penned by his brother, Giulio Cesare.

a conservative stance that seeks to uphold the presumably universal values of the platonic tradition and a deracinated position that sacrifices the certainties of the scholastic past on the altar of individual free will.[2]

Our sympathies have always tilted toward Monteverdi, in part because most of us have little investment in the cultural agendas pursued under Artusi's régime, in part because of a conditioned predisposition toward evidence of progress. But Monteverdi and his brother, Giulio Cesare, author of the expanded version of the composer's original manifesto, did not truly respond to the specificities of Artusi's objections; rather, they changed the floor of the argument, citing Cipriano and others as precedents for this "second practice,"[3] referring to their own favorite passages from Plato for philosophical support, and asserting expressivity as their governing principle. Music historians have tended to follow suit, casting Artusi as an antiquated curmudgeon, Monteverdi as a daring rebel defying all petty regulations. Thus the genuinely outrageous passages signaled by Artusi get valorized as transgressions per se, and Artusi's pointed critiques receive the sneers we reserve for the obtuse. Even this particular term of abuse dates from the moment of the debate, for our Wagnerian hero of 1600 actually punned on his Hanslickian opponent's name, twisting it to Ottuso—"the obtuse one."

This chapter will deal more directly with present-day interpretations of musical details than do previous chapters, because Monteverdi's pioneering efforts in music drama have made him appear to be "one of us" and thus susceptible to the tools of tonal music theory and analysis. The other madrigals considered thus far have been relegated to antiquity: no one except the occasional specialist cares enough to worry about them. But Monteverdi—for better or worse—has been put into a different historiographic category, and much modernist ink has been spilled in defense of the madrigals attacked by Artusi, especially "Cruda Amarilli." Any attempt at repositioning these embattled madrigals has to engage with now-dominant readings, which remove the music from its cultural and modal allegiances in order to redeem it.

---

2. See Claude V. Palisca, "The Artusi-Monteverdi Controversy," in *The New Monteverdi Companion,* ed. Denis Arnold and Nigel Fortune (New York: Norton, 1968), 133–66. For a particularly astute rhetorical analysis of this debate, see Suzanne Cusick, "Gendering Modern Music: Thoughts on the Monteverdi-Artusi Controversy," *JAMS* 46.1 (Spring 1993): 1–25.

3. Oddly enough, Artusi expressly praises the treatments of dissonance not only in the works of Cipriano but also in those of Wert. Monteverdi too will claim Wert for his side. See Carol MacClintock, *Giaches de Wert (1535–1596): Life and Works* (n.p.: American Institute of Musicology, 1966), 12.

I want to return to the Monteverdi/Artusi controversy and take up, for a change, Artusi's cause.[4] Artusi deserved a better, more musically nuanced response than the one the Monteverdi brothers offered. And even Monteverdi—the apparent winner of the fight—did not serve his own interests as a composer very well by appealing exclusively to the overriding dominance of the words he set. For he obviously cared deeply about the particularities of his pitches, even if they functioned to intensify the affects of his chosen lyrics. In fact, Monteverdi shared much more with Artusi than is commonly acknowledged, including a scrupulous concern with the musical integrity of his compositions. Moreover, the cultural ambivalences manifested in this debate—the desire to maintain the known in the face of radical discontinuity versus the exigencies of a world in which anything goes, with no higher authority than the whims of isolated individuals—continue to characterize modernity even to this day.

The torment voiced by Monteverdi's Mirtillo and Amarilli through their dissonances and contorted modal strategies does not simply proclaim the right of the composer to flout the guidelines of the *prima prattica;* it stems also from the internalized struggle between the desire for formal security and the impossibility of living any longer within the Eden—the pastoral *locus par excellence*—of tradition. If Monteverdi attempts in Books IV and V to revive the tight allegories of centered subjectivity challenged decades earlier by Cipriano, he does so with full knowledge and use of the expanded harmonic palette that had accumulated over the intervening years. Like Brahms, he tries to reinhabit earlier formal procedures but with the sonorities unleashed by those who had called the viability of such procedures severely into question with their chromatic and dissonant experiments. This pouring of new wine into old bottles produces the ruptures Artusi targets in his diatribe, even as it signals (as with Brahms) that the center will not

---

4. For historical purposes, I may as well mention that my debut with the American Musicological Society occurred in 1975 at the annual meeting in Los Angeles, with a paper titled "A Belated Answer for Artusi." A mere graduate student at the time, I found myself speaking before a packed room of musicologists, apparently enraged by the arrogance of my title. The discussion that followed foreshadowed the hysteria that seem to have characterized most of my contributions to the field. I am ever in debt to the late Claude Palisca, who stood up and called for the attacks to cease. Much water has passed under the bridge since 1975: I did not notice gender at the time, for instance (such events began to draw my attention to this aspect of both music and my own career). But my formal readings of the pieces in question have changed very little from the ones that appear in my dissertation, "The Transition from Modal to Tonal Organization in the Works of Monteverdi" (Harvard University, 1976).

hold. Monteverdi himself pulled the plug on this last-ditch effort soon after he composed these pieces. But for the time being, he places his ambivalences within the mouths of Guarini's star-crossed lovers.

Within the context of Guarini's *Il pastor fido*, Mirtillo and Amarilli love each other desperately. But the oracles have destined Amarilli for someone else (or so it seems). Throughout the play—until its dénouement, in any case—Mirtillo repeatedly rails against Amarilli's cruelty, and she in turn retreats into private monologues that disclose her true feelings, which she cannot confess openly. Mirtillo vents his grievances publicly, in the time-honored style of troubadours, whereas Amarilli can bring her sorrows to light only with the greatest of effort and only in the absence of anyone to hear her. Mirtillo makes his first entrance in the play in Act I, scene ii, with the famous "Cruda Amarilli." Later, in Act III, scene iii, he launches his self-pitying "Ah, dolente partita." Amarilli has all of the following scene to herself, and she begins with "O Mirtillo" and ends with "Anima mia, perdona."

Artusi features all of these except "Ah, dolente partita" prominently in his hit list: "Anima mia, perdona" appears along with "Ah, dolente partita" in Monteverdi's Book IV, and Book V opens with "Cruda Amarilli" followed immediately with "O Mirtillo." We know that all of these circulated together before the publication of either book, because they appear in Artusi's diatribe of 1600, yet Monteverdi chose to distribute them in an order that diverges significantly from that of the play. Moreover, as he proceeds through his particular reordering, he moves into increasingly rarified musical strategies, producing an internal logic of increasingly greater angst.

I began *Modal Subjectivities* with "Ah, dolente partita" because it abides so faithfully inside the constraints of modal practice, even as it pushes to an extreme limit the ambiguities and self-divisions available within diatonic Aeolian. Amarilli's response in Book IV similarly adheres to modal convention, though it violates rules of voice leading and thus shows up on Artusi's radar screen. The two madrigals that open Book V both flaunt their modal and part-writing transgressions flagrantly. Consequently, in my treatment of these pieces, I will follow not Guarini's but rather Monteverdi's ordering, with its musical logic of miscommunication and psychological unraveling.

I will also pay considerable attention to the gender dynamics of the four madrigals—all sung, to be sure, by five mixed voices, but representing nevertheless alternately a male and a female subject. As in the exchange of vows between Monteverdi's Orfeo and Euridice,[5] as well as in the case of the lovers in Rore's "Da le belle contrade d'oriente" (see again Chapter 5), gender matters enormously in these pieces. Indeed, Monteverdi's uncanny abilities to invent complex, multifaceted characters for the operatic stage already manifests itself here in this series of madrigals.

Yet neither Mirtillo nor Amarilli can be reduced to a particular stereotype of gender construction. Rore's precedent involved a learned, controlled male narrator and a distraught, nearly hysterical woman, and the wedding scene in L'Orfeo grants the eponymous protagonist supreme rhetorical abilities, his bride the modest, self-abnegating speech expected of domestic partners at the time (her friend the Messenger receives far more air time). In his settings of the Mirtillo/Amarilli controversy, Monteverdi does much more than mine Guarini's verses for their emotive content. He offers us insights into the interiorities of two fictional personae whose anguish pushes the capabilities of his musical language to their extreme.

ANIMA MIA, PERDONA

"Anima mia, perdona" does not follow "Ah, dolente partita" immediately in Book IV, but it constitutes a kind of answer to Mirtillo's opening madrigal. A much longer verse (seventeen lines as opposed to Mirtillo's eight), it evidently requires a series of two parts (this not including "O Mirtillo," which occurs within this same speech in Il pastor fido) to respond adequately to his parting shot.

Anima mia, perdona
a chi t'è cruda sol dove pietosa
esser non può, perdona a questa,
nei detti e nel sembiante
rigida tua nemica, ma nel core
pietosissima amante;
e se pur hai desio di vendicarti,
deh, qual vendetta aver puoi tu maggiore
del tuo proprio dolore?

5. See my discussion of this exchange in "Constructions of Gender in Monteverdi's Dramatic Music," *Feminine Endings: Music, Gender, and Sexuality*, 2nd ed. (Minneapolis: University of Minnesota Press, 2002), chap. 2.

Che se tu se' 'l cor mio,
come se' pur malgrado
del cielo e de la terra,
qualor piagni e sospiri,
quelle lagrime tue sono il mio sangue,
que' sospiri il mio spirto e quelle pene
e quel dolor, che senti,
son miei, non tuoi, tormenti.

My soul, forgive
her who is cruel to you only where
pity cannot be, pardon her, who only
in her words and appearance
is your rigid enemy, but in her heart
your most compassionate lover;
and if you still desire to avenge yourself,
ah! what greater revenge could you have
than your own sorrow?

For if you are my heart,
as you truly are, despite
both heaven and earth,
whenever you weep and sigh,
those tears of yours are my blood,
those sighs my spirit, and those pains
and that sorrow that you feel
are my—not your—torments.

Here, insulated from any onstage auditors, Amarilli can finally express what she cannot say directly to her beloved himself. Mirtillo's "Ah, dolente partita" concentrates heavily on the simultaneity of irreconcilable sentiments, each of which has the potential to cancel the others out; he indulged in histrionics—his authentic Aeolian requiring the frequent engagement of the shrieking high A at the top of the modal octave and frequent cadences on the "wrong" pitch. Amarilli's strategies too operate on the usual madrigalian premise of divided subjectivity. But in contrast to Mirtillo, Amarilli knows her own mind and understands only too well the circumstances still opaque to her lover; she seeks only to articulate her position in clear, linear speech— almost all circumscribed modestly within the D-D octave. Her duality stems from the arduous task of wrenching her explanation from the very depths

FIGURE 25. G-Hypodorian

division at G   division at A

of her being, where, as a dutiful daughter and proper female subject, she has buried as unspeakable her forbidden passions.

Monteverdi locates Amarilli's essence for this madrigal in G-Hypodorian, the most stable of modal types. He pursues, moreover, only the most basic of ambiguities offered by this mode: the possibility of dividing the D-to-D octave at A rather than at G, thus suggesting the lower D as an alternative final (Fig. 25).

Of course, most modal compositions (Aeolian and Phrygian aside) allow for tonicized arrivals on the fifth degree; fugal points of imitation rock back and forth between these two positions without producing the slightest puzzlement. Over the course of her speech, however, Amarilli maintains a double image, as she rehearses internally how to put words to her anguish, then pivots through A to state them in her more public register. Unlike her equivalent in Guarini's play, Monteverdi's Amarilli constantly stammers—she tries out fragments of lines first low in her alternative range (i.e., in the D-A diapente) then repeats them "aloud" (in the G-D diapente); only rarely does she superimpose contrary ideas polyphonically (Mirtillo's favored strategy in "Ah, dolente partita"), and these few instances serve primarily to cast doubt on certainties or to elevate timid admissions to the level of bold speech. She finally voices—though only with exquisite struggle—the fantasy of mutually acknowledged and shared love pangs that blossoms only at the end of the *seconda parte.* In her concluding section, we witness a simulation of their love fully consummated, even if poor Mirtillo has no knowledge of (much less share in!) the much-desired event (see Ex. 20).

Monteverdi's opening page already sets the terms of Amarilli's negotiation between inside and outside. The canto begins forthrightly enough, outlining in her first internal the boundaries of the G diapente before deflecting back up to A for a half cadence. The bass's E♭ creates a powerful dissonance against the canto's reiterated D, forcing it to move—though it ought rightly to resolve by step to C (a pitch the quinto supplies) rather than to jump down to G, a detail that galls Artusi. But Amarilli isn't in this business in order to comply with voice-leading correctness; her leap to G both defies propriety and announces unambiguously her true Hypodorian Self (as does the alto's minimalist presentation of the bare modal species).

But after this courageous start, Amarilli shifts into a different gear. As the tenor takes up and repeats the canto's opening gambit, canto and quinto murmur low in their registers an admission of cruelty. The confident F♯ of the half cadence, which pointed unequivocally to G as final, gives way to F♮. Consequently when the tenor arrives at its termination, it seems to have served merely as a bass (a slight alteration of its middle pitch gives it precisely the contour of the basso in the first three measures), and its A (now harmonized with C♯ in the canto) functions not as an indicator of G but as the cadential dominant in D. In other words, Amarilli's most clear articulation of Selfhood gets drawn back into the interior, her confession of guilt buried deep in the mix.

A new configuration of voices—the three lowest ones—takes up and mulls over this confession, pivoting through A first to V/G, then to G, then through an excruciating *fauxbourdon* back to V/G. This clumsy, equivocal statement (though back in G) does not satisfy her, but it does lend her courage, allowing the top voices to come back in m. 11 with a full-throated plea for pardon. The canto returns to the contour of its first statement, and it now receives much stronger articulation as it moves toward G before deflecting back up to A, once again clearly acting as $\hat{2}$. For harmonizing her line, Monteverdi makes use of the most forceful progression available to him: that of the Romanesca, a pattern that will persist throughout this madrigal. What began as an abject self-acknowledgment of culpability works its way at first awkwardly, then powerfully to external pronouncement. If eavesdroppers were hiding in the bushes onstage, they would observe Amarilli talking to herself under her breath, then hear some half-intoned muttering, and finally comprehend fully this last statement, which would come through loud and clear.

But Renaissance ladies cannot express themselves so boldly. Amarilli suddenly recalls why she is prohibited from responding to Mirtillo, why she cannot even ask the forgiveness that this madrigal rehearses so fervently. Back to the D diapente she goes in m. 13 for an internal statement, followed this time in short order by an emphatic statement in her upper register (through A as pivot). From the authoritative position of the upper boundary, D, she traces her most direct diapente descent yet in mm. 21–22.

Occasionally Monteverdi modifies her pattern: for instance, on the words "ma nel core / pietosissima amante" he sounds the return from D to G in the three lowest voices alone. Moreover, although the arrival that occurs in m. 44 constitutes the first full cadence in the madrigal (the others, all of which have asked for pardon, end on half cadences), it resolves onto a bare octave. This, then, is the unadorned truth of the matter, Amarilli's moment of greatest rhetorical risk, and she nearly swallows this confession in shame when she finally utters it. One ought to be able to hear a pin drop in the concert space at this moment.

Immediately she rallies, changing the subject from her own private feelings to a prolonged conceit concerning how Mirtillo might avenge himself. We hear her gathering her energies, shaking herself free from that quietistic nadir at which she had arrived for "pietosissima amante"; she cranks herself up through a standard Hypodorian formula, from G to B♭, then pushes onward for an audacious parallel statement in D/F. Note particularly in m. 46 the canto's E♮ (a tritone away from the B♭ sonority that precedes it), which exceeds her modal range and stands in place of the E♭ that usually appears to top off the fifth degree. She clearly means business: "You want revenge? All right—I'll show you revenge!"

But when it comes time to explain, her pugnaciousness evaporates. Despite her delaying tactics (a cavalier flourish on "deh," a contrary-motion expansion mechanism on "qual vendetta aver," an excruciating suspension chain), she traces her way down through the D diapente. Another deeply internalized admission, again punctuated with an open octave. Rallying once again, she throws this speech into her public register. The cavalier flip gets her up to F in m. 60, but the gravitational forces of the previous statement bring about a powerfully resisted cadence on G for the conclusion of the *prima parte*.

A word about that expansion mechanism. The five-voice setting of "qual vendetta aver" quite understandably arouses Artusi's ire: the second sonority in m. 61, for instance, includes simultaneously the pitches C, D, E, and F. One doesn't have to be a curmudgeon to wonder about the propriety of such part writing! Monteverdi's response to Artusi's attacks would merely point us to the lyric situation, to Amarilli's anguish, which presumably justifies whatever crunching dissonances the composer sees fit to serve up.

Yet Monteverdi does not suddenly begin writing atonal music at this point; his response operates entirely within a set of techniques available to him for expressive purposes. In this case, he seizes onto a device that will prove crucial for articulating some fundamental changes in cultural notions of temporality at this turn of the century. Although the voices correspond on a one-to-one basis and favor each pitch with a new syllable of text (making them sound "real" rather than ornamental), the contrary motion starting

FIGURE 26. Expansion process

Romanesca

Romanesca with expanded $\hat{5}$

from B♭ announces a sudden hiatus from the harmonic rhythm of the pre-vious passages; we wait in a highly animated suspended state until the next principal harmonic arrival—in this case, F. *Seconda prattica* composers (in-cluding Frescobaldi, who loves inserting such passages of contrary-motion discords into his toccatas) rarely do this outside the framework of a stan-dard formula to guide the ear through this radical deflection forward in time. In this case, Monteverdi banks on the Romanesca (already heard repeatedly undergirding Amarilli's statements): a G-Hypodorian diapente descent har-monized with B♭-F-G-D-G. But by virtue of this device (as well as the in-tricately managed knot of suspensions for "proprio dolore"), Monteverdi al-lows us to share in the experience of Amarilli's searing pain (Fig. 26).

In the *seconda parte,* Amarilli refocuses her argument, starting with the word "Che" ("For") that draws one by one the logical consequences from her equation of Mirtillo with herself. The A that had already emerged as a crucial pivot between her interiority and her externalized speech now comes to the fore. Descartes theorized the pineal gland as the spot where body and soul attach as though through a Velcro strip, and as Amarilli turns A every which way, demonstrating how it functions as a conduit between in-side and outside, she presses her argument to its climax.

Consider her first line, for instance. The *prima parte* had concluded—perhaps prematurely—on G, as though she had achieved closure. The stark D-minor triad that opens the second half announces the necessity of greater elaboration. It is as though Amarilli stops, satisfied at her double bar, only to realize in the interim the latent fecundity of her conceit. If the alternation between thought and speech occurred at a relatively leisurely rate in the *prima parte,* it now acquires an almost feverish urgency. She begins with her D-minor triad, but when she repeats those words in mm. 73–74, she has hiked it up into the G diapente, only to drop back to subaudible murmuring for her poignant "come se' pur." But she immediately vaults that confession into the G realm, leading to a powerful reiteration of the entire complex, until it comes to a screeching halt on a preparation for a cadence on D in m. 86. Note that this V/D sets up an arrival not in the lowest part of the G-Hypodorian range but rather at its octave—a crucial distinction in music based on modal species. No longer buried deep in the ensemble, this indicator of D boldly shouts its intentions from the rooftops, in defiance (as she says) of heaven and earth—or (as we might say) hell and high water.

For the first time in the two-part madrigal, Amarilli ceases to stammer. The next several lines, in which she enumerates the points of identification (tears, sighs) linking her lover and herself, she twists back and forth by means of A between her two dimensions. The more rapid rate of declamation and the dizzying series of half cadences in quick succession push forward to the final line: "e quelle pene / e quel dolor, che senti, / son miei, non tuoi, tormenti." And here Monteverdi begins an extravagant point of imitation on a standard diapente descent—very much like the fabled conclusion of "Il bianco e dolce cigno," except that it lasts nearly as long as Arcadelt's entire composition as it milks its dissonances for every last drop of affective power. Like the speaker in "Il bianco e dolce cigno," Amarilli has maintained tight homophonic control over her declamation up until this point. But at this moment, her dammed-up fantasy overwhelms rational speech, and the inside spills out in luxuriant torrents. Again as in the Arcadelt, each would-be cadence finds itself canceled out at its arrival point by another wave that pursues in turn its own desire trajectory.

Monteverdi has raised the stakes, however, through his premises of two rival modal areas, and that demands some kind of resolution independent of Guarini's verse. Recall that Amarilli has operated on the basis of a stark binary opposition between G and D, without any third party to break the tie. The most obvious candidate would be C, which would tip the balance toward G as it broke the dominance of the D-A axis that has pushed the piece forward. As the madrigal approaches its conclusion, Amarilli pauses to give "non tuoi, tormenti" its own concentrated point of imitation—now favoring G and C in dynamic tension. If D still appears prominently, it does so in proximity to B♮, which makes it sound like a second degree ready to confirm C—an eventuality that occurs in m. 120. But overlapping that excruciatingly achieved cadence is a tenor line starting on E♭, tracing its way back to G, and the consequent E♭s cancel out the viability of C as a termination (the secondary area on the fourth degree in the Dorian modes being major in quality), even as they add tremendous poignancy to its failure.

Rising from the ashes of that anguish, the canto enters with unprecedented audacity into her top range—starting on E♮, which lies above the modal octave and in defiance of the fictive E♭ required by both the B♭ in the tenor, with which it forms a particularly aggressive tritone, and the *una nota super la* injunction that should put a cap at the top of the diapente. This interval of D to F in excess of the mode has occurred before in the piece, though usually as ornamental pitches. Here Amarilli leaves no doubt. She seizes control of those renegade pitches, bringing them in through that flagrantly resistant E♮ for a decisive cadence on D, and only then relenting (albeit reluctantly—she ends by descending to the mediant rather than the final) to a final resolution on G. A character who started her speech with trepidation, rehearsing her ideas beneath her breath before trying them out loud here not only confesses her desire but depicts them in graphic detail. Monteverdi transforms a timid maiden into a woman with formidable self-knowledge and self-command. The ambivalences within which Mirtillo still wallowed at the end of "Ah, dolente partita" have no place in Amarilli's self-presentation, whose only quandary involves whether or not to speak her true mind in the face of societal prohibitions.

CRUDA AMARILLI

Alas, poor Mirtillo. In the sequence as presented by Monteverdi, his frustration has only intensified with Amarilli's cold disregard. Having held his peace since 1603, the publication date of Book IV, he bursts forth at the beginning of Book V (1605) with the infamous "Cruda Amarilli"—the composition that raised Artusi's dander more than any other, his invectives causing this to become the most heavily anthologized madrigal of the entire repertory.

> Cruda *Amarilli*, che col nome ancora,
> d'*amar*, ahi lasso, *amaramente* insegni!
> Amarilli, del candido ligustro
> più candida e più bella,
> ma de l'àspido sordo
> e più sorda e più fera e più fugace,

poi che col dir t'offendo,
i' mi morrò tacendo.

Cruel Amarillis, who even with your name,
alas! bitterly teach me to love!
Amarillis, than the white privet
whiter and more beautiful,
but than the deaf asp
deafer, fiercer, and more evasive,
since in speaking I offend you,
I will die in silence.

Although this speech first introduces the character Mirtillo and the name
Amarilli in the opening act of Guarini's *Il pastor fido,* Monteverdi's reordering makes it follow Amarilli's intimate explanation, making it seem even more
petulant than it does in its original context. Mirtillo's multiple puns on his
beloved's name—in which "amar" resonates with both love and bitterness—
and his comparisons of her with a delicate white flower and a poisonous serpent lead up to a threat of suicide. At least Guarini's Amarilli does not have
to listen to his insults; he utters them only in the presence of his confident,
Ergasto. In Monteverdi's implicit staging, however, she responds immediately to this outburst, indicating quite clearly that she does hear it. And, as
we shall see, it wounds her deeply. Deaf as a snake, indeed!

In my discussion of this madrigal, I want to avoid two of the most common approaches: the first castigates Artusi for not simply acknowledging
the legitimacy of ninth chords (an entity not truly recognized by theorists—
cantankerous or otherwise—before the late nineteenth century), and the
second (unfortunately encouraged by Monteverdi himself) relies on the celebrated "the words made me do it" defense. With respect to the first, I see
no purpose in bringing in musical concepts nearly three centuries removed
from the music in question. If this composition makes sense, it has to do
so within the framework of early seventeenth-century practice, even if it
pushes the envelope quite a bit; moreover, interpreting these collisions as
chords masks the contrapuntal and modal forces that generate them. Concerning the second approach: although Monteverdi's dissonances in "Cruda
Amarilli" undeniably occur in response to his reading of Guarini's text, he
does not thereby drop all sense of musical responsibility. As with all the
other madrigals we have considered, "Cruda Amarilli" produces its reading of the poetry in tandem with the modal matrix.

Finally, I will not deal here with Luca Marenzio's setting of this text, even though Monteverdi borrows several striking musical images from him. Marenzio's "Cruda Amarilli"—especially its chromatic twists and extensive battery of deceptive moves—deserves full treatment on its own, but it would detract from the dramatic sequence Monteverdi produces for his particular setting. If many of these madrigals allude to others (clearly an important cultural project at the time), they also have to make sense in and of themselves.

My argument will hinge on an idea that has been dismissed as anachronistic: a commitment to the correspondence between surface details and structural unfolding that many musicologists associate exclusively with nineteenth-century "organicism." I hope that by this point in *Modal Subjectivities* I do not have to explain how the Romantics did not own this ideal, that it underscores madrigalian allegories from the very beginning of the genre. But this is especially true for Monteverdi, whose music reveals a deep-seated desire to bring the experimental harmonies of the more adventurous Mannerists together with the powerful sense of formal integrity typical of *prima prattica* composers such as Willaert. The two madrigals that comprise Mirtillo's and Amarilli's second exchange—the ones that drew most of the critical fire—count as his most extraordinary ventures (see Ex. 21).

If we focus exclusively on the canto at the beginning of "Cruda Amarilli," we witness the most lucid of patterns: a diapente descent in G-Mixolydian, followed immediately by another descent, this one tracing out the remainder of the Mixolydian octave from G, ending, however, on C rather than the rightful divisor, D. In the endless discussions of Monteverdi's dissonance treatment in his opening statement, few have noted that Artusi also complains that this madrigal has too many cadences on C for a composition ostensibly in Mixolydian. Indeed, the composer announces that problem right from the outset: not only does the parallel version in C follow immediately on the heels of the proper presentation, but its higher tessitura, its powerfully articulated initial pitch (which jumps the gun and holds for much longer than its predecessor), and its incisive arrival on its implied final (in contrast with the deflected cadence on G in m. 4) make it far more formidable.

In the discussion of Mirtillo's "Ah, dolente partita" in Chapter 1, I noted a tendency for Mirtillo to become hysterical—to shriek in the highest register of his authentic mode. He continues that propensity in "Cruda Amarilli," as he cranks up the volume, aggressively nails that premature G, and broadcasts his malediction at the top of his lungs. It is as if he were shouting: "Cruel Amarillis, CRUEL AMARILLIS, YOU BITCH!" (Most commercial recordings of this passage have the soprano sweetly croon the high pitches of the first fourteen bars—especially the offending A and F of m. 13. But that performance decision does not match the energy vectors Monteverdi seems to demand—nor does it sound much like the transgression that pushed Artusi to mount his critique.)

The composer's choice of Mixolydian for this bitter denunciation may be lost on modern listeners, who tend to read such pieces as G major with F♯ leading tones cumbersomely added along the way instead of established once and for all by a key signature. But G-Mixolydian occupies the hard hexachord, and its wide-tuned interval between its final and mediant give it a harsh quality reserved at this time for particularly unpleasant affects.[6] Moreover, Mixolydian brings with it certain structural predispositions: the above-mentioned tendency to divide the G octave at C rather than D and also a minor-mode secondary area on D, the fifth degree, in keeping with the F♯ of its entirely accurate signature. These details that distinguish Mixolydian from Ionian persist well into the seventeenth century (Fig. 27).

Amplifying exponentially the bitterness of the opening eight bars are the grinding dissonances targeted by Artusi. In his much later treatise on *seconda prattica* contrapuntal techniques, Heinrich Schütz's associate Christoph Bernhard demonstrates how to take a perfectly conventional progression and ratchet up its expressivity through anticipations, displaced resolutions, or accented ornamental tones.[7] But Artusi himself offered similar reductions of Monteverdi's objectionable passages within his own dialogue; he simply did not believe that such musical misbehaviors should become acceptable in civilized society. Nor, I think, did he approve of the shrillness of Mirtillo's brutal assault as Monteverdi voices it.

Yet we might hear those dissonances as mitigating factors against the single-

---

6. For an extensive discussion of Monteverdi's manipulations of hard and soft hexachords, see Eric Chafe, *Monteverdi's Tonal Language* (New York: Schirmer Books, 1992). Chafe perceives the tendency toward C in "Cruda Amarilli" as evidence of Monteverdi's tonal inclinations. But Mixolydian had long operated this way in practice, as opposed to theory, which frequently prizes consistency over observation. Mixolydian will continue to display this proclivity toward its fourth degree quite late in the seventeenth century in, for instance, the works of Carissimi, where it stands in stark contrast to the emerging tonal structures attached to Ionian. In many respects, however, my reading of this madrigal and Chafe's complement each other.

7. Christoph Bernhard, "The Tractatus," in *The Treatises of Christoph Bernhard*, trans. Walter Hilse, Music Forum, vol. 3 (New York: Columbia University Press, 1973).

FIGURE 27. Mixolydian with subregions

diapente descent   division at C ($\hat{4}$)   subregion on $\hat{5}$

minded determination of the canto's double diapente descent. If the leading voice drives home its grievance without equivocations, the others reveal an inner torment that nearly justifies the cries of anguish Mirtillo hurls against his unresponsive mistress. Or we might even perceive the unbearable discords of the lower voices as wrenching those cries from Mirtillo, despite his best intentions. In either case, the basso's E in m. 2 produces a seventh against the canto's D—a seventh that, moreover, does not receive proper resolution, for just as the top voice finally relents, the bass moves on, creating an even more intolerable stack of pitches: G, A, B, C, D. The same pattern repeats for the presentation on C, its few modifications (e.g., the quinto line, with its added dissonances and its conclusion shrieking up on that high G) only exacerbating the situation.

A homophonic presentation of "che col nome ancora, d'amar" in m. 9 makes a bid for a return to rational, focused speech, especially as the outer voices collude to pull forcibly back from C to the proper G boundaries; the canto even pushes up to conquer the octave through F♯, and the arrival in m. 11 counts as a moment of hard-won victory. But despite herculean efforts, the center will not hold. One by one, the voices lose their grasp, cascading down in nightmarish slow motion to a seemingly inevitable V/C and a devastating cadence on C in m. 14. At first, the quinto rises up through F♯ to try to shore up, along with the strung-out canto, the common-tone G, but it too eventually plummets. The cause of this spectacular cataclysm? A parenthetical "ahi lasso," which barely inflected the line in Guarini, becomes in Monteverdi's hands the pretext for a complete psychic meltdown.

Those infamous canto pitches in m. 13 qualify, of course, as part of the meltdown. If we persist in hearing them as a mere ninth followed by a seventh over the bass, then they simply enhance the demand for resolution onto C. But these extraordinarily exposed pitches—including the A that exceeds the modal octave—do not behave that way. Glancing forward through the rest of the madrigal, we might note that that same high A appears four more times, each time more strongly articulated as a significant function in and of itself, culminating in the piece's climactic turnaround in mm. 52–55.

I have already mentioned that "Cruda Amarilli" tends to highlight its upper register more than is (to Artusi) seemly, and that this activity in the modal diatessaron not only amplifies Mirtillo's shrill accusations but also tips D, the proper fifth degree, toward C as divider of the octave and would-be finale. On a purely formal level, Monteverdi will need to enhance D so that it operates as a defining species boundary rather than as $\hat{2}$ about to resolve to C, and he will do this eventually by giving D its own temporary diapente from A to D to counterbalance C. When we arrive at m. 13, he has still given few hints of this longer-term strategy, which will loom large indeed at the end, though the quinto in mm. 9–11 does trace the ascent to A before dropping to D. And in m. 13, he transfers those enigmatic sore pitches to a range we cannot fail to notice.

In the madrigals examined earlier in *Modal Subjectivities,* composers have sometimes smuggled in crucial modal lines but harmonized them so that their true substance goes unrecognized temporarily. Recall, for example, the tenor's transcendental ascent to its cadence on F in "Il bianco e dolce cigno"—an arrival hidden by a "misharmonization" in D minor. But at least Arcadelt's accompanying voices surrounded the misunderstood tenor with consonances and well-behaved counterpoint. I would ask the canto singing mm. 13–14 in "Cruda Amarilli" to perform this line as though it were $\hat{5}$-$\hat{3}$-$\hat{2}$ in an interrupted descent to D,[8] as though in its desperate efforts at rechanneling the dynamic of the piece it only manages to enact an uncushioned head-on collision between rival dimensions of the mode. The canto receives no support whatsoever from the other voices, all of which prove deaf to the canto's plea, and the attempt ends impotently on E, the second degree of its implied D diapente—now heard in harmonic context as a mere mediant of C. Nonetheless, this head-on collision precipitates such a degree of psychological trauma that the madrigal grinds to a halt halfway through its poetic line—a violation that would have horrified literary theorist Pietro Bembo.

But what precisely is this other force that derails Mirtillo's speech? As we have seen, he crawls up to the subregion on C to deliver his invectives, his resentment of Amarilli, at full volume. As always, however, he does so with mixed feelings, for he also adores her to the point of wishing self-

8. Note the powerful difference this produces from the usual reading, in which A serves as an ornamental escape tone against the defining bass, skipping irregularly to a seventh before resolving. If that top note, A, is the hinge on which the modal life of this madrigal depends, it will have to be embraced as a last-ditch effort, not a cute escape tone.

annihilation. These warring factions—fervent love on the one hand, vituperative loathing on the other—fight it out within the battlefield of poor Mirtillo's interiority. Monteverdi here takes advantage of that slight fissure, the whimpered "ahi lasso," that bubbles up as if involuntarily in the middle of Mirtillo's recrimination. He seizes this hint of vulnerability, which becomes increasingly prominent over the course of the speech, and dilates it to the point where the line ruptures and collapses in on itself, the hatred and self-pity canceling each other out. Performed in this way, the yawning abyss that opens in mm. 11–14 of "Cruda Amarilli" ought not just to disturb a conservative like Artusi but any listener who expects some modicum of order in musical process. We do Monteverdi no honor by minimizing the violence of this horrendous event.[9] Whatever this complex moment represents, it is emphatically *not* just a V/C with an added ninth.

How to begin speaking again after such an implosion? The bottom three voices pick up the thread of the argument from before it snapped, and once again we proceed through a tug-of-war between C and G. But this time, just when the cadence on C seems unavoidable, the quinto puts up a show of resistance with a sudden rush up to F in m. 19. As slight as that gesture might be, it suffices to hold the door open when bass and tenor collude to slam it shut. With the greatest care, quinto and tenor grope their way, step by gingerly step, through those pitches that can tilt in any of the available directions, finally bringing the entire complex in (against grinding dissonances in the contrary-motion bass line) to a unison cadence on G. For a moment anyway, Mirtillo speaks without either the hostility or the self-pity that fuels his outbursts. In view of the text, we might say that Mirtillo has learned his bitter lesson and resigned himself to some sense of reality.

The lull does not last for long, however, for a recollection of Amarilli's name awakens both these subdued emotions, now mixed together as C major gets shunted twice to D, complete with high A (quinto in mm. 27 and 29, canto in m. 28) and even a Dorian-oriented B♭ for good measure. Anger yields to despair, rage to anguish with no middle-ground G to serve as referee. If the arrival on G in m. 25 had to be negotiated with the utmost caution, Monteverdi's setting of the line comparing Amarilli with the white flower that bears her name sounds as though it walks on egg shells. From

---

9. Ahi, lasso, I am reminded inevitably of the point of recapitulation in the first movement of Beethoven's Ninth—the head-on collision that I so notoriously described as violent. Schenkerian sleight-of-hand tricks cannot—and should not—erase the traumatic effect of that moment in Beethoven or this one in Monteverdi.

moment to moment we tilt toward C or toward D (A even receives its own leading tone to shore it up) before finally settling obliquely on G.

The provisional quality of the arrival on "bella," however, already forecasts the "but" that has to follow. Jumping the gun, the quinto jumps to "ma" on a held G reminiscent of the high G that opened up the previous cataclysm. The canto picks up the gesture and holds G while the voices ricochet around through the space that opens up within a sustained C chord. Mirtillo's stifled rage returns here with a vengeance, untempered by the ambivalences that had gradually crept into his discourse. If he completes his harsh comparison of his beloved with an asp on G, it is through exclusive alternation with the C side. A sniggering setting of "e più fugace" traces the entire G-Mixolydian scale, thus restoring his equilibrium, and another abortive presentation of the D diapente—the canto's "e più fera"—becomes an ironic twist of the knife, a recollection of earlier weakness, now thoroughly converted to the enhancement of Mirtillo's hatred.

He has not truly succeeded in walling off the other side, however, and it emerges now starkly with a subdued plea for mercy on D. The very abjectness of that plea, however, conjures forth its opposite; once again, it is as if he says: "But if my speaking offends you, BUT IF MY SPEAKING OFFENDS YOU, BITCH!" as the complex gets transferred up to the C region for a harshly amplified reiteration. Buried under the assault, the bass utters the consequence: "I will die in silence." The self-pity that creeps in with that single line becomes the impetus for the move toward a powerful confirmation of the D side ("OK, I'll just kill myself!"), with the canto now presiding with A rather than G. From here to the end, Monteverdi puts these motivic and poetic lines together in a dizzying variety of ways, each one canceling out the vectors of the others until the voices quite literally die out. One last flare-up on C occurs in mm. 60–61, but the conviction that had compelled previous outbursts no longer exists, and the complex arrives at the end, too depleted for either anger or hysterical suicide threats, on an exhausted G. At last, he shuts up.

O MIRTILLO

In response to Mirtillo's confused anguish in "Ah, dolente partita," Amarilli labored over the course of "Anima mia, perdona" to bring her deeply buried feelings to articulate speech, but she never lost her bearing. As Monteverdi stages this second exchange, however, she must come to terms not only with Mirtillo's pain but also with the rage with which he has just lashed out at her in "Cruda Amarilli." She no longer has access to the generosity and sensuality that elevated the final section of her earlier madrigal. Now she must contend with the undeserved violence of her lover's verbal assault, and she scarcely knows how to begin—or to continue, for that matter.

O Mirtillo, Mirtillo, anima mia,
se vedessi qui dentro
come sta il cor di questa
che chiami crudelissima Amarilli,
so ben che tu di lei
quella pietà, che da lei chiedi, avresti.

O anime in amor troppo infelici!
Che giova a te, cor mio, l'esser amato?
Che giova a me l'aver sì caro amante?

Perché, crudo destino,
ne disunisci tu, s'Amor ne strigne?
E tu, perché ne strigni,
se ne parte il destin, perfido Amore?

O Mirtillo, Mirtillo, my soul,
if you could only see here inside
how fares the heart of her
whom you call "cruelest Amarilli,"
I know well that you would have for her
that pity which you ask of her.

O souls too unhappy in love!
What good to you, my heart, to be loved?
What good to me to have so dear a lover?

Why, cruel destiny,
do you separate us if Love binds us?
And you, why do you bind us,
if destiny parts us, treacherous Love?

The modal center of this madrigal has perplexed analysts beginning with Artusi. Carl Dahlhaus uses this madrigal as *prima facie* evidence that mode no longer obtains in Monteverdi's music, but he mounts his critique with the assumption that G must be the final for "O Mirtillo," then goes on to show how that does not work.[10] In his *Monteverdi's Tonal Language,* Eric Chafe correctly identifies the mode as D-Dorian, supporting his argument by pointing to an almost identical passage to the opening of "O Mirtillo" in the middle of the much clearer "Cor mio, mentre vi miro" (Book IV).[11] Only D-Dorian has available to it both B♭ and B♮, which play such crucial roles in this madrigal. But whereas "Cor mio" begins and ends firmly grounded in D-Dorian before the interpolated parenthesis here under consideration, Amarilli effectively turns the normal process inside out: she opens in the position of greatest ambiguity, voices her true feelings quickly in the middle of the piece, then lapses back into ambivalence for her conclusion. As in "Anima mia, perdona," she struggles to acknowledge her inner beliefs. But those have been driven by Mirtillo's rage deep inside. So dumbstruck is she by the sentiments expressed in "Cruda Amarilli" that she can approach her damaged feelings only obliquely and with tremendous reticence (see Ex. 22).

Accordingly, she starts her stammered response on a B♭ triad: a triad based on the unlikely position of the lowered sixth degree—available in D-Dorian as the upper auxiliary capping the diapente but rarely raised to the status of a harmony or (as in this case) an implied final. More in incredulous sorrow than in anger, she utters her lover's name beginning melodically on D, but harmonized with pitches so tentative that they scarcely even belong to her. Starting on B♭ does give Monteverdi the opportunity to scroll through the entire modal gamut, however, and he does so immediately: B♭-F-C-G, all the way to V/A (an E major triad) in mm. 7–8. But however logical a circle of fifths may be with respect to each successive progression, it does not carry any ballast: it could stop anywhere or nowhere, it has no center. Dahlhaus is easily forgiven for grasping at the G that seems confirmed in m. 5, for without that potential anchor we must retain that state of dislocation for a very long time. Yet the B♭ so prominently displayed in the opening sonority and elsewhere has no place within G-Mixolydian, except occasionally as a means of shoring up the area on the fifth degree (recall "Cruda Amarilli," m. 28).

In "Anima mia, perdona," however, Amarilli took a very long time to get up the nerve to speak her feelings. How much more so now in her trau-

---

10. Carl Dahlhaus, *Untersuchungen über die Entstehung der harmonischen Tonalität* (Kassel, 1968), 257–66; trans. as *Studies on the Origin of Harmonic Tonality* by Robert O. Gjerdigen (Princeton, NJ: Princeton University Press, 1990).

11. Chafe, *Monteverdi's Tonal Language,* 67–75.

matized condition! If she groped for words before, she at least knew her own mind. But the scrolling through the circle of fifths at the beginning of this madrigal represents an agonizingly slow emergence from the position of retreat to which Mirtillo's words had driven her. Her articulation of G in m. 5 responds to Mirtillo on his turf, but it does not constitute her own home base, to which she can gain access only with extreme difficulty. Her first attempt at explanation—"se vedessi qui dentro"—is riddled with discontinuities: that V/A in mm. 7–8 merely clunks down to V/G a step lower (fancy part-writing footwork prevent this from sounding like the parallel fifths and octaves it truly is), and a provisional approach to G drops to F in m. 10. Amarilli's discomfort does not allow for a direct statement yet, and her mixed signals match rhetorically the subjunctive grammar of her sentence.

Amarilli's first modally coherent statement occurs in mm. 11–14. With her words buried deep in her range, with only the top three voices participating, she operates here exclusively within D-Dorian. She says nearly inaudibly: "If you only knew . . . " But Guarini's verse does not allow her to disclose her true thoughts; rather, he requires Amarilli to take onto herself as her own identity the insults Mirtillo has hurled at her. And Monteverdi makes it clear that Amarilli has heard not only the invective "cruelest Amarilli" but the music that had intensified those words in the previous madrigal (she evidently perceived the "you bitch" part). She returns to Mirtillo's mode and presents a near-quotation of his diapente descents, his suspension chains, his illicit dissonances. By far the most extravagant section in her madrigal, this passage throws back in Mirtillo's face his hurtful imagery, even as it lacerates Amarilli all over again: note, for instance, that at m. 23, the point of greatest discord, she returns to D (ostensibly to reproduce Mirtillo's Mixolydian diapente descent) with the bass on B♭, the enigmatic sonority that opened her madrigal. The searing counterpoint at this moment also results in simultaneous A and C (along with the D and B♭), creating a snarl of heaped seconds, sevenths, and ninths worthy of Ligeti.

Following the luxuriant cadence on G in m. 29, Amarilli returns to her own D-Dorian orientation. Once again by means of a highly reduced texture and deep in the mix she states plainly her own position. No stammering, no extravagance, no ambiguities: "I know well that you would have for her / that pity which you ask of her." But Guarini couches this sentence, too, in the subjunctive, and Amarilli harbors no false hopes. Her statement cannot reach an authentic cadence, just as she knows Mirtillo cannot know the secret that holds them apart. Instead of the closure we expect, her V/D in m. 35 gives rise to a howl of anguish that revisits Mirtillo's G mode and tries to reconcile it with her D.

Her lucid encapsulation of the dilemma follows: Mirtillo's G cannot succeed, as it gets shunted to A (m. 46), while her own arrival on D (m. 51) seems ridiculously arbitrary. From here to the end, she demonstrates how neither side can win, as B♭-oriented passages empty out onto G, and G-based gestures end inconclusively on D, which can mean either D as final or V/G. And so it goes, even to the very last cadence.

In her part of their earlier exchange, Amarilli fantasized in great sensuous detail the eventual consummation of their love. With "O Mirtillo," she surrenders her agency to the greater power of fate. She can no longer envision a way out, for every conceivable recourse finds itself stymied by another of equal force. Accordingly, she abandons the kind of modal clarity that stands for a viable center, a plausible and rational procedure; the ambiguities of her position paralyze her. Yet even this extreme moment underscores—even more than those pieces that rely on convention—the capacity of mode to simulate complex subjectivities. Monteverdi may turn the entire set of norms every which way but loose to present Amarilli's paradoxical diagnosis, but they still matter enormously.

The internal convulsions of "O Mirtillo" bring my historical survey to its end. The composition of polyphonic madrigals continues, of course—in the capable hands of Monteverdi and many others—for several more decades.[12] But other cultural practices begin to compete for attention during the first decade of the seventeenth century. Indeed, the heightened sense of theatricality in the exchanges between Mirtillo and Amarilli already anticipates Monteverdi's matchless ability to construct psychologically complex, realistic characters for the stage.

Yet nothing he accomplishes within the realm of the *dramma per musica* surpasses in quality what he already achieves in the Mirtillo/Amarilli controversy. Of all his heroines, for instance, only Arianna competes with Amarilli in terms of depth and power.[13] If Monteverdi assumes other means of

12. See the illuminating chart in Lorenzo Bianconi, *Music in the Seventeenth Century*, trans. David Bryant (Cambridge: Cambridge University Press, 1987), 2.

13. I am not forgetting Poppea as I write this. Poppea has extraordinary complexity and rhetorical power. Yet for strategic reasons, she refuses to allow us to hear her interiority (though she does offer Nero mock-ups, which he takes to be evidence of genuine depth).

representation, they count merely as different—not better, and the question of why someone of his stature would make such a change is not answered by appeals to the necessary evolution toward tonality. I will take those new procedures up in my next book, for which this one serves as the unexpectedly long prequel.

NINE

I modi

Music theorists today usually define mode strictly in terms of scale; we teach our undergraduates that Dorian, for instance, comprises the white keys on the piano stretching from D to D. Aeolian (or tonal minor), by contrast, stretches from A to A, with a half step between its fifth and sixth degrees, whereas Dorian has a whole-step interval in that position—difference more easily seen at a glance if Aeolian is transposed down a fifth to D (Fig. 28). Because present-day musicians distinguish between modes on the basis of such details, scalar purity seems crucial to identity. But even the most cursory review of the madrigals included for discussion in this book reveals that none of them lives up to such standards; to greater or lesser degrees, they all employ sharps or flats, especially at cadential moments when what tonal musicians call dominant-tonic progressions suddenly lock in.

Mode first developed, however, not as a collection of empty pitch class sets but as a pragmatic means of sorting into categories the liturgical music that had long circulated through the oral tradition. In response to Charlemagne's injunction that the musicians on his staff devise ways of standardizing and preserving the melodies of the Divine Service, they decided to adopt as their model the ready-made structures left behind by the Greeks. An eight-mode system, corresponding to the number designated by the Greeks (though not actually the same, owing to errors in translation), was thereby consolidated under political pressure, and it was transmitted to fu-

FIGURE 28. Dorian vs. Aeolian

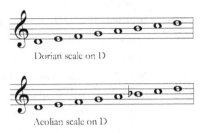

Dorian scale on D

Aeolian scale on D

ture generations along with the repertories it served. Because many of the melodies in question took shape without the benefit of such theories, they often resisted the new conceptual categories. Sometimes these tunes retained their anomalous features, and sometimes they were modified so as to fit the beds the procrustean theorists had prepared for them. But however ad hoc its origins and arbitrary its deployment, "mode" acquired nearly the same degree of authority as liturgical chant itself.

At the same time that scholastic music theorists were formulating modal theory, their colleagues were embarking on a new set of practices involving two or more simultaneously sounding voices: polyphony. Theorists involved with polyphony concerned themselves for many generations with the means of coordinating those lines, with respect to both rhythm (through the development of mensural notation) and pitch (through the refinement of the voice-leading principles that regulated the flow of consonance and dissonance). Because polyphonic compositions were often based on preexisting liturgical melodies, their larger-scale structural features seemed to require no particular discussion. Pedagogical texts frequently presented chant-oriented modal theory cheek by jowl with rules of counterpoint, as though they simply belonged together. In Chapter XXIV of his treatise on mode, *Liber de natura et proprietate tonorum* (1476), Johannes Tinctoris mentions quite casually that traditional modal categories also obtain for polyphony, and although he sprinkles in two-voice examples throughout the treatise, he does not expand on this principle.[1]

---

1. Johannes Tinctoris, *Liber de natura et proprietate tonorum,* trans. Albert Seay (Colorado Springs: Colorado College Music Press, 1967). The chapter that addresses polyphony directly is titled "That mixture and mingling of tones may be made not only in simple song but also in composed." Incidentally, Tinctoris qualifies as one of the most hilarious prose stylists in the history of Western music theory. Witness, for instance, his prologue to this treatise.

The next generation of music theorists, however, began to interrogate the music composed by their own contemporaries—a change of orientation actually suggested by Tinctoris, who famously claimed that no one paid any attention to music more than forty years old.[2] (If we were to adopt such a policy, we would no longer bother with music written before the mid-1960s!) Tinctoris's modernist manifesto emerges not only out of new attitudes transforming scholarship across Europe but also from the kinds of musical enterprises appearing in the fifteenth century; he praises in particular the contributions of Ockeghem, Régis, Busnois, Caron, and Faugues, along with those of their teachers, Dunstable, Binchois, and Dufay. Although artists continued to produce songs following relatively simple formal designs and masses based on previously existing materials, they also increasingly wrote freely composed motets that sought to elevate the meanings of the words. Eschewing the aid of the cantus firmus to dictate structure in advance, they began to shape their pieces with an eye toward signification and rhetorical effect. Within this context, mode became a feature actively exploited for purposes of formal design and even complex allegorical meaning.[3]

As free composition came to the fore, theorists returned to the question of mode, now explicitly as it pertained to the musics of their own moment. In his *Trattato della natura e cognitione di tutti gli tuoni di canto figurato* (1525), Pietro Aron brought the standard eight categories to bear on early monuments of music printing, ranging from Petrucci's *Odhecaton* (1501) to a collection of motets published as recently as 1521, and in doing so, he encountered several points of discrepancy between this repertory and his inherited theories. By hammering away at those problem areas, he called attention to the inability of conventional theory to account for some of the

2. "In addition, it is a matter of great surprise that there is no composition written over forty years ago which is thought by the learned to be worthy of performance." Johannes Tinctoris, *Liber de arte contrapuncti* (1477), trans. Albert Seay (Rome: American Institute of Musicology, 1961), 14.

3. For modally oriented analyses of fifteenth-century music, see Leeman L. Perkins, "Modal Species and Mixtures in a Fifteenth-Century Chanson Repertory," in *Modality in the Music of the Fourteenth and Fifteenth Centuries,* ed. Ursula Günther, Ludwig Finscher, and Jeffrey Dean, Musicological Studies and Documents 49 (Neuhausen-Stuttgart: Hänssler-Verlag, 1996), and "Modal Strategies in Okeghem's Missa Cuiusvis Toni," *Music Theory and the Exploration of the Past,* ed. Christopher Hatch and David W. Bernstein (Chicago: University of Chicago Press, 1993). For an approach that works particularly through modal allegories, see Kate Bartel, "Portal of the Skies: Topologies of the Divine in the Latin Motet" (Ph.D. diss., UCLA, in progress).

most esteemed polyphony of his day.[4] Heinrich Glareanus took up the challenge raised by Aron's demonstration, and in classic Kuhnian fashion, he used those apparent anomalies to bring about a paradigm shift. He also opened the doors to humanistic music criticism, as he interpreted whole compositions by Josquin according to their idiosyncratic structures.[5] In his turn, Gioseffo Zarlino picked up the twelve-mode system introduced by Glareanus's *Dodecachordon* and located it within an elaborate compendium for all musical knowledge, *Istitutioni harmoniche* (1558), thereby presuming to supplant Boethius. Zarlino used the music of his own mentor, Adrian Willaert, for most of his examples and objects of analysis.[6]

These three theorists of polyphonic mode—Aron, Glareanus, Zarlino—do not concur on all details: Aron persists with the traditional eight categories, Glareanus increases the number to twelve, Zarlino adopts (without citation) Glareanus's twelve but changes the principle of numbering. Thus when Aron refers to Mode 1, he means (as does Tinctoris) a configuration with a final on D, while Glareanus designates A and Zarlino C as the finals for their Mode 1. A set of categories that had at least offered some kind of international consensus thus becomes hopelessly confused, all the more so when seventeenth-century theorists devise a typology based on the eight modes they actually use—which are not the same as either the traditional system or any of the internally consistent versions produced by the sixteenth century.

If the theorists of the time could not themselves agree on something as basic as the number of categories, then we might well conclude that their efforts were desperate attempts at shoring up an intellectual paradigm that had outlived its practical plausibility. At least this is the conclusion drawn by many prominent scholars of our own time. In place of this cluster of competing models, none of which seems to offer clear guidance for the sep-

---

4. Pietro Aron, *Trattato della natura e cognitione di tutti gli tuoni di canto figurato* (Venice, 1525); partial translation in Oliver Strunk, *Source Readings in Music History,* rev. ed. (New York: Norton, 1998), 415–28. I work principally from a facsimile. For an examination of Aron's analyses, see Cristle Collins Judd, "Reading Aron Reading Petrucci: The Music Examples of the *Trattato della natura et cognitione di tutti gli tuoni* (1525)," *Early Music History* 14 (1995): 121–52.

5. Heinrich Glareanus, *Dodecachordon* (Basle, 1547), trans. Clement A. Miller (Rome: Musicological Studies and Documents, 1965). I have modeled *Modal Subjectivities* on the *Dodecachordon* in so far as I include complete scores of the compositions I discuss. My thanks to the University of California Press for allowing me to do so.

6. Gioseffo Zarlino, *Istitutioni harmoniche* (Venice, 1558). I make use of the facsimile edition of a revised version published in 1573 (Ridgewood, NJ: Gregg Press, 1966).

aration of sixteenth-century repertories into distinct categories, Harold Powers has proposed instead a system of what he calls "tonal types," which allows for objective classification on the basis of such features as clefs and final pitches.[7] His solution, which has been adopted by many Renaissance scholars during the last twenty-five years, avoids mode altogether as an incoherent project.

Anyone familiar with my work will not expect me to balk at anachronism per se. If I insist in this book on the pragmatic viability of mode, it is not just because I want to correspond with the testimony of the native informants. I do so rather because classification turns out to be only a minor aspect of sixteenth-century modal theory. For although my principal informants quibble among themselves about how to assign numbers, they concur wholeheartedly about how modes actually operate to structure complex compositions—and this is something Powers in his substitution of tonal types for modes does not address.

Zarlino begins his discussion of mode not with music as his target but with a much broader definition: mode is a way of doing something.[8] And here I would like briefly to bring in a book extremely famous and influential in Zarlino's day, Giulio Romano's *I modi*—a collection that deals not with scales or clefs or reciting tones but rather with drawings of an astonishingly wide variety of sex acts (engravings published in 1524). Romano's graphic depictions of couples, threesomes, and much more, later accompanied by erotic verses *(Sonetti lussuriosi)* by Pietro Aretino, invite readers to consider the ways their bodies might engage with those of others—ways that move far beyond the "mode" sanctioned by the church and imported to the heathen as "the missionary position."[9] Like Romano, Zarlino envisions a wide range of modal possibilities not in order to shove them into

---

7. Harold Power, "Tonal Types and Modal Categories in Renaissance Polyphony," *Journal of the American Musicological Society* 34 (1981): 428–70. See also his entry on "Mode" in the *New Grove Dictionary.*

8. "Si debbe adunque avertire, che questa Parola Modo . . . significa propiamente la Ragione; cioè quella Misura, or Forma, che adoperiamo nel fare alcuna cosa, laqual ne astrenge poi a non passar più oltra; facendone operare tutte le cose con una certa mediocrità, o moderatione." ("Note, then, that this word *mode* . . . properly signifies the logic, the measure, or the form which we adopt in doing anything and which keeps it from going too far, making everything function with a certain moderation.") Zarlino, *Istitutioni,* 359. My translation.

9. Giulio Romano, *I modi* (Rome, 1524). For a translation of Aretino's sonnets and insightful commentary concerning Romano, see Bette Talvacchia, *Taking Positions: On the Erotic in Renaissance Culture* (Princeton: Princeton University Press, 1999).

pigeonholes, but so as to expand imaginatively on what had become a rather mechanical modus operandi. Zarlino exalts the music of his own mentor, Adrian Willaert, precisely because (as we saw in Chapter 4) Willaert had so systematically explored so many of these options in his settings of motet texts and Petrarch sonnets. I propose that whenever we hear the word *mode* in relation to sixteenth-century polyphony, we keep in mind how the word resonates with the title and licentious subject matter of Romano's and Aretino's erotica—the *Kama Sutra* of the Italian Renaissance.

As I have demonstrated over the course of this book, the modal ambiguities of madrigals do not result from the breakdown of an old system nor from a relatively primitive (i.e., pretonal) approach to composition; rather it qualifies as a deliberate and highly complex set of strategies for delineating self-divided subjectivities. When we listen to Beethoven's *Große Fuge* (which somehow begins on G even though it turns out to be grounded in Bb), we trust that Beethoven knows what he is doing. And although he clearly is subjecting the premises of tonality to extreme stress, no one would imagine throwing away our tonal tools for analysis in the face of his onslaught;[10] nor would we want to make up, for the sake of consistent classification, a new category or tonal type of "pieces that start in G even though they're really in Bb." Many of the madrigals discussed in the preceding chapters resemble Beethoven's Op. 133 in their daring manipulations of inherited materials. If composers such as Rore depart from convention and relocate coherence within their own invented clusters of correspondences, they do not thereby operate in a discursive void.

One of the problems with defining *mode* in scalar terms is that it places these categories in binary opposition against tonality, for which we have internalized justifications for all the chromatic deviations, all the loopholes that make a composition interesting as it goes about satisfying its tonal duties. Too often, scholars act as though a cadential leading tone or a lowered sixth degree in Dorian demolishes modal purity and moves the piece closer to what will (at long last!) become tonality. We do not hold tonal minor to the same rigid standards, however, for we know about the functional flexibility of the sixth and seventh degrees. Such flexibility of sensitive pitches also obtains in sixteenth-century modality. And far from weakening the identities of the modes, these inflections (as in tonal minor) act as crucial

10. See the discussion of Beethoven's Op. 132 in my *Conventional Wisdom: The Content of Musical Form* (Berkeley and Los Angeles: University of California Press, 2000), chap. 4.

markers for energy vectors and for definition itself. Thus, oddly enough, the two available versions of the sixth degree in Dorian (as opposed to Aeolian, which normally has available to it only the position a half step above the fifth degree) counts as one of its distinguishing characteristics.

A species-oriented conception of mode, by contrast, allows for dynamic process. It is sufficiently baggy in definition that it liberally accommodates all the imaginative strategies pursued by the composers of the sixteenth century. Moreover, the theorists of the sixteenth century, however much they may differ in their approaches to numbering, agree in their accounts of how mode actually operates. If they offer too little detail for our tastes, they do so in part so as to maintain the bagginess that empowers their theoretical construct, for more rigid criteria would only serve to narrow the options. Armed with little more than knowledge of a mode's species of octave, fifth, and fourth and a sense of how those inform everything from melodies to background structures in a composition, the artist can produce infinite numbers of coherent pieces, and the analyst can make sense of their details.

Throughout this book I have followed J. L. Austin's performative models of understanding discursive processes rather than relying on the ontologically oriented scales that greatly restrict our usual approaches. In this final section, I want to turn things around and proceed through the various modes individually, explaining quickly their particular guidelines and distinguishing characteristics. But I will also follow the lead of my Renaissance theorists in offering a smattering of pieces belonging to each of the modes—in this case, the very madrigals considered in detail in previous chapters. Instead of treating them as extraordinary cultural texts, however, I will now engage them as examples of formal types, thus exploiting them this time around for theoretical purposes.

Because sixteenth-century theorists differed with each other with respect to the numbering of their modes, they left no obvious order for me to follow. Consequently, I will take up first the eight orthodox categories—those located on D through G—and only afterward consider the ones added by Glareanus and Zarlino: those with finals on A and C. I do this in part in order to delay until last discussing the modes that most resemble the major and minor scales of eighteenth-century tonality, to avoid giving them pride of place. I hope that by the time I reach these too-familiar configurations they will appear more clearly as what they are at this time: additional modal categories rather than the advent of something quite different. In keeping with the practice I have followed throughout *Modal Subjectivities,* I will make

FIGURE 29. Dorian species

FIGURE 30. Dorian subregions

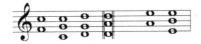

use of the old Greek names for the modes in order to avoid the confusion over numbering practices that developed along with the theoretical inclusion of the four new modes in the sixteenth century.

DORIAN

Probably the most versatile and inclusive of modes, Dorian occupies the D diapason, with its division at A and final on D (Fig. 29).

As theorists of the sixteenth century indicate, cadences in Dorian tend to occur on D and A (the boundary pitches of the diapente) and on F, also a forceful means of harmonizing A. For the sake of theoretical consistency among modes, my native informants only occasionally mention the frequent internal cadences that occur in Dorian practice on G and even on C, both of which emphasize the fourth degree and threaten to divide the D octave arithmetically. On the other end of the spectrum, Phrygian cadences on E may also emerge. But such cadences—those on G, C, and E—belong more properly to the realm of critical interpretation than to generalized theory per se: that is, they come into play at the level of compositional strategy rather than of abstract modal constitution. Alone of the modes, however, Dorian allows for the easy and intelligible incorporation of all other configurations as secondary regions (Fig. 30).

Stable melodic activity occurs largely within the D-A diapente, usually circumscribed on top with a B♭—added to prevent the tritone that would emerge between the mediant, F, and the sixth degree, but also to enhance the status of A as species boundary. The custom of lowering the sixth degree for stable melodies in this mode dates all the way back to the first liturgical chants captured by notation and theoretical models: thus, the typical

FIGURE 31. D diapente with B♭

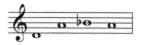

FIGURE 32. G functions within Dorian

area on $\hat{4}$ (G)   iv as harmonization

Dorian formula leaps from the final to the fifth degree, circumscribed by B♭ before returning to A and the continuation of the melody (Fig. 31).

But the natural Dorian sixth degree—that is, B♮—exerts its power on the level of structural development. As counterintuitive as this may seem to tonally oriented musicians, scalar purity in Dorian does not obtain within stable passages, but it does so with respect to available secondary regions. Thus the B♮ encourages strong cadences on the fifth degree, for which B♮ functions as the necessary $\hat{2}$, and it also permits Phrygian arrivals on E, bounded melodically and/or harmonically with B♮. Moreover, the hardwired B♮ means that the secondary region on G, the fourth degree, has a major rather than minor mediant. Yet the chord on G within stable Dorian contexts usually harmonizes B♭ (Fig. 32).

Many Dorian compositions will play on these subtle differences and produce their allegories by means of them. Recall, for instance, that in *L'Orfeo,* Monteverdi locates his idyllic pastoral world in G circumscribed with B♭; when the lead character begins to push the envelope and move beyond that protected space, he moves to the region on G with B♮. And within the intensely paranoid universe Monteverdi has created, the hard-G region progresses arrogantly to C, which then—by means of a short circuit of C's mediant, E, that forges an unexpected link to the other extreme, A—suddenly lands Orfeo in the realm of tragedy and lamentation. Apollo will eventually lead his contrite son back to the neutral position of D, which reigns omnipotent over the entire affective spectrum (Fig. 33).

Over the course of this book, we have encountered three Dorian madrigals, each exploiting the resources of this mode in its own way for its own purposes. Verdelot's "Chi non fa prova, Amore" eschews the potential am-

FIGURE 33. *Orfeo* synopsis

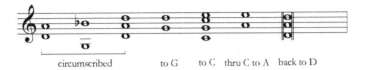

circumscribed   to G   to C   thru C to A   back to D

FIGURE 34. 6̂ in D-Hypodorian

natural 6̂   lowered 6̂

biguities latent within Dorian but relies rather on its capacity for extreme stability. For purposes of setting Machiavelli's preachy text on the dangers of love, Verdelot chooses to drive home over and over again this lesson by means of the descending Dorian diapente; he includes only a couple of cadences on the fifth degree, which make even clearer the narrow limits of this moral sermon. Note that the canto and tenor in this madrigal present different arrangements of the species: the tenor makes use of the entire D octave and even stretches beyond as far as F, while the low-lying canto maintains from the very outset a plagal design, with its diatessaron residing below the final. When the canto's initial motive stretches up from the fifth degree to the final, it does so through B♮, very far away from the B♭ that would mark the boundary at the other extreme of the scale (Fig. 34).

One could quite properly label "Chi non fa prova, Amore" as what Zarlino terms a "common" mode, because its lead voices bring both Dorian and Hypodorian arrangements to bear.[11] I am including it as Dorian, however, because the tenor (the voice part usually singled out as the mode bearer by theorists) seems to me more responsible for directing the piece and because the madrigal is located within D rather than G with signed-in B♭—the more typical configuration for Hypodorian. Verdelot does not use both versions of Dorian arbitrarily, however. In keeping with Machiavelli's unrelieved message, these two voices manage to hem us in all the more inescapably: the canto catches us from below, the tenor from above,

11. Zarlino, *Istituzioni*, 385–6.

and both converge as though through absolute necessity on the diapente from A to D.

Willaert's "Giunto m'à Amor," on the other hand, makes full use of the different spellings of the sixth degree as he twists and turns in search of relief from the lovesick condition Petrarch presents in his sonnet. If the placid beginning appears to ground us in G-Hypodorian (with signed in B♭), the shriek of protest that enters with the second line of text ("chi m'ancidono a torto") jumps to the high register and reveals its authentic (if transposed) Dorian identity. In that higher register, E♮ resists strenuously the pull back to the diapente, and the inevitable collapse through E♭ announces defeat. If that initial move to the area on the fifth degree brings no lasting refuge, then our persona also tries to move in the other direction—to arrive on the fourth degree, again with E♮, which cannot hold indefinitely either. In this madrigal, the power of Dorian's flexible sixth degree makes itself palpable, as E♮ continually stands as a mirage of false consciousness, E♭ as inexorable reality.

The conceptual leap from "Giunto m'à Amor" to Monteverdi's "O Mirtillo" is enormous, though both actually exploit the same Dorian resources. At least Willaert presents stable Dorian passages at the beginning before he begins to explore other regions, and he returns on a regular basis to his principal species. By contrast, Monteverdi throws us without preparation into the most extreme of positions: the lowered sixth degree, B♭, becomes the root of the first sonority we hear. As the opening lines unfold, we also get subjected to regions reliant on B♮. As we have seen, this kind of passage belongs at best to the middle sections of compositions. But Monteverdi has turned the usual process inside out to portray Amarilli's wounded soliloquy: only in the middle of the madrigal does the mode get presented in an unambiguous fashion, after which it comes unraveled for a highly equivocal ending.

The strategy for "O Mirtillo" is unthinkable without decades of properly behaving Dorian pieces backing it up. Connoisseurs at the time (sympathetic ones, in any case, if not Artusi) would have known how to supply the missing center of this mode, how to construe D as the necessary mediator between the extremes presented so baldly in Amarilli's opening gambit. It is as if the entire affective range of Monteverdi's *L'Orfeo* were to find itself compressed within the scope of a three-minute madrigal. The linear exposition of the music drama helps to make its allegorical tensions intelligible, whereas "O Mirtillo" simultaneously resists modal orthodoxy and depends upon Dorian's dynamics for all it is worth.

FIGURE 35. G-Hypodorian species

FIGURE 36. 6̂ in G-Hypodorian

natural 6̂   lowered 6̂

HYPODORIAN

Hypodorian most frequently appears in transposition to G with one flat, and it qualifies as one of the most stable, least ambiguous of the modes. It shares the same species of fifth and fourth as authentic Dorian, but it arranges them with the diapente on top, the diatessaron situated below the final (Fig. 35). Because of this arrangement, the alternate versions of the sixth degree that so often characterize Dorian rarely become an issue in Hypodorian: the natural sixth degree occurs in ascents to the final or in confirmations of the fifth degree as a temporary final, the lowered version does little more than serve as upper auxiliary to the fifth degree. They do not, in other words, tend to appear in proximity to one another (Fig. 36).[12]

Although conflicts over chromatic alterations do not usually emerge as the focus of Hypodorian pieces, the plagal mode does have its own characteristic strategies. Foremost among these is the potential division of the octave at A, such that the heavily weighted fifth degree becomes a rival final. Note that whereas arrivals on the fifth degree in Dorian engage the upper part of the modal range, those in Hypodorian involve a descent into the lower part of the octave. A floor seems to open up beneath the final, and we are drawn down into another realm (Fig. 37). Reestablishing the final then requires an increase of energy and the reconquest of the upper region; by contrast, the arrival on the final in authentic Dorian entails moving down

12. Note that this example (Fig. 36) is the same as Figure 34, except for the transposition. The point being made in the previous context is that Verdelot's canto behaved as though it were in Hypodorian.

FIGURE 37. Divisions of D octave

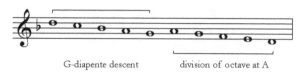

G-diapente descent   division of octave at A

to the lower part of the range. Put differently, authentic and plagal modes differ in terms of their centers of gravity.

The trapdoor dimension of Hypodorian proves especially useful for the presentation of inside and outside so crucial to the cultural task of the madrigal. If the diapente continues to function as the public voice, the lower part of the Hypodorian diapason can be made to sound like a hidden aspect of the Self. And this is, in fact, how both Arcadelt and Monteverdi (among so many others) exploit Hypodorian.

In Arcadelt's "O felic' occhi miei," for instance, the eloquent melody in the canto operates for the first half of the madrigal strictly within the diapente. Its rational control, however, is undermined by the licentious eyes, which continually peek up unbidden from the lower recesses of the mode. Eventually, we witness the dethroning of that serene authority, as the mind is dragged against its will over and over again down to the bottom of the scale: the lower fifth degree. In this context, the performers have the option of playing with the two versions of the sixth degree as a means of enhancing or resisting the abjection implied in Arcadelt's slippery slope: maintaining the natural sixth degree, E♮, will apply a bit of resistance against the skid, while lowering the sixth degree to E♭ at the end through *musica ficta* will make the arrival on $\hat{5}$ sound as though the brakes have failed utterly. Either choice makes sense, and both qualify as legitimate within the system: it all depends on the spin one wishes to put on this devastating conclusion. In either case, Arcadelt's "O felic' occhi miei" harnesses the tensions of Hypodorian and exploits them to create an extraordinary simulation of the lofty mind undone by the impulses of the lower body.

Monteverdi's Amarilli makes use of the same set of dynamic tensions in "Anima mia, perdona," but her mapping of the Hypodorian species produces a very different set of stakes. For Amarilli can express herself by means of speech only with the greatest effort. If the lower range of her octave also represents a kind of interiority, it does not represent the lower body but rather that place where she conceals that which she cannot say out loud. She shifts constantly between her two modal regions: the G diapente standing for public utterance, the D diapente for those buried truths that she can only gradually bring to light—that is, into the G diapente. But first she must rehearse those admissions below the level of audibility, down in the bottom of the octave. The resulting dualism, then, simulates her own internal struggle, her attempt to come to terms with her denied feelings—first to herself and eventually (even if no one hears) in full voice.

One more of the madrigals discussed in previous chapters, Wert's setting of "Tirsi morir volea," operates within a kind of Dorian or Hypodorian transposed through a signed-in B♭ to G. Much like Verdelot's "Chi non fa prova, Amore," however, it rarely ventures beyond the diapente itself. As in the Verdelot, Wert's tenor does extend up as far as a third above the upper boundary of the diapente, but it does not (as does Verdelot's) produce actual cadences on $\hat{5}$. Whereas Verdelot stayed largely within his diapente in order to present Machiavelli's single-minded warning, Wert does so as a means of delivering his streamlined, breathless account of Tirsi's sexual encounter with his Ninfa. They too prove to be single-minded: they want desperately to reach climax (thus their forceful—if incomplete—diapente descents all the way through), but they want to hold off the moment itself until both parties are ready (thus the many half cadences, overlapped cadences, temporary breathers in B♭ as the other standard support of the fifth degree, and other extension devices that do not detract from the goal but merely delay its gratification).

Ahem, back to the matter at hand—namely the modal theories of Zarlino rather than those of Giulio Romano's *I modi,* where Wert seems to have drawn us. Zarlino has classificatory terms for pieces that do not fill out an entire octave (he calls them "imperfetti" or "diminuti"), and he hastens to add that such irregularities should not affect our analyses, which still ought to rely on the final and the ways the modal species underscore the formal process.[13] In other words, it makes little difference whether we label pieces like Wert's "Tirsi morir volea" (or Verdelot's "Chi non fa prova, Amore") as plagal or authentic or as some subset of Dorianish pieces. I have provisionally placed the Verdelot in my discussion of D-Dorian, Wert with G-Hypodorian. But in fact both elect to concentrate their activities almost exclusively within the diapente itself, which does not truly tip its hat in one direction or the other. What is of greater consequence, however, is *why* they act the way they do, and that I hope to have explained.

13. Zarlino, *Istitutioni,* 385.

FIGURE 38. Phrygian species

FIGURE 38. Phrygian species

FIGURE 39. Second degree above E

dominant-tonic arrival on E   Phrygian with F♮

PHRYGIAN

Technically speaking, Phrygian should operate much as does Dorian, but with its species bounded by E and B (Fig. 38). It rarely does so, however, because of a peculiarity hardwired into the diapente itself: its second degree sits a half step above the final, which precludes strongly harmonized (i.e., dominant-tonic) arrivals (Fig. 39). Indeed, even within monophonic music genuine Phrygian is relatively uncommon in Western music. Before the advent of distinct modal categories on A, many compositions that hover around A were ordinarily classed as Phrygian (see the following section). But with Glareanus's designation of modal types grounded on A came the problem of separating out which of the pieces thrown into the Phrygian catchall were truly Phrygian and which were Aeolian *avant la lettre* (though they often ended, dutifully enough, on E so as to fit into some orthodox pot or other).

Of course, Phrygian occurs quite frequently in other musics. Peter Manuel has written extensively on the Andalusian modes—most familiar to most of us through flamenco—that trace a descending tetrachord down through a half step to the final. He also notes that European art composers employing this device usually convert that final at the bottom to a dominant that resolves back (as the Christian God no doubt meant it to) to A.[14] Of all Western musicians, heavy metal bands seem to have come to terms most comfortably with Phrygian, in part because the guitar is still tuned with E at the

---

14. Peter Manuel, "From Scarlatti to 'Guantanamera': Dual Tonicity in Spanish and Latin American Musics," *Journal of the American Musicological Society* 55 (Summer 2002): 311–36. See also the discussions concerning Bizet's tendency to do this in *Carmen,* in my *Georges Bizet: Carmen* (Cambridge: Cambridge University Press, 1992), especially 90–91.

bottom (you can take the guitar out of Andalusia, but not Andalusia out of the guitar).[15] Yet although Western art composers have flirted with Phrygian qualities—most evidently in the Neapolitan device that emerges in the seventeenth century to mark grief—bona fide Phrygian pieces remain rare beasts.

Viewed from the vantage point of standard European music theories, Phrygian has an unsolvable problem: it cannot support strong cadences on its own final, but it also undermines the efficacy of all other options within its orbit. It either sits paralyzed on its species boundaries, thus insisting on its identity, or it ranges as though arbitrarily through other subregions and returns back at the end, as though by mere fiat, to embrace its final. But Metallica and other such bands have realized that this "problem" turns into a strength if one wishes to simulate such an uncomfortable affective realm.[16] As centered, rational subjectivity becomes increasingly the assumption underlying musical procedures, Phrygian gets squeezed out of the picture. Yet the existence of such a category lured some number of sixteenth-century composers to inhabit it from time to time. Never a happy place, Phrygian infuses its pieces with equivocations that sound more than any other group as though they are constructed from arbitrary premises.

Willaert chooses an uncompromising Phrygian for his setting of Petrarch's hateful "Lasso, ch' i' ardo": if the poet showers his lady with the conventional encomium (and Willaert responds with the whole array of modal types), he does so only in order to reduce her all the more effectively to cinders (the inevitable moment of closure on E). Freedom of motion seems to obtain from time to time within the madrigal, but it always drains away, back to that bitter pill, the cadence on the final. No other mode could produce this spirit of glum sniping, the musical equivalent of Richard III's winter of discontent. Comfortable neither with itself nor with any other possibilities, Willaert's Phrygian final in this madrigal functions like a black hole, sucking the light out of everything around it.

Not too surprisingly, Gesualdo also finds this affective realm particularly congenial to his explorations of unrequited (or is it, rather, requited?) anguish. In his self-parody " 'Mercè,' grido piangendo," he steps over the line

15. For more on the uses of Phrygian in heavy metal, see Robert Walser, *Running with the Devil: Power, Gender, and Madness in Heavy Metal Music* (Hanover, NH: Wesleyan University Press, 1993). Glenn Pillsbury theorizes the impact of the guitar itself on this configuration in his dissertation, "Pure Black, Looking Clear: Genre, Race, Commerce, and the Music of Metallica" (Ph.D. diss., UCLA, 2003).

16. See again Walser and Pillsbury.

and engages the raised second degree, which is ordinarily off-limits for Phrygian; indeed, he begins his pseudoscreed on a B-major triad, thus exacerbating the agony he professes. This illicit F♯ drains away at crucial moments, however, reverting to the impotent F♮ that characterizes Phrygian. Use of the altered second degree does occur in this repertory and with increasing frequency, but it always qualifies as a gesture outside the bounds of rational discourse, and Gesualdo counts on our knowing this for the full histrionic impact of his madrigal.

PHRYGIAN/AEOLIAN

The positing of independent modes on A, which often found themselves cast into the Phrygian category by default, solved many theoretical problems and also cleared the way for genuinely and consistently Aeolian pieces, such as Monteverdi's "Ah, dolente partita." But it did not always apply retroactively to repertories that predated the conceptual separation, which often relied primarily on the Aeolian species for rational mobility, even if the pieces had to revert in the end to type—or at least to conclude on E, a legitimate final (Fig. 40). Nor did it obliterate the attractions of what came to be theorized as "mixed modes," for this particular combination continued to offer affective strategies not available within any other configuration. Hovering on the cusp between Aeolian and Phrygian, these compositions refuse to declare themselves one way or the other. So attractive is this particular mixture for the sixteenth-century cultural agenda of divided consciousness that it becomes an important category in and of itself.

Two such madrigals in our collection emerged before the theoretical separation, both Verdelot settings of Machiavelli texts. The first, "Sì suave è l'inganno," operates almost entirely within what would later be labeled Aeolian, though it concludes on E. It does so, I would claim, not because it had to do so, which would make this just a Phrygian composition, but because Verdelot wants to make the canzona sound as though it ends up in the air, making us wait for the inevitable other shoe to drop. The other, "O dolce notte," revels in the oblique quality of mixed modalities, starting as it does with a deceitful major chord on the transposed Hypophrygian final. The canzona relies on its Aeolian side to explain its conceit, but it ends back in that impossible position, pregnant with meanings it refuses to divulge. Clearly, Verdelot did not write these compositions out of ignorance of proper procedure: his strategies exploiting the Janus-faced properties of this configuration reveal the very highest level of sophistication.

FIGURE 40. A-process ending on E (= Phrygian?)

When Marenzio returns to this mixture for his setting of "Tirsi morir volea," he gives it the task of rendering the shepherd's desire (for a cadence on A) and his commitment to postponing as long as possible his climax. The three-section madrigal ends and begins with Tirsi strung out on E—the last time by choice, as he commits himself to another round; only when the lovers come together at the end of the *seconda parte* do we (and they) get the long-awaited arrival on A—the event that grounds the entire sequence, even as it can appear in all its glory only the one time, given the allegory underpinning the madrigal. "Tirsi morir volea" is for all practical purposes an Aeolian composition that ends on its fifth degree; it even traffics in divisions of the A octave at D, which seems to be where Tirsi's Ninfa resides (they meet together—the extremes of E, where Tirsi begins, and her D—on A). Still, the strong Phrygian qualities of Marenzio's setting and its persistent ambiguities recall that cluster of earlier pieces, such as Verdelot's, that embraced the mixture as a recognized type.

LYDIAN

A consideration of Lydian brings with it one of the modal tradition's great inconsistencies—or so it seems to us today, as well as to the sixteenth-century theorists who began to posit independent modes on C. The species themselves have F and C as boundaries (Fig. 41). If it followed the pattern of all the other diatonic modes, the diapente on F would have a B♮, which produces a tritone with the final (Fig. 42). Yet right from the beginning of chant notation—even before reliable staff lines came into use—this diabolical interval was corrected with the addition of a flat; indeed, Greek theory itself offered the option of a pitch that had two versions, allowing for mutation. So fundamental was this configuration to medieval theory that the hexachord on F contained the B♭ as the most crucial part of its essence, ergo its name: the soft hexachord (Fig. 43). Consequently, there existed an enormous number of compositions based on F with signed-in B♭, but labeled as Lydian—one of the core categories available.

To those accustomed to the notion of transposition, these pieces share

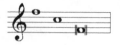

FIGURE 41. Lydian species

FIGURE 42. Lydian diapente

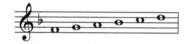

FIGURE 43. Soft hexachord

the same scale—and surely, then, the same mode—as those grounded in C. When Pietro Aron started scrutinizing his repertory for purposes of modal analysis, he realized that he could explain away the C pieces by labeling them as F pieces transposed. But the notion of transposition, applied across the board, got him into trouble when he examined pieces on D with signed-in B♭: what had appeared merely as quirky Dorian now appeared as transposed . . . what? Glareanus will posit a new category, Aeolian, for such compositions, and he will also move toward a consistent model of transposition, by virtue of which the flat in whatever mode moves the whole system by a fifth. But that theoretical advance also leaves the Lydian category high and dry, with virtually no compositions to call its own. It becomes an empty set: theoretically feasible but almost never encountered in practice. (Beethoven's *Heiliger Dankgesang* does not so much resurrect an archaic tradition as explore the possibilities within a tonal context of a configuration nearly unknown to the Renaissance; George Russell's Lydian approach to jazz deliberately wrenches apart the tendency of the "normal" fourth degree to pull down to the tonic, thus liberating his musical language from the enforced allegiances of tonal hierarchies.)[17]

17. George Russell, *Lydian Chromatic Concept of Tonal Organization* (New York: Concept Publishing,1953).

I could postpone the discussion of F-based madrigals for my section on Ionian, and I would thereby satisfy both our craving for scalar consistency and that of some sixteenth-century theorists. Yet a substantial body of music operated within F with signed-in B♭, before the new category came into being and along side an also substantial number of pieces based in C. Were these, in fact, the same? Or did some kind of distinction exist in practice— a distinction that got collapsed when the theoretical rezoning ordinance occurred?

Judging on the basis of the madrigals discussed in the previous chapters, it would appear that composers choose the soft hexachord deliberately. Arcadelt's "Il bianco e dolce cigno," Willaert's "I' vidi in terra," the narrative frame of Rore's "Da le belle contrade d'oriente," and even Gesualdo's "Luci serene e chiare" all seek to simulate a kind of pastoral tranquility. The strong cultural association of F with the pastoral topic persists in works by Handel and, most famously, in Beethoven's Sixth Symphony. This is where the practice of numbering the modes proves preferable to that of giving them Greek names: no one would balk if we called these pieces in Mode 5, but "Lydian" carries with it the expectation of that edgy, too-high fourth degree. On the other hand, we probably should hesitate before lumping these in with the pieces on C in the natural hexachord, which seem to carry a significantly different affective charge: the two discussed in this book— Arcadelt's "Ahime, dov' è 'l bel viso" and Wert's "Solo e pensoso"—have little in common with the serenity of the ones on F.

I will leave my discussion of these F-based madrigals for my section on Ionian, largely because the formal constraints imposed by their species are identical. But because of this complicated history, I will deal with those on F separately from those on C. As Giulio Romano would remind us, even if these scales are physiologically the same, they have distinctly different preferences and predispositions.

MIXOLYDIAN

Mixolydian, with species boundaries on G and D (Fig. 44), sets up shop in the hard hexachord (Fig. 45), making it conceptually and with respect to tuning a much harsher terrain than diapente on either on F or C. If to our equal-tempered ears these three qualify as interchangeable, they did not do so in the sixteenth century. The choice of Mixolydian signifies much more, in other words, than major with a lowered seventh degree (which performers usually raised to F♯ at cadences, in any case). Eric Chafe has demonstrated

FIGURE 44. Mixolydian species

FIGURE 45. Hard hexachord

at length how Monteverdi made use of the contrast between the softness of flat-oriented modes and the hardness of Mixolydian—the mode of choice for cruel, unyielding ladies.[18]

A few comments on Mixolydian's formal predispositions before we turn to examples. If the F♮ normative to this mode disappears through *musica ficta* at cadences, it makes itself felt at the structural level, for the secondary region on the fifth degree, D, is minor in quality (Fig. 46). Moreover, the very wide interval between the modal final and mediant, between G and B, almost insists on resolving to C for relief. Consequently, the G octave tends to divide more congenially on C, and the mode requires heroic effort to counterbalance that tendency through plausible assertions of D as the proper boundary (Fig. 47).

Monteverdi's "Cruda Amarilli," with all its puns on bitterness, hardness, deafness, and cruelty, stands as a model for Mixolydian. Its overwhelming desire to have done with it all and collapse onto C (as all but the resistant canto do on the infamous "ahi lasso!") meets its match in Mirtillo's outraged suicide threats on D. They cancel each other out, and at the end he announces his retreat into silence—on G, which still speaks its bitterness loud and clear. As we saw, Amarilli's response, "O Mirtillo," although itself in a highly extenuated Dorian, quotes Mirtillo's words and his Mixolydian framework as part of her rebuttal. One should never make the mistake of confusing Mixolydian with G major!

The other Mixolydian madrigal discussed in the previous chapters is Marenzio's setting of "Solo e pensoso," which makes use of this mode in

18. Eric Chafe, *Monteverdi's Tonal Language* (New York: Schirmer Books, 1992).

FIGURE 46. Area on D (5̂)

FIGURE 47. Octave divided at C

response to the harshness of the wilderness with which Petrarch's persona has thrown his lot. Although he does not pursue in this piece the tight modal allegories typical of Willaert or Monteverdi (or even his own "Tirsi morir volea," for that matter), Marenzio does design his structure with cadence points on C and D battling, with G as the final point of nonrepose; grammatically, in other words, his "Solo e pensoso" counts as relatively orthodox Mixolydian, chromatic flare-ups aside. But his attention focuses less on the level of competing species or on problematizing the basis of his musical language than on the stunning images that he unfolds along with the succeeding lines of Petrarch's sonnet. Mixolydian simply serves to hold it all together into some semblance of background organization—but given the centrifugal eclecticism of the surface, that's a tall order.

AEOLIAN

The opening chapter of *Modal Subjectivities* dealt in some detail with the formal proclivities of Aeolian, with species boundaries on A and E (Fig. 48), and the section above on Phrygian addressed many of the fundamental issues related to this mode. Under normal circumstances, Aeolian cannot shore up its fifth degree through a dominant-tonic arrival, and it tends instead to tilt toward the area on the fourth degree (Fig. 49). The area on the mediant (also available and common in Dorian and Hypodorian compositions) alleviates this lack to some extent, in that it supports the fifth degree. And several apparently Aeolian pieces end on E (see the discussion of Phrygian/Aeolian above) (Fig. 50).

Still, the tendency of Aeolian to divide the octave at the fourth degree fuels most of the pieces in this mode we have examined. Recall how Mir-

FIGURE 48. Aeolian species

FIGURE 49. Octave divided at D ($\hat{4}$)

FIGURE 50. Harmonizations of $\hat{5}$

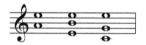

tillo in "Ah, dolente partita" drifts ever more disastrously toward D until the diapente on A and D reach a kind of standoff at the end to match his internal dilemma. Cipriano's "Mia benigna fortuna" heightens the stakes enormously by giving the opposing tendencies separate key signatures—a tension that becomes even more exacerbated in the *seconda parte* when the alto joins the enemy faction. This madrigal takes the polarities native to Aeolian and raises them to the level of meta-critique. Thus the stage is already set for Gesualdo's "Moro, lasso," which likewise takes the basic impulses of Aeolian but hides them under the perverse harmonizations for which he is justly celebrated. Yet with respect to the background structure of cadence points, "Moro, lasso" behaves quite properly—far more so, in fact, than does Cipriano.

Perhaps as a renegade mode, with its roots in Phrygian, Aeolian invited sixteenth-century radicals to perform some of their most transgressive experiments within its framework. In a sense, Monteverdi—dyed-in-the-wool classicist that he always really is—attempts in "Ah, dolente partita" to put Humpty together again, to show what can be accomplished within a scrupulously diatonic version of Aeolian. But it's too little too late.

Incidentally, although it shares the same scale with tonal minor, Aeolian does not contribute as much to the development of later practices as does Dorian. Throughout the seventeenth century and even up through early Bach, minor-key pieces usually sported Dorian signatures. Moreover, the common strategy of modulating to the fifth degree in tonal minor—especially in the highly formulaic binary dance forms—betrays its descent from Dorian. To the very great extent that tonal minor emerges from an expanded diapente descent, it does not have to be labeled as either Dorian or Aeolian. But throughout the seventeenth-century, when middle sections of pieces still function in terms of modal formal relationships, the priorities of Dorian continue to make themselves heard.

IONIAN

Which brings us to Ionian, often considered the equivalent of tonal major (Fig. 51). To be sure, Ionian and tonal major share the same scale, and Ionian even has a hardwired leading tone, greatly facilitating its sense of centeredness and transparency. But this feature proved something of a liability within the cultural enterprise of the madrigal, which traded on ambiguity and internal conflict. As theorists acknowledge, the self-assured complacency of Ionian found its place far more regularly at this time within the context of light songs and dances. The dynamism we associate with tonal major results not so much from the strategies of Ionian as from, once again, the expansion of the diapente descent.

Still, two of the most complex madrigals in my previous chapters operate within C-Ionian. The first, Arcadelt's "Ahime, dov' è 'l bel viso," locates its final outside the frame of the piece as the face of the now-departed Beloved. The Ionian leading tone continues to point toward its object of desire, which—within the economy of this madrigal—can never materialize. The fact that Ionian usually resists ambiguity makes Arcadelt's achievement all the more remarkable.

For his version of Petrarch's "Solo e pensoso," Wert chooses C-Ionian, which provides a stable backdrop for his extraordinarily spectacular surface. As with Marenzio's setting of the same sonnet, this madrigal inhabits its mode largely for convenience rather than for allegorical or metacritical purposes. Even so, its distance from tonal major ought be fairly clear.

These two madrigals operate within the natural hexachord, grounded on C, as opposed to the soft hexachord on F (Fig. 52). As I mentioned above in my truncated discussion of Lydian, this distinction matters to Renaissance musicians, and they opted most often for F when trying to evoke pastoral qualities. Once again, the always-available leading tone (E♮ in this case) ensures stability and decreases the likelihood of fundamental internal conflicts, making it ideal for producing affects such as serenity, as in Cipri-

FIGURE 51. Ionian species

FIGURE 52. Natural hexachord

FIGURE 53. $\hat{4}$ harmonized with VII♭

ano's frame for "Da le belle contrade d'oriente," with its depiction of the morning star and intertwining ivy.

Occasionally, the leading tone will itself be lowered to VII♭ in Ionian (Fig. 53). This is, of course, the principal progression in Arcadelt's "Ahime, dov' è 'l bel viso." Moreover, the lowering of the seventh degree often has the effect of pulling the line forcibly down from a fifth degree that threatens to become too stable for the strategy at hand. It also produces the bruised sonority on "piangendo" in Arcadelt's F-Ionian "Il bianco e dolce cigno" and the E♭ that brings us repeatedly back to earth in Willaert's angelic vision, "I' vidi in terra." For the most part, such deviations do little more than ruffle the otherwise placid surface. Gesualdo has to work very hard indeed to make his F-Ionian "Luci serene e chiare" take on a tinge of mysterious depth. But as Philip Gossett demonstrated in his classic article on the sketch books for the Pastoral Symphony, so did Beethoven.[19]

Accounts of sixteenth-century musical style usually trace a trajectory toward ever greater tonal sensitivity, with Monteverdi already showing signs in Books IV and V of his imminent plunge into tonality itself. To be sure,

19. Philip Gossett, "Beethoven's Sixth Symphony: Sketches for the First Movement," *Journal of the American Musicological Society* 27 (1974): 248–84.

the madrigals of Marenzio, Wert, and Monteverdi generally sign in chromatic pitches at cadences rather than leaving them to the whims of performers, making their scores appear more similar to those produced by later practices. But tonal analysis achieves very little for even these pieces except the occasional island of tonality awash in a sea of inexplicable stuff. To my ear, the homophonic madrigals of Arcadelt actually sound more tonal than most of Monteverdi's—largely because they stick so closely to the directionality of the diapente, harmonized in the least ambiguous fashions.

By contrast, a neomodal framework allows not only for consistent formal analysis but also for interpretations, especially for the very large number of madrigals that work on the basis of modal allegories. To be sure, musical style changes over the course of the sixteenth century: the opacity of Willaert's dense web of independent voices seems very far indeed from the powerfully articulated structures of Monteverdi. But this need not be understood as a linear evolution, for Josquin had already pioneered that means of delineating text in the late fifteenth century. Willaert thus represents not so much a throwback as another branch of Mannerism, in his case, the simulation of intensive soul searching by Florentine exiles striving to reconstitute their beloved city on the inside.

A vast change in musical syntax will occur in the first decade of the 1600s. It does not, of course, emerge *ex nihilo*—and to that extent, those who search for the roots of tonality in the sixteenth century are justified. But neither does it descend directly from the polyphonic madrigal, which remains to the end a creature of the neomodal movement. If the madrigal becomes increasingly marginalized over the course of the following decades, its gradual eclipse has nothing to do with any technological failings on its part. To be sure, something we later call tonality displaces the spectrum of modes that underlie the madrigal. But that change has far more to do with the new temporalities demanded by an emerging social order than with the grammar for arranging pitches. New conditions developed and, along with them, different cultural needs, foremost among them a radically altered conception of temporality and, consequently, subjectivity.

The hothouse environments for and to which the madrigal spoke so eloquently themselves disappeared, rather like the *fin de siècle* salons Proust describes so lovingly just as they begin to vanish like ghosts in the harsh light of twentieth-century industrialism. The intensely introspective gaze cultivated by the madrigal, even as it demanded the participatory energies of noble amateurs, became a luxury no longer viable in the theatricalized and propagandistic arena of seventeenth-century cultural politics. Put simply, the seventeenth-century Self literally had no time for the contemplative introversion of the polyphonic madrigal.

I suppose that our impatience with this repertory—our longing to hear it getting closer and closer to something we can identify as our own way of understanding the world—underscores how alien from us are the sixteenth-century artists who invested these pieces according to their own sensibilities. We cannot attain Ranke's historical ideal of knowing how it really, really was. But we can get much closer than we have if we take the trouble to learn the musical languages of the Renaissance instead of scouring its repertories for embryonic traces of later cultural priorities.

We may well mourn the passing of the exquisite court sensibilities that sustained the madrigal over the course of the sixteenth century, just as we mourn the retreat from immediate relevance of so many other great traditions. My elegy, however, does not mean to stop time, to return us to a world long since supplanted by others, even though I hope to have offered some unfamiliar whiffs and glimpses of Renaissance Italy. As a historian, my task is to bring to the table evidence of how people in the past arranged and understood their lives. As a musicologist, I draw much of my evidence from the elusive medium of music—the ways cultures sculpt images of ideal Selves within sound. The madrigal offers us an incomparable source if we will but listen.

Examples

EXAMPLE I. Monteverdi, "Ah, dolente partita"

(continued)

EXAMPLE I *(continued)*

EXAMPLE I *(continued)*

(continued)

EXAMPLE I *(continued)*

EXAMPLE I *(continued)*

(continued)

EXAMPLE I *(continued)*

EXAMPLE I *(continued)*

EXAMPLE 2. Verdelot, "Chi non fa prova, Amore"

EXAMPLE 2 *(continued)*

(continued)

EXAMPLE 2 *(continued)*

EXAMPLE 3. Verdelot, "Sì suave è l'inganno"

(*continued*)

EXAMPLE 3 *(continued)*

EXAMPLE 3 *(continued)*

EXAMPLE 4. Verdelot, "O dolce notte"

EXAMPLE 4 *(continued)*

(continued)

EXAMPLE 4 *(continued)*

EXAMPLE 5. Arcadelt, "Il bianco e dolce cigno"

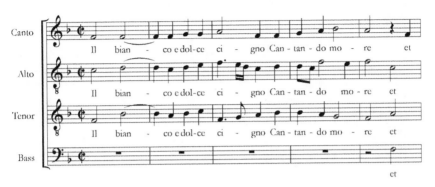

(continued)

EXAMPLE 5 *(continued)*

EXAMPLE 5 *(continued)*

EXAMPLE 6. Arcadelt, "O felic' occhi miei"

EXAMPLE 6 *(continued)*

(continued)

EXAMPLE 6 *(continued)*

EXAMPLE 7. Arcadelt, "Ahime, dov' è 'l bel viso"

(continued)

EXAMPLE 7 *(continued)*

EXAMPLE 7 *(continued)*

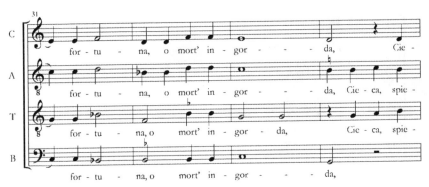

(continued)

EXAMPLE 7 *(continued)*

EXAMPLE 8. Willaert, "Giunto m'à Amor" (parts 1 and 2)

(continued)

EXAMPLE 8 *(continued)*

EXAMPLE 8 *(continued)*

(continued)

EXAMPLE 8 *(continued)*

EXAMPLE 8 *(continued)*

(continued)

EXAMPLE 8 *(continued)*

SECONDA PARTE

EXAMPLE 8 *(continued)*

(continued)

EXAMPLE 8 *(continued)*

EXAMPLE 8 *(continued)*

EXAMPLE 9. Willaert, "I' vidi in terra" (parts 1 and 2)

EXAMPLE 9 *(continued)*

(continued)

EXAMPLE 9 *(continued)*

EXAMPLE 9 *(continued)*

(continued)

EXAMPLE 9 *(continued)*

EXAMPLE 9 *(continued)*

EXAMPLE 9 *(continued)*

EXAMPLE 9 *(continued)*

(continued)

EXAMPLE 9 *(continued)*

EXAMPLE 9 *(continued)*

SECONDA PARTE

(continued)

EXAMPLE 9 *(continued)*

EXAMPLE 9 *(continued)*

(continued)

EXAMPLE 9 *(continued)*

EXAMPLE 9 *(continued)*

(continued)

EXAMPLE 9 *(continued)*

EXAMPLE 10. Willaert, "Lasso, ch' i' ardo" (parts 1 and 2)

(continued)

EXAMPLE 10 *(continued)*

EXAMPLE 10 *(continued)*

(continued)

EXAMPLE 10 *(continued)*

EXAMPLE 10 *(continued)*

(continued)

EXAMPLE 10 *(continued)*

SECONDA PARTE

EXAMPLE 10 *(continued)*

(continued)

EXAMPLE 10 *(continued)*

EXAMPLE 10 *(continued)*

(continued)

EXAMPLE 10 *(continued)*

EXAMPLE 11. Rore, "Da le belle contrade d'oriente"

(continued)

EXAMPLE II *(continued)*

EXAMPLE II *(continued)*

(continued)

EXAMPLE II *(continued)*

EXAMPLE II *(continued)*

(continued)

EXAMPLE II *(continued)*

EXAMPLE II (*continued*)

EXAMPLE 12. Rore, "Mia benigna fortuna" (parts 1 and 2)

EXAMPLE 12 *(continued)*

(continued)

EXAMPLE 12 *(continued)*

EXAMPLE 12 *(continued)*

SECONDA PARTE

(continued)

EXAMPLE 12 *(continued)*

EXAMPLE 12 *(continued)*

(continued)

EXAMPLE 12 *(continued)*

EXAMPLE 13. Wert, "Solo e pensoso" (parts 1 and 2)

(continued)

EXAMPLE 13 *(continued)*

EXAMPLE 13 *(continued)*

(continued)

EXAMPLE 13 *(continued)*

EXAMPLE 13 *(continued)*

(continued)

EXAMPLE 13 *(continued)*

SECONDA PARTE

EXAMPLE 13 *(continued)*

(continued)

EXAMPLE 13 *(continued)*

EXAMPLE 13 *(continued)*

EXAMPLE 14. Marenzio, "Solo e pensoso" (parts 1 and 2)

EXAMPLE 14 *(continued)*

(continued)

EXAMPLE 14 *(continued)*

EXAMPLE 14 *(continued)*

(continued)

EXAMPLE 14 *(continued)*

EXAMPLE 14 *(continued)*

(continued)

EXAMPLE 14 *(continued)*

EXAMPLE 14 *(continued)*

SECONDA PARTE

(continued)

EXAMPLE 14 *(continued)*

EXAMPLE 14 *(continued)*

(continued)

EXAMPLE 14 *(continued)*

EXAMPLE 15. Marenzio, "Tirsi morir volea" (parts 1, 2, and 3)

(continued)

EXAMPLE 15 *(continued)*

EXAMPLE 15 *(continued)*

(continued)

EXAMPLE 15 *(continued)*

SECONDA PARTE

EXAMPLE 15 *(continued)*

(continued)

EXAMPLE 15 *(continued)*

EXAMPLE 15 *(continued)*

TERZA, ET ULTIMA PARTE

(continued)

EXAMPLE 15 *(continued)*

EXAMPLE 15 *(continued)*

EXAMPLE 16. Wert, "Tirsi morir volea"

EXAMPLE 16 *(continued)*

(continued)

EXAMPLE 16 *(continued)*

EXAMPLE 16 *(continued)*

(continued)

EXAMPLE 16 *(continued)*

EXAMPLE 16 *(continued)*

(continued)

EXAMPLE 16 *(continued)*

EXAMPLE 16 *(continued)*

(continued)

EXAMPLE 16 *(continued)*

EXAMPLE 17. Gesualdo, "Luci serene e chiare"

(continued)

EXAMPLE 17 *(continued)*

EXAMPLE 17 *(continued)*

(continued)

EXAMPLE 17 *(continued)*

EXAMPLE 17 *(continued)*

(continued)

EXAMPLE 17 *(continued)*

EXAMPLE 18. Gesualdo, "'Mercè,' grido piangendo"

(continued)

EXAMPLE 18 *(continued)*

EXAMPLE 18 *(continued)*

EXAMPLE 19. Gesualdo, "Moro, lasso, al mio duolo"

EXAMPLE 19 *(continued)*

(continued)

EXAMPLE 19 *(continued)*

EXAMPLE 19 *(continued)*

EXAMPLE 20. Monteverdi, "Anima mia, perdona" (parts 1 and 2)

EXAMPLE 20 *(continued)*

(continued)

EXAMPLE 20 *(continued)*

EXAMPLE 20 *(continued)*

(continued)

EXAMPLE 20 *(continued)*

SECONDA PARTE

EXAMPLE 20 *(continued)*

(continued)

EXAMPLE 20 *(continued)*

EXAMPLE 20 *(continued)*

(continued)

EXAMPLE 20 *(continued)*

EXAMPLE 20 *(continued)*

EXAMPLE 21. Monteverdi, "Cruda Amarilli"

EXAMPLE 21 *(continued)*

(continued)

EXAMPLE 21 *(continued)*

EXAMPLE 21 *(continued)*

(continued)

EXAMPLE 21 *(continued)*

EXAMPLE 22. Monteverdi, "O Mirtillo"

(continued)

EXAMPLE 22 *(continued)*

EXAMPLE 22 *(continued)*

(continued)

EXAMPLE 22 *(continued)*

EXAMPLE 22 *(continued)*

INDEX

Page numbers in italics denote musical examples.

CPSIA information can be obtained
at www.ICGtesting.com
Printed in the USA
JSHW020009261021
19848JS00001B/7